Pocket Rough Guide

İstanbul

written and researched by

TERRY RICHARDSON

Contents

<< THE BLUE MOSQUE AND THE GOLDEN HORN
< BÜYÜK MECIDIYE CAMII, ORTAKÖY

INTRODUCTION TO İstanbul

Few of the world's cities capture the imagination quite like İstanbul, superbly situated at the confluence of predominantly Christian Europe and the largely Muslim Middle East. It is a booming megalopolis of more than fifteen million people, standing astride both the Asian and European sides of the Bosphorus strait, the vibrant cultural and economic powerhouse of a resurgent Turkish Republic. Of course İstanbul has been a major city for over two thousand years, and it is the incredible legacy of the two great empires which made it their capital, the Christian Byzantines and Muslim Ottoman Turks, that make it so appealing today.

GALATA

Best places for a perfect kebab

Forget that soggy late-night kebab at your local takeaway. Real kebabs come in many forms in the land of their birth and eating them is a seriously enjoyable business. Try a metre-long special at *Akendiz Hatay Sofrası* (see p.78), a lunchtime stand-up treat at *Dönerci Şahin Üsta* (see p.77), a southeast Turkish delight at *Develi* (see p.91) or a *rakı*-enhanced kebab feast at *Kenan Üsta Ocakbaşı* (see p.114).

For most visitors, İstanbul is a city of two, albeit rather uneven, halves. The first is the old city, strategically located on a peninsula pointing east across the Bosphorus towards Asia, and cut-off from the European mainland to the west by the substantial remains of the monumental Byzantine-era land walls. The peninsula is bound to the south by the glimmering waters of the Sea of Marmara, to the north by the curving inlet of one of the world's finest natural harbours, the Golden Horn. Like ancient Rome, which Constantinople superseded as the Roman Empire's major city, it was built on seven hills. There is so much to see and do in the old city that you could spend weeks exploring its many sights, but even with just a few days at your disposal it's possible to get a real flavour of this great metropolis. Fortunately, the majority of the major sights, such as the Haghia Sophia (Aya Sofya), Topkapı Palace and Blue Mosque, are located within a short distance of each other in compact Sultanahmet. By far the best way to explore is on foot, especially as there are so many smaller, easily missed sights tucked-in between the major ones, from Byzantine cisterns to historic Turkish baths. The buzzing waterfront around the Golden Horn-spanning Galata Bridge is unmissable, and offers superb views up to the old city's exotic skyline of domes and slender minarets. Try, too, to get a taste of the conservative parts of the old city by walking a section of the land walls or exploring the backstreets of the northwest quarter. Although the language barrier may be formidable and street signage less than perfect, don't be afraid to wander off the beaten path and temporarily mislay yourself. After all, with water on three sides and the towering land walls on the fourth you'll eventually reach an unmissable landmark.

RUMELI HISARI

The second half of the city is the European quarter of Beyoğlu and Galata, north across the Golden Horn from the old city and easily reached by tram or metro. As well as being home to the famous Galata Tower and a host of wonderful, mainly nineteenth-century buildings, it is İstanbul's entertainment hub. Even if you've no interest in the hedonistic delights of cinema-going, gallery-gazing, shopping, bar-hopping, puffing on a water pipe or clubbing, you should come here to challenge your preconceptions of what a predominantly Muslim city is like, dine at one of the myriad (usually excellent) restaurants or simply join the Friday or Saturday crush of people surging down İstiklal Caddesi. Then, if there's time, a bargain ferry ride to Asia awaits.

When to visit

Hot, humid summers and cold, damp winters mean spring and autumn are the best times to visit, with May–June and September–October offering the (usually) dry, warm weather ideal for exploring on foot. Needless to say, this is also the most expensive time for accommodation. Midsummer is more than bearable, however, with maximum temperatures rarely exceeding 28 degrees – avoid long tramps during the hottest part of the day and enjoy the benefits of warm evenings in a rooftop bar or restaurant. One downside of midsummer visits is that many İstanbulites decamp to Aegean resorts and some clubs close for the duration. Winters can be snowy, most likely in January or February, or more usually simply cold, wet and windy (the downside of the city's proximity to so much water means it has a maritime climate). Fog can also be a problem in winter, sometimes closing the Bosphorus to shipping. On the plus side, hotel rates are cheaper and the arts and cultural scene vibrant.

İSTANBUL AT A GLANCE

>> EATING

İstanbulites are fussy and demanding when it comes to food. Whether choosing a humble *simit* (sesame-coated bread ring) from a street barrow or a freshly-caught fish in a stylish Bosphorus-front restaurant, they'll only accept the best. Fish is highly prized, but more regular foods include all kinds of *sulu yemek* (stews), served-up from big steamtrays, the Turkish "pizzas" *pide* and *lahmacun*, a bewildering array of savoury pies and breads, soups and, inevitably, kebabs – either grilled on skewers over charcoal at an *ocakbaşı* or sliced from a rotating spit at a *dönerci*. However tempting for ease, don't just dine in tourist-dominated Sultanahmet, head across to **Galata/Beyoğlu**, further west in the old city – or across to **Asia**.

>> DRINKING

Turkey may be predominantly Muslim but there are plenty of places to enjoy a drink in İstanbul. The most lively area by far is buzzing **Galata/ Beyoğlu**, where student bars rub shoulders with hip licensed cafés and the well-heeled sip cocktails at expensive rooftop establishments. **Nevizade Sokak** in Beyoğlu is particularly noted for its raucous drinking (and eating) scene, particularly madcap on a Friday and Saturday night. The old city is much quieter, though there are plenty of places on Divan Yolu and Akbıyık Caddesi for a beer, glass of wine or the national drink, *rakı*, an aniseed spirit.

>> SHOPPING

With some four thousand shops in a mall over five hundred years old, the **Grand Bazaar** is a shopping experience few visitors will want to miss. There's everything from fake designer jeans to centuries-old Turkish rugs and plenty of cafés to take the weight off your feet for a while. The **Spice Bazaar** in Eminönü is much more manageable and equally historic, the streets around it are wonderful for foodstuffs. The **Arasta Bazaar** near the Blue Mosque is good for quality Turkish souvenirs; for more food shopping, head to **Kadıköy** in Asia or into conservative Fatih for the Çarşamba Pazarı (Wednesday Bazaar). For fashion, **İstiklal Caddesi** is the focus.

>> NIGHTLIFE

The old city has very little in the way of genuine nightlife. The real action is across the Golden Horn, primarily in and around **İstiklal Caddesi** in **Beyoğlu**, where there are clubs catering to every taste, from hard rock to dance and jazz to blues. **Galata** has a few small bohemian venues, as does **Kadıköy** in Asia. For pop glitz, head down to the Bosphorus-front in Ortaköy/ Kuruçeşme. For something more Turkish, try a *meyhane*, a kind of tavern, where the food (usually fish) takes second place to drink and the locals sing and dance to traditional Turkish music, as in **Kumkapı** in the old city.

OUR RECOMMENDATIONS FOR WHERE TO EAT, DRINK AND SHOP ARE LISTED AT THE END OF EACH CHAPTER.

Day One in İstanbul

1 Haghia Sophia > p.36. The mosaic-clad interior of the domed Haghia Sophia (Aya Sofya), for a thousand years the largest enclosed space in the world, still impresses today.

2 Basilica Cistern > p.32. Beautifully lit and atmospheric underground Byzantine cistern, famed for its Medusa-head carvings and lazy carp.

Lunch > p.46. Grilled meatballs are a Turkish favourite, and *Tarihi Sultanahmet Köftecisi*, overlooking the heart of the old city, does them to perfection.

3 Blue Mosque > p.43. With its cascade of domes and plethora of the gorgeous blue tiles from which its name derives, the Blue Mosque is unmissable.

4 Hippodrome > p.42. A relatively tranquil square, in Roman and Byzantine times a chariot-racing circuit, dominated by the splendid Egyptian obelisk.

5 Sokullu Mehmet Paşa Camii > p.40. A quite beautiful Ottoman mosque tucked away in the backstreets near the Hippodrome.

6 Church of St Sergius and Bacchus > p.40. Below the Hippodrome, this former early-Byzantine church is today the Küçük Aya Sofya Camii (Little Haghia Sophia), a working mosque.

Dinner > p.48. Sample a multitude of delicious cold and hot *meze* morsels (starters) at *Giritli* before a fish main washed down, if you you go for the fixed-meal deal, with an unlimited amount of wine, *rakı* or beer.

Day Two in İstanbul

1 Topkapı Palace > p.54. Make an early start to explore this fascinating palace complex, ranged around a series of attractive courtyard gardens.

2 Archeology Museum > p.51. Receiving far less attention than it deserves, this fine museum exhibits a wealth of artefacts from the former Ottoman domains.

Lunch > p.64. Grab a fish sandwich from *Tarihi Eminönü Balık Ekmek* and enjoy the vibrant chaos of Eminönü waterfront.

3 Spice Bazaar > p.60. Admire the beautifully arranged spices for sale in this covered Ottoman market – but make your purchases in the streets round about.

4 Rüstem Paşa Camii > p.62. A gem of a mosque in the bustling bazaar quarter of Eminönü, noted for its gorgeous İznik tiles.

Coffee > p.77. After toiling up the third hill, stop in the "hidden" *Ağa Kapısı* café for incomparable views down to the Galata Bridge and Bosphorus.

5 Süleymaniye Külliyesi > p.66. This mosque complex is the masterwork of the Ottomans' greatest architect – unmissable.

6 Süleymaniye Hamamı > p.67. Part of the mosque complex, unwind after your heavy day in this steamy and attractive *hamam*.

Dinner > p.48. For a tender charcoal-grilled kebab, *Khorasani*, a fashionable place in the heart of Sultanahmet, is perfect.

Backstreet İstanbul

The biggest and best concentration of traditional backstreets in the city is in the conservative northwest quarter. Winding their way along the old city's fourth, fifth and sixth hills, they are home to many seldom-visited sights and afford great views across the Golden Horn.

1 Aqueduct of Valens > p.74. You can't miss the two-tiered arches of this Byzantine engineering marvel spanning traffic-clogged Atatürk Bulvarı.

2 Yavuz Selim Camii > p.84. Beautifully austere imperial mosque atop the old city's fifth hill, offering grand views over the Golden Horn.

3 Church of the Pammakaristos > p.84. The funerary chapel of this little-visited Byzantine jewel is today a museum with some fine mosaics.

Lunch > p.91. Noted for updated versions of traditional Ottoman dishes, *Asitane* is right next to the Kariye Museum.

4 The Kariye Museum > p.80. Every picture tells a story at the former Church of St Saviour in Chora, one of the best collections of Byzantine mosaics anywhere.

5 The land walls > p.87. Follow the mighty land walls down to the Golden Horn, past the once-grand Palace of the Porphyrogenitus.

6 Ferry to Asia > see map p.86 & p.155. A ferry from the jetty at Ayvansaray runs down the Horn and across the Bosphorus to Üsküdar.

Dinner > p.133. Eat at *Kanaat*, a very traditional (and dry) restaurant in conservative Üsküdar.

The European quarter

The old city may have all the major historic sights, but for a hint of fin-de-siècle decadence, a generous slice of the contemporary arts and a no-holds-barred night on the town try the European quarter. The three million or so people who throng İstiklal Caddesi on an average Saturday – most İstanbulites – can't all be wrong.

1 İstanbul Modern > p.96. Great introduction to modern Turkish art and plenty of temporary exhibitions at this Bosphorus-front retort to London's Tate Modern.

2 Galata Tower > p.93. Ascend to the balcony of this landmark Genoese tower for superb vistas.

2

Lunch > p.99. The views from the popular rooftop *Galata Konak* café-cum-patisserie are just wonderful.

3 Galata Mevlevi Lodge > p.94. See the hall where the dervishes whirled in this fascinating little museum.

4 İstiklal Caddesi > p.102. Formerly the Rue de Pera and lined with fine nineteenth-century buildings, this is the city's premier shopping and entertainment street.

3

Tea > p.106. The tearooms of the grand *Pera Palace Hotel* are a period delight.

5 Pera Museum > p.106. Fine gallery-cum-museum housed in a beautifully restored nineteenth-century building.

Dinner > p.114. A lively İstanbul-Greek *meyhane* (taverna), *İmroz* is great for a raucous meal out.

6 Venue > p.101. *Nardis*, a short hop from the Galata Tower, is a cool and sophisticated jazz club.

4

BEST OF İSTANBUL

Big sights

1 Blue Mosque One of the most famous, most visited mosques in the world.
> **p.43**

2

2 Süleymaniye Mosque Complex Built by the Ottoman Empire's greatest architect for its greatest Sultan, Süleyman the Magnificent. > **p.66**

3 Bosphorus cruise A bargain ferry ride up the continent-dividing Bosphorus strait is a great day out. > **p.134**

3

4

4 Haghia Sophia (Aya Sofya) The most important church of the Byzantine world was converted into a mosque in 1453, a museum in 1934. > **p.36**

5

5 Topkapı Palace Home to the intriguing *harem* and nerve centre of the Ottoman Empire, which once spanned three continents. > **p.54**

Museums and galleries

1 Archeology Museum Three museums for the price of one and a staggering wealth of beautiful and intriguing exhibits. > **p.51**

2 Saklp Sabancı Museum This former Bosphorus-front mansion attracts genuine international-standard exhibitions. > **p.136**

3 Museum of Turkish and Islamic Art Priceless Turkish carpets, rare ceramics and much more in a former grand vizier's palace. > **p.41**

4 Mosaic Museum Quite charming collection of mosaics from the long-gone Byzantine Great Palace. > **p.39**

5 İstanbul Modern The name says it all, a real contrast to the sights of the old city. > **p.96**

Byzantine legacy

1 Church of the Pammakaristos A typical late Byzantine church-turned-mosque adorned with stunning mosaics. > p.84

2 Basilica Cistern Incredible to think something so prosaic as a cistern could be so beautiful. > **p.32**

3 Church of St Sergius and Bacchus (Küçük Aya Sofya Camii) This former Byzantine church retains some gorgeous original features. > **p.40**

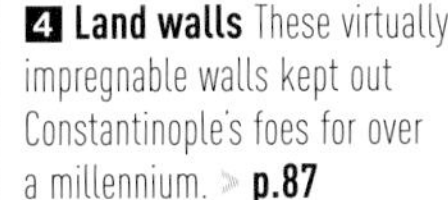

4 Land walls These virtually impregnable walls kept out Constantinople's foes for over a millennium. > **p.87**

5 Kariye Museum The fabulous frescoes and mosaics of the former Church of St Saviour in Chora tell biblical tales in near cartoon fashion. > **p.80**

Ottoman architecture

1 The Grand Bazaar This fifteenth-century covered market boasts 66 streets and over 4000 shops – the ultimate mall. > **p.70**

2 Rüstem Paşa Camii The interior of this small mosque has a carapace of finest period İznik tiles. > **p.62**

3 Ayasofya Hürrem Sultan Hamamı Ottoman *hamams* were temples to hygiene, godliness and gossip. > **p.39**

4 Sokullu Mehmet Paşa Camii Sinan masterpiece enhanced by the restrained use of exquisite tiles. > **p.40**

5 Traditional houses Vulnerable to fire, few Ottoman houses have survived the city's many blazes. > **p.38**

Viewpoints

1 Galata Tower Gaze across the busy waters of the Golden Horn to the exotic skyline of the old city. > **p.93**

2 360 bar-restaurant This swanky rooftop establishment delivers what its name promises – at a price. > **p.116**

3 Ortaköy boardwalk Trendy waterfront promenade with a classic view of a venerable mosque backed by the 1970s Bosphorus suspension bridge. > **p.123**

4 Arcadia Blue Terrace Head-up here for the best possible views of the old city's star sights, the Bosphorus and Asia. > **p.49**

5 Ağa Kapısı café Stunning window on the Golden Horn, Bosphorus and Asia from this traditional café. > **p.77**

Eating out

1 Sweet time Syrup-soaked and nut-stuffed pastries such as *baklava* are İstanbul institutions – try *Saray*. > **p.113**

2 Meyhane Culture A *meyhane* is a lively taverna for fish, *rakı* (aniseed spirit), wandering Roma musicians and carousing İstanbulites – there are dozens in vibrant Beyoğlu. > **p.102**

3 Kebab Head to *Kenan Üsta's* for succulent charcoal-grilled kebab. > **p.114**

4 Breakfast al Turca A full Turkish is tempting – numerous places across the city put on sumptuous Sunday buffets – try *Galata Konak*. > **p.99**

5 Street Cart Snacks Sesame-coated bagels, roast chestnuts and sweetcorn are among the goodies pushed around Sultanahmet's streets. > **p.32**

Shopping

1 Kadıköy Narrow lanes with a permanent market ideal for authentic foodstuff souvenirs. > **p.128**

2 İstiklal Caddesi High-street shops, historic arcades, a mall and much more. > **p.102**

3 Galata Great for chic little boutiques and alternative clothing stores. > **p.92**

4 Grand Bazaar Browse, haggle and appreciate the architecture of this historic bazaar. > **p.70**

5 Spice Bazaar A centuries-old waterfront bazaar packed with spices, herbs and Turkish delight. > **p.60**

On the water

1 The Maiden's Tower Sweeping views from a former lighthouse in the middle of the Bosphorus. > **p.127**

2 Up the Golden Horn Watch the old city's skyline unfold from the deck of a ferry plying this busy waterway. > **p.155**

3 Fishing from the Galata Bridge Watch the ever-hopeful massed anglers trying their luck. > **p.62**

4 Europe to Asia The return ferry ride to Asia is little over a couple of euros. > **p.155**

5 Swimming off the Princes' Islands The blue waters of the Sea of Marmara are a delight in summer. > **p.137**

PLACES

Sultanahmet

Once the fulcrum of both the Christian Byzantine and Muslim Ottoman empires, Sultanahmet is the heart of old İstanbul. The essence of its grand, imperial past is distilled in two truly great, domed buildings facing each other imperiously over an attractive park – the monumental sixth-century church of Haghia Sophia, today the Aya Sofya Museum, and the equally impressive Blue Mosque, built a thousand years later. There are plenty more, notable historic buildings scattered across the crown of the peninsula and in the old alleys running down to the shipping-filled blue waters of the Sea of Marmara, and you could easily spend two or three days sightseeing in Sultanahmet alone. Inevitably, tourism is Sultanahmet's *raison d'être* today, and there are legions of hotels, cafés and restaurants catering to visitors' needs.

MILION

Divan Yolu Ⓣ1 Sultanahmet. MAP P.34–35, POCKET MAP H11

Unfortunately, most visitors, in their rush to get to the nearby Haghia Sophia, walk by the remains of the Milion without noticing it, hardly surprising given that it is a mere stump of marble lost in a verge at the eastern end of busy Divan Yolu. This is all that's left of the Milion, a once-magnificent **triumphal arch** surmounted by a cross, flanked on either side by a statue of the Emperor Constantine and his mother Helena, beneath which was a milestone measuring distances to all corners of the Roman Empire. The crudely built stone tower next to it is actually an Ottoman-era water regulator for the Basilica Cistern (Yerebatan Sarnıcı) below your feet.

THE MILION

BASILICA CISTERN *YEREBATAN SARNICI*

Yerebatan Cad 13 Ⓣ1 Sultanahmet
Ⓣ0212 522 1259, Ⓦyerebatan.com.
Daily 9am–6.30pm. ₺20, audio-guide ₺10.
MAP P.34–35, POCKET MAP H11

The Yerebatan Sarnıcı or "Sunken Cistern", just downhill from the Milion, is better known to foreigners as the

BASILICA CISTERN

Basilica Cistern. Reached by a long flight of stairs and atmospherically lit, it proves a major hit with most visitors. Built originally under Emperor Constantine when he was re-founding the city as his new imperial capital, it was much modified in the sixth century. It could hold up to 80,000 cubic metres of water, used to supply the Great Palace of Byzantine-era Constantinople and, in the Ottoman period, the Topkapı Palace. The attractive roof, comprising a series of brick-built domes, is supported by a veritable forest of 336 columns arranged in 12 rows of 28, each topped by a capital, the most attractive of which are of the elaborately carved, acanthus-leaf Corinthian variety. Walkways lead through the columns, allowing visitors to admire the carp swimming in the shallow, clear and subtly illuminated waters, as well as wonder at the massive amount of work its 1987 restoration must have been, when some 50,000 tonnes of mud were dredged out of the 140m long by 70m wide cistern. At the far end of the cistern are two massive capitals, both carved into the form of the snake-haired mythological creature **Medusa** and each supporting a pillar. Almost certainly reused from much earlier structures, one Medusa is upside down, the other laid on its side, possibly because the Medusa was a pagan symbol and the cistern was built in the Christian period. A scene from the 1963 James Bond film, *From Russia with Love*, was shot here.

CAFER AĞA THEOLOGICAL SCHOOL *CAFER AĞA MEDRESESİ*

Caferiye Sok Ⓣ1 Sultanahmet. Daily 8.30am–7pm. MAP P.34–35, POCKET MAP H11

In the shadow of the Haghia Sophia, this former Islamic theological school was designed by the prolific Ottoman master architect Sinan in the sixteenth century. The domed rooms ranged around the attractive courtyard, formerly the cells of the theology students, are now home to the studios of craftspeople maintaining traditional Ottoman arts such as *ebru* (marbling), calligraphy and the painting of miniatures. Many of their wares are for sale and the whole enterprise is surprisingly low-key given that it is situated in the most heavily touristed part of the city.

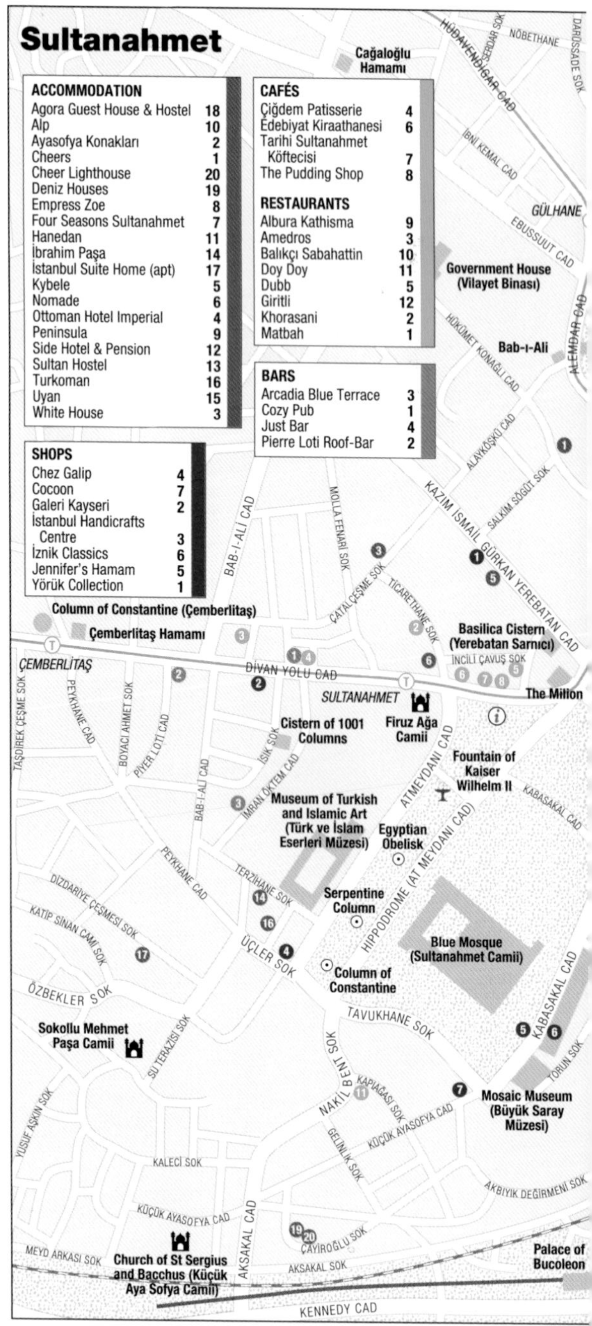
Sultanahmet
ACCOMMODATION
Agora Guest House & Hostel 18
Alp 10
Ayasofya Konakları 2
Cheers 1
Cheer Lighthouse 20
Deniz Houses 19
Empress Zoe 8
Four Seasons Sultanahmet 7
Hanedan 11
İbrahim Paşa 14
İstanbul Suite Home (apt) 17
Kybele 5
Nomade 6
Ottoman Hotel Imperial 4
Peninsula 9
Side Hotel & Pension 12
Sultan Hostel 13
Turkoman 16
Uyan 15
White House 3
SHOPS
Chez Galip 4
Cocoon 7
Galeri Kayseri 2
İstanbul Handicrafts Centre 3
İznik Classics 6
Jennifer's Hamam 5
Yörük Collection 1
CAFÉS
Çiğdem Patisserie 4
Edebiyat Kiraathanesi 6
Tarihi Sultanahmet Köftecisi 7
The Pudding Shop 8
RESTAURANTS
Albura Kathisma 9
Amedros 3
Balıkçı Sabahattin 10
Doy Doy 11
Dubb 5
Giritli 12
Khorasani 2
Matbah 1
BARS
Arcadia Blue Terrace 3
Cozy Pub 1
Just Bar 4
Pierre Loti Roof-Bar 2
Cağaloğlu Hamamı
HÜDAVENDİGAR CAD
SERDAR SOK
NÖBETHANE
DARÜSSADE SOK
İBNİ KEMAL CAD
GÜLHANE
EBUSSUUT CAD
Government House (Vilayet Binası)
ALEMDAR CAD
HÜKÜMET KONAĞI CAD
Bab-ı-Ali
ALAYKÖŞKÜ CAD
SALKIM SÖĞÜT SOK
KAZIM İSMAİL GÜRKAN YEREBATAN CAD
BAB-I-ALİ CAD
MOLLA FENARİ SOK
ÇATALÇEŞME SOK
TİCARETHANE SOK
Column of Constantine (Çemberlitaş)
Çemberlitaş Hamamı
Basilica Cistern (Yerebatan Sarnıcı)
İNCİLİ ÇAVUŞ SOK
ÇEMBERLİTAŞ
DİVAN YOLU CAD
SULTANAHMET
The Milion
TAŞDİREK ÇEŞME SOK
PEYKHANE CAD
BOYACI AHMET SOK
PİYER LOTİ CAD
Cistern of 1001 Columns
Firuz Ağa Camii
Fountain of Kaiser Wilhelm II
İŞIK SOK
İMRAN ÖKTEM CAD
ATMEYDANI CAD
KABASAKAL CAD
BAB-I-ALİ CAD
Museum of Turkish and Islamic Art (Türk ve İslam Eserleri Müzesi)
Egyptian Obelisk
HIPPODROME (AT MEYDANI CAD)
PEYKHANE CAD
TERZİHANE SOK
Serpentine Column
DİZDARİYE ÇEŞMESİ SOK
KATİP SİNAN CAMİ SOK
Blue Mosque (Sultanahmet Camii)
ÜÇLER SOK
Column of Constantine
ÖZBEKLER SOK
TAVUKHANE SOK
KABASAKAL CAD
Sokollu Mehmet Paşa Camii
SU TERAZİSİ SOK
NAKİL BENT SOK
KAPIAĞASI SOK
TORUN SOK
Mosaic Museum (Büyük Saray Müzesi)
YUSUF AŞKIN SOK
GELİNLİK SOK
KÜÇÜK AYASOFYA CAD
KALECİ SOK
AKBIYIK DEĞİRMENİ SOK
KÜÇÜK AYASOFYA CAD
AKSAKAL CAD
ÇAYIROĞLU SOK
MEYD ARKASI SOK
Church of St Sergius and Bacchus (Küçük Aya Sofya Camii)
AKSAKAL SOK
Palace of Bucoleon
KENNEDY CAD

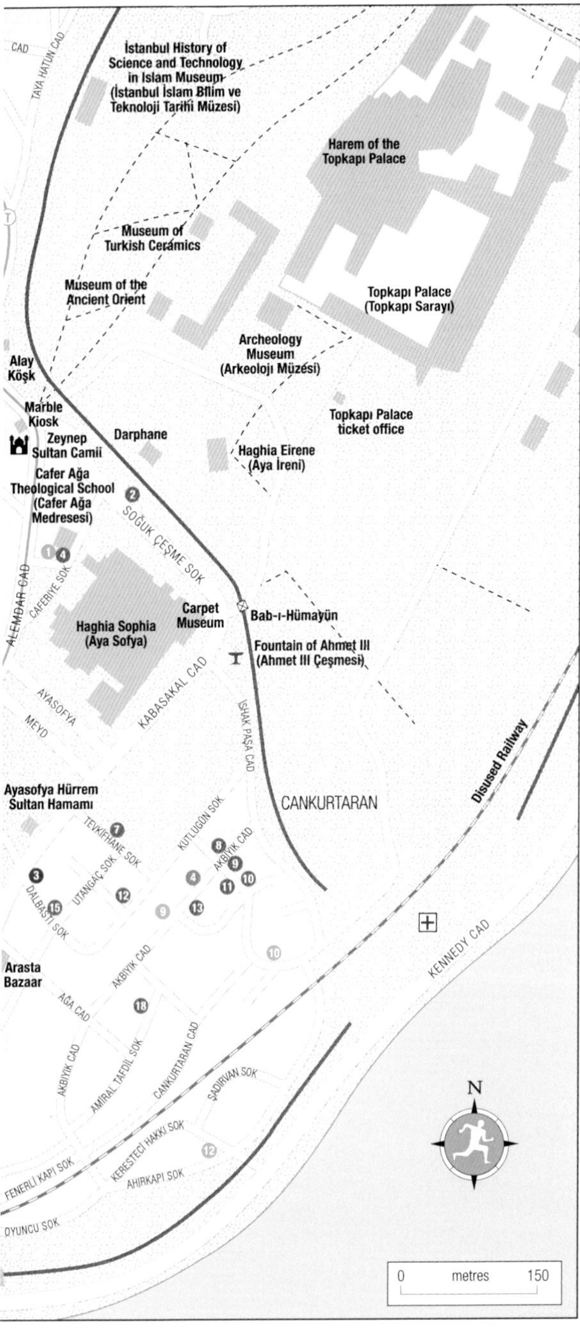
CAD
TAYA HATUN CAD
İstanbul History of Science and Technology in Islam Museum (İstanbul İslam Bilim ve Teknoloji Tarihi Müzesi)
Harem of the Topkapı Palace
Museum of Turkish Ceramics
Museum of the Ancient Orient
Topkapı Palace (Topkapı Sarayı)
Archeology Museum (Arkeoloji Müzesi)
Alay Köşk
Marble Kiosk
Topkapı Palace ticket office
Zeynep Sultan Camii
Darphane
Haghia Eirene (Aya İreni)
Cafer Ağa Theological School (Cafer Ağa Medresesi)
SOĞUK ÇEŞME SOK
ALEMDAR CAD
CAFERIYE SOK
Haghia Sophia (Aya Sofya)
Carpet Museum
Bab-ı-Hümayün
Fountain of Ahmet III (Ahmet III Çeşmesi)
KABASAKAL CAD
AYASOFYA MEYD
İSHAK PAŞA CAD
Disused Railway
Ayasofya Hürrem Sultan Hamamı
CANKURTARAN
TEVKIFHANE SOK
KUTLUGÜN SOK
AKBIYIK CAD
UTANGAÇ SOK
DALBASTI SOK
KENNEDY CAD
Arasta Bazaar
AKBIYIK CAD
AĞA CAD
AKBIYIK CAD
AMIRAL TAFDIL SOK
CANKURTARAN CAD
ŞADIRVAN SOK
KERESTECI HAKKI SOK
FENERLI KAPI SOK
AHIRKAPI SOK
OYUNCU SOK
N
0 metres 150

HAGHIA SOPHIA
AYA SOFYA

Sultanahmet Meydanı 1 Ⓣ1 Sultanahmet Ⓣ0212 528 4500, Ⓦayasofyamuzesi.gov.tr. Tues–Sun: April–Oct 9am–7pm, last entry 6pm; Nov–March 9am–4.30pm. ₺30, audio-guide ₺10. MAP P.34–35, POCKET MAP H11

Representative of the Byzantine Empire at the peak of its power in the sixth century, the Haghia Sophia, or **Church of the Holy Wisdom**, still inspires awe today. Two previous churches of the same name had stood on the site before being razed, the latter in a riot in 532. Justinian, determined to bolster his temporal and spiritual authority, ordered a rebuild on a scale not realized before. The architects, Greek mathematician Anthemius and geometer Isidore, came up with an innovative and much-imitated design – covering a near-square building with a dome of unprecedented height and impressive diameter.

Sunk a few metres below current ground-level at the entrance to Justinian's masterpiece is the stepped base of the second church, along with a series of blocks which once adorned its facade, relief-carved with sheep symbolizing the Twelve Apostles. The so-called "Beautiful Gate", the central door of five, leads to the **inner narthex**, a vaulted vestibule containing the sarcophagus of the Empress Irene. Further doorways lead to the inner narthex, its ceiling glittering with gold mosaics and containing, above the imperial portal leading to the nave, a stunning mosaic panel depicting an all-powerful Christ being beseeched by Emperor Leo IV.

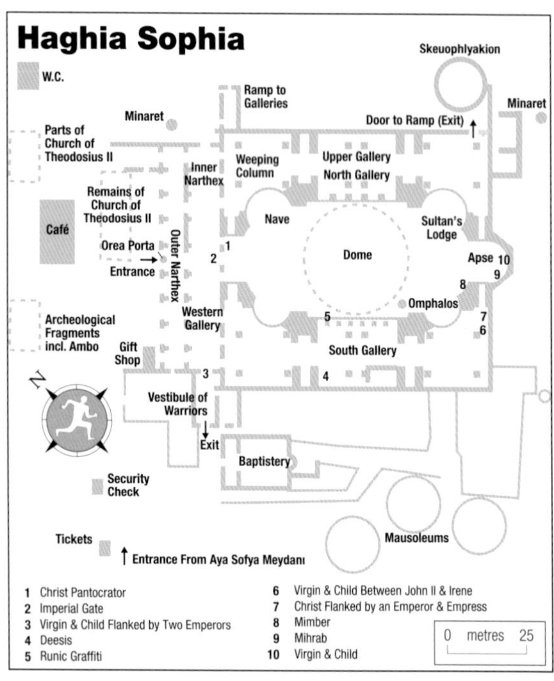

HAGHIA SOPHIA INTERIOR

It is the **nave** of the church, however, that is truly inspiring. Here the 32m-diameter central dome, towering 55m above floor level, appears to be suspended in mid-air, its supporting piers cleverly concealed in the twin line of pillars separating the nave from the aisles. Two half-domes join the central dome to the west and east, emphasizing the sense of space, an effect aided by light filtering in from the forty windows puncturing the dome. Also on the ground floor are the **weeping column**, so-called because it "sweats" water and supposedly cures all ills, and the omphalos, a marble-inlay floor panel where coronations took place.

Following the 1453 Ottoman Turkish conquest of the city, this church became, as the **Aya Sofya Camii**, the city's major mosque. Thus the apse is pierced by a Mecca-facing niche (*mihrab*), flanked to one side by a prayer-platform (*mimber*). There's also the loge, a platform used by the Sultan at Friday prayers, and eight large plaques below the dome adorned with Arabic calligraphy. Outside, the four minarets at each corner of the building were added post-Ottoman conquest. It was turned into the Aya Sofya museum in 1934.

Reached by a stone ramp from the inner narthex's north end are the **upper galleries**. The south gallery is the most interesting as it contains several beautifully executed and preserved Byzantine mosaic panels, including one depicting John the Baptist and the Virgin Mary beseeching an impassive-looking Christ to save humanity. Scratched into the marble balustrade here is some Viking graffiti, probably scrawled by a member of the Varangian Guard, bodyguards to the Byzantine emperors recruited from Scandinavia. Exiting via the south end of the inner narthex, in the **Vestibule of Warriors**, is the pick of the church's mosaic panels. Executed in the late tenth century, it depicts the Virgin and Child. On her right, Emperor Justinian offers a model of the Haghia Sophia church; to her left, an even more munificent Emperor Constantine presents her with a model of his city, Constantinople.

SOĞUK ÇEŞME SOKAĞI

Ⓣ1 Sultanahmet. MAP P.34–35, POCKET MAP H11

In Turkish, Soğuk Çeşme Sokağı means "street of the cold fountains", though the cobbled alley is notable today not for its fountains but for the attractively restored nineteenth-century wooden houses lining its cobbled course. It's worth strolling down this pedestrianized lane to see a version of how the old city would have looked before the modern era, when the then-standard wooden houses, subject to frequent fires, were rebuilt in brick and concrete. The houses are attractively painted, with traditional overhanging upper floors.

FOUNTAIN OF AHMET III
AHMET III ÇEŞMESİ

Bab-ı Hümayün Cad Ⓣ1 Sultanahmet. MAP P.34–35, POCKET MAP J11

Situated just in front of the Bab-ı Hümayün gateway leading to the outer court of the Topkapı Palace (see p.54), this splendidly ornate, eighteenth-century Turkish Rococo fountain is the most attractive in the city. The building is almost square, with stylized, massively overhanging eaves topped by five small domes. At each corner are counters covered by ornate, curved marble window grilles, from which refreshments such as iced water and sherbets would have been handed to passers-by in the Ottoman period. These water dispensers, known as *sebil* in Turkish, were found throughout the city and often, as here, also had wall-mounted taps (*çeşme*) to provide that most basic of necessities to a local populace whose homes lacked running water.

CARPET MUSEUM
HALI MÜZESİ

Bab-ı Hümayün Cad Ⓣ1 Sultanahmet, Ⓦ halimuzesi.com. Mon-Fri 9am-noon & 1pm-5pm; ₺10. MAP P.34–35, POCKET MAP H11

Located in the domed soup-kitchens attached to the Haghia Sophia (Aya Sofya) the Carpet Museum, opened in 2013, displays a fantastic range of fine carpets and kilims woven between the fourteenth and twentieth centuries. The exhibits, many of them taken from mosques across Anatolian Turkey, are well-labelled, and there is plenty of information both on how the rugs were made and the significance of the patterns with which they are decorated.

FOUNTAIN OF AHMET III

AYASOFYA HÜRREM SULTAN HAMAMI

Bab-ı Hümayün Cad 1 Ⓣ1 Sultanahmet ⓣ0212 517 3535, ⓦayasofyahamami.com. Daily 7am–midnight. Bath packages from €86. MAP P.34–35, POCKET MAP H12

Built by Sinan in 1556 for Sultan Süleyman the Magnificent, appropriately enough on the site of the Roman Baths of Zeuxippus, this beautiful *hamam* (**Turkish baths**) was originally intended for the faithful attending the Aya Sofya Camii. It was named after Süleyman's wife, known to Turks as Haseki Hürrem, though better known in the west as Roxelana. In 2011, following many years of restoration, it became a working *hamam* once again. The building comprises two separate baths, for men and women, with entry from either end into the large, domed *camekan* or reception/changing area. Beyond this lies the main bath chamber, the *hararet*, where bathers sluice themselves down with water from a basin or "steam" on the hot *göbek taşı* ("navel stone").

MOSAIC MUSEUM *BÜYÜK SARAY MÜZESİ*

Torun Sok 103 Ⓣ1 Sultanahmet ⓣ0212 518 1205. Tues–Sun April–Oct 9am–7pm, last entry 6pm; Nov–March 9am–5pm. ₺8. MAP P.34–35, POCKET MAP H12

The mosaics exhibited on the floor in this museum are actually *in-situ*, and once formed part of a huge panel adorning the courtyard of one of the royal residences within the Great Palace complex of the Byzantine period, which sprawled all the way down the hill to the Sea of Marmara. Sections have been taken up and wall-mounted to make viewing easier, and some are so finely executed they contain

MOSAIC, MOSAIC MUSEUM

40,000 *tesserae* (mosaic pieces) per square metre. They depict quite charming scenes from everyday **Byzantine life**. In one a stubborn goat resists the efforts of a shepherd to drag it along by its tether, in another an equally stubborn donkey turns its head away from a basket of food. Less cute are the hunting dogs bringing down a bloodied hare, leopards feasting on the carcass of an antelope and a lion tangling messily with an elephant. Although most of the mosaics here probably date from the firmly Christian sixth century, some of the scenes are pagan, Classical-era in nature, including the mythological hero Bellerophon taking on the monstrous fire-breathing Chimera.

ARASTA BAZAAR

Arasta Çarşısı 143 Ⓣ1 Sultanahmet ⓣ0212 517 6813, ⓦarastabazaar.com. MAP P.34–35, POCKET MAP H12

Originally, this long bazaar of small shops was part of the early seventeenth-century Blue Mosque complex and the revenues from it helped pay for upkeep of the mosque. An attractive market area, it's far less hassle to browse here than in the much larger Grand Bazaar. Today, there are 77 shops, selling everything from traditional Turkish carpets and kilims through to İznik tiles and Meerschaum pipes.

SOKULLU MEHMET PAŞA CAMİİ

CHURCH OF ST SERGIUS AND BACCHUS
KÜÇÜK AYA SOFYA CAMİİ

Küçük Aya Sofya Cad Ⓣ1 Sultanahmet.
MAP P.34–35, POCKET MAP G9

The "small mosque of Aya Sofya", as it is known in Turkish, is presumably so called because of its resemblance, on a miniature scale, to the Aya Sofya itself. It is located down the hill from the Blue Mosque and Arasta Bazaar, close to the Sea of Marmara, and was originally the church for the nearby **Palace of Hormisdas**, a part of the Great Palace complex. Commissioned by Justinian and his consort Theodora, the church slightly predated that of Haghia Sophia, having been begun in 527 and completed in 536. The ground plan of the church is an irregular octagon, with beautiful marble columns supporting an encircling gallery, itself topped by a shallow dome oddly corrugated with alternate convex and concave ribs. Some of the capitals helping transfer the weight of the roof onto the columns are deeply incised with stylized plant motifs and the monogram of Justinian and Theodora can still be seen on a few. Converted into a **mosque** in the sixteenth century, nothing remains of its original mosaics, though a frieze inscribed with Greek letters honours Justinian, Theodora and St Sergius (the latter one of the two **Christian martyrs**, both soldiers who later became patron saints of the Roman army, after whom the church was named). The proportions of the largely brick-built church have been spoiled by the addition, after its conversion to a mosque, of a five-domed "last prayer place" porch. Opposite the main door is a pleasant courtyard medrese with a teahouse.

SOKULLU MEHMET PAŞA CAMİİ

Mehmet Paşa Yokusu Ⓣ1 Sultanahmet.
MAP P.34–35, POCKET MAP G8

Tricky to find in the narrow lanes a short walk uphill from

the Church of St Sergius and Bacchus, this small mosque, designed by the brilliant **Sinan** and finished in 1571, is exquisite. The courtyard, very large in proportion to the prayer hall, has at its centre a pretty ablutions fountain. It is ringed on three sides by dome-topped colonnades, beneath which are ranged the cells of a still-active boys' Koran school. The intimate prayer hall is almost square and covered by a high dome supported by four semi-domes. This interior is a model of restraint, with the finest-period İznik tiles used, sparingly, to enliven the pale stonework. Soft light filters in through the coloured glass in the tracery-work windows, and worked into the lintel above the door and embedded in the *mimber* are pieces of stone said to be from the sacred Kaaba in **Mecca**. The mosque was built for Süleyman the Magnificent's last grand vizier, Sokullu Mehmet Paşa.

MUSEUM OF TURKISH AND ISLAMIC ART
TÜRK VE İSLAM ESERLERİ MÜZESİ

Atmeydanı Sok 6 Ⓣ1 Sultanahmet ⓘ0212 518 1805. Tues–Sun: April–Oct 9am–7pm; Nov–March 9am–5pm. ₺20.
MAP P.34–35, POCKET MAP G17

Located a little west of the Blue Mosque and flanking the Hippodrome, this impressive museum houses exhibits from the Islamic world including oriental **carpets**, illuminated Korans, calligraphy, Ottoman and Persian miniatures, tiles, ceramics, metalwork, intricately carved wooden doors and mother of pearl inlaid furniture as well as ethnographical artefacts. The building is a former-palace, originally home to İbrahim Paşa, grand vizier to the greatest Ottoman sultan, Süleyman the Magnificent. Completed in 1524, it was rebuilt following a devastating fire in 1843. İbrahim was the empire's most successful grand vizier and during his thirteen years in office he amassed enormous wealth. Eventually incurring the mistrust of Süleyman, the unfortunate statesman was strangled in the Topkapı Palace. Today, the museum is home to over **40,000 exhibits** dating from the earliest years of Islam in the late seventh century to today, though the main focus is on the Selçuk Turkish (eleventh to thirteenth centuries) and Ottoman (fourteenth to nineteenth centuries) periods. The major exhibition room, once the Great Hall of the palace, houses stunning Turkish carpets ranging from threadbare thirteenth-century rugs to superbly preserved giants weighing thousands of kilograms that once graced the Topkapı Palace. In the basement, the fascinating ethnography section is home to a **black goat-hair tent** woven by the nomadic *Yörük* tribes of the Taurus Mountains, descendants of the Turkoman nomads who poured into Anatolia from the eleventh century onwards.

BOWL, MUSEUM OF TURKISH AND ISLAMIC ART

HIPPODROME *AT MEYDANI*

Ⓣ1 Sultanahmet. MAP P.34–35, POCKET MAP G11–12

Set between the landmark Blue Mosque and the Museum of Turkish and Islamic Art, this paved, rectangular public park area was, in the Roman and Byzantine periods, a **stadium**. The original incarnation dates to 203 AD, when Emperor Septimius Severus rebuilt the city, but it was enlarged when Constantine made it the imperial capital in 330. Used during the Byzantine period for court ceremonies and games – most notably chariot racing – it was some 480m long and 117.5m wide and held up to 100,000 spectators. Spectacles in the Hippodrome were presided over by the emperor and his entourage from the *kathisma* or royal box, situated in the vicinity of what today form the grounds of the Blue Mosque. At the northeast end of the Hippodrome, close to the tramway on Divan Yolu, is the attractive domed **Fountain of Kaiser Wilhelm II**, gifted to the then Ottoman sultan by the German leader in 1898 and located where the starting gates for the chariot races used to be. Southwest of this, following what was the central line or *spina* of the course, is the **Egyptian Obelisk**. Shipped here from Egypt in the fourth century, it is covered in hieroglyphic symbols and dates back to the sixteenth century BC. Intriguingly, it is mounted on a sandstone block carved on all four sides with images of Theodosius I, the emperor responsible for its erection, overseeing the chariot races from the royal box.

Continuing down the *spina* you'll find the **Serpentine Column**, comprising three intertwined bronze snakes, today sadly headless, though one is displayed in the city's Archeology Museum. Cast to celebrate a Greek victory over the invading Persians in 479 BC, it was brought here from Delphi by Constantine I. The last monument is a crude stone obelisk, the **Column of Constantine**, which also served as a race marker. Beyond this was a raised semicircular seating area lining the curved end of the course where the chariots turned. Known as the **sphendrome**, the seating has been subsumed by more modern buildings, but its massive substructure is visible from Naklibent Sokak below. The course of the Hippodrome was used for state ceremonies in Ottoman times, hence its Turkish name **At Meydanı** or "square of the horses".

EGYPTIAN OBELISK, HIPPODROME

THE BLUE MOSQUE AT NIGHT

BLUE MOSQUE
SULTANAHMET CAMİİ

Sultanahmet Meydanı Ⓣ1 Sultanahmet. Closed to non-Muslims at prayer times and Friday mornings to noon. MAP P.34–35, POCKET MAP G12

Properly known as the Sultanahmet Camii in Turkish, after the Ottoman sultan Ahmet I who commissioned it, this is probably the single most visited sight in İstanbul. Completed in 1616 after seven years' labour, the mosque takes its more tourist-friendly name from the carapace of predominantly **blue İznik tiles** liberally adorning its interior. Along with the Haghia Sophia it dominates the skyline of Sultanahmet, its majestic flow of domes and half-domes encompassed by six slender, cylindrical minarets (the latter reviled by the pious at the time of construction for consciously imitating the Great Mosque in Mecca) quite breathtaking to behold – especially when atmospherically illuminated at night. The best approach is from the Hippodrome, where a splendid doorway leads into the *avlu* or courtyard, which covers virtually the same ground area as the prayer hall itself. Only Muslims can enter the prayer hall via the main, northwest-facing door; other visitors must exit the courtyard and enter via the southwest portal, where there are often long queues. Even though non-Muslims are kept back from much of the prayer hall by a rope barrier, the cavernous interior, with its large **central dome**, 23.5m in diameter and 43m high, flanked by four smaller semi-domes and supported by four enormous ribbed columns, is impressive. The twenty thousand-plus İznik tiles vie with each other for the visitor's attention and the prayer wall at the southeast end is pierced by the standard Mecca-facing prayer niche, the *mihrab*. To the right is the *mimber* or pulpit, used by the *imam* to lead prayers. To the left the loge, a raised platform for the sultan and his entourage, is connected to a royal pavilion attached to the easternmost corner of the building. Only visible from outside, this contains a suite of rooms used by the sultan on days he visited, and was reached by a sloping ramp, allowing access by horse. **Sultan Ahmet I's tomb** (Tues–Sat 9am–4pm; free), an attractively domed structure, stands in the northern corner of the grounds, accessible from Mimar Mehmet Ağa Caddesi. The sultan was buried here with his wife and three of his sons.

FIRUZ AĞA CAMII, DIVAN YOLU

CISTERN OF 1001 COLUMNS

İmran Öktem Cad Ⓣ1 Sultanahmet. Ⓣ 0212 518 1000. ₺10. MAP P.34–35, POCKET MAP G11

Despite the fact that it has been turned into a posh function space used for business meetings, gala events and weddings among other things, it's well worth having a look inside another of those great covered cisterns so crucial to the growth of Byzantine Constantinople. At around 64m by 56m, it's not quite as large as the much better known Basilica Cistern, not far to the east along Divan Yolu, but it is still the second largest in the city. The pretty, herring-bone-patterned brick domes of the vault are supported by 224 columns erected in 16 rows of 14. The total height of the interior is nearly 15m, though it is difficult to get a true impression of this as the false wooden floor, inserted when it was converted into a function space, is raised well above the original ground level. Opening hours are generally 9am-8pm daily but it is closed when there's a function taking place.

DİVAN YOLU

Ⓣ1 Sultanahmet.

Just north of the Cistern of 1001 Columns is Divan Yolu, today Sultanahmet's busiest thoroughfare as, despite being semi-pedestrianized (watch out for speeding service vehicles), it carries the incredibly useful T1 tramline. In Roman and Byzantine times it was the most important street in the city. Then known as the Mese or Middleway, it could be followed from the Milion (see p.32) west out of the city and on to the Adriatic. It became Divan Yolu in the Ottoman period as it led visitors and petitioners to the Divan (council) chamber in the Topkapı Palace.

On the south side of Divan Yolu is the **Firuz Ağa Camii**, one of the city's earliest mosques. Built in 1491, compared to the nearby Blue Mosque it is a model of architectural restraint, being little more than a square prayer hall surmounted by a dome attended by a single minaret. It is well used by the local faithful, and like all mosques in the city has (useful for visitors) public toilets attached.

Shops

CHEZ GALİP

At Meydanı 78 Ⓣ1 Sultanahmet. Daily 9am–8pm. MAP P.34–35, POCKET MAP G12

Selling pottery crafted in the central Anatolian pottery town of Avanos, the most intriguing items are those based on ancient Hittite designs, though there is plenty of decent-quality İznik pottery on show as well.

COCOON

Küçük Aya Sofya Cad 13 Ⓣ1 Sultanahmet. Daily 9am–7pm. MAP P.34–35, POCKET MAP G12

A positive cornucopia of richly hued artefacts made from felt – bags, hats, figurines and the like, plus an array of carpets, kilims and throws from Central Asia.

GALERİ KAYSERİ

Divan Yolu 58 Ⓣ1 Sultanahmet. Daily 9am–8.30pm. MAP P.34–35, POCKET MAP G11

The best bookshop in the old city, this is the place to come if you want to pick up a specialist book on the city (or Turkey) – though prices are considerably higher than at home. There's another branch diagonally opposite, with both stocking English-language novels as well.

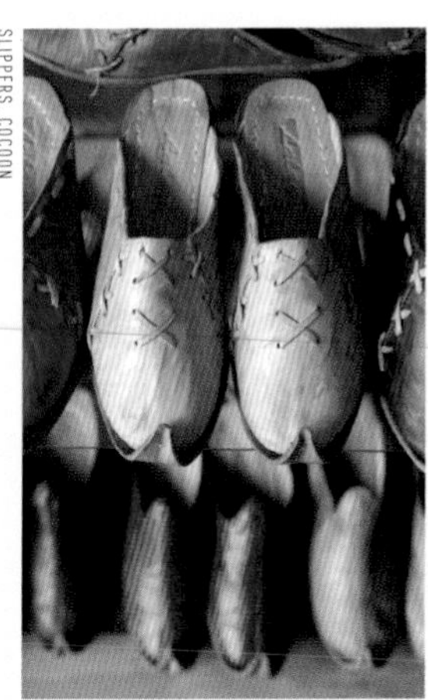

SLIPPERS, COCOON

İSTANBUL HANDICRAFTS CENTRE

Kabasakal Cad 5 Ⓣ1 Sultanahmet. Daily 9am–8pm. MAP P.34–35, POCKET MAP H12

Housed in a restored medrese (Islamic theological school), this centre keeps alive traditional crafts such as book-binding, marbling and calligraphy. It's worth visiting to see the building and the artisans at work even if you don't buy anything.

İZNİK CLASSICS

Arasta Çarşısı Ⓣ1 Sultanahmet. Daily 9am–7pm. MAP P.34–35, POCKET MAP H12

İznik ceramics were, at their best, among the finest wares produced in the Ottoman Empire. The gorgeous tiles sold here today are handcrafted in the same traditional way by studio potters – and are very expensive as a result.

JENNIFER'S HAMAM

Arasta Çarşısı Ⓣ1 Sultanahmet. Daily 9am–8pm. MAP P.34–35, POCKET MAP H12

Run by a friendly Canadian, the big draw here is that all the textiles are hand-woven from organic cotton, linen or silk. Choose from a bewildering range of all-cotton *peştemals*, Turkish bath wraps very popular as lightweight beach towels, traditional fluffy towels and scarves.

YÖRÜK COLLECTION

Yerebatan Cad 35 Ⓣ1 Sultanahmet. Daily 9am–9pm. MAP P.34–35, POCKET MAP G11

A well-laid-out shop that tries, and mostly succeeds, in being all things to all people, with all manner of traditional (and modern interpretations of) Turkish handicrafts, from carpets to silver jewellery and Ottoman miniatures to cushion covers.

Cafés

ÇİĞDEM PATISSERIE

Divan Yolu Cad 62 Ⓣ1 Sultanahmet
0212 526 8859. Daily 8am–11pm.
MAP P.34–35, POCKET MAP G11

This busy, continental-style patisserie is as popular with locals as visitors. Temptingly arrayed in the window are savoury snacks such as *poğaça*, soft bread rolls stuffed with cheese or a slightly spiced potato mixture; semi-sweet *tahinli ekmek*, a bread spiral coated in sweetened sesame paste; and a huge range of sweets ranging from nut-stuffed *baklava* to *acıbadem*, Turkey's monster-sized answer to Italy's Amaretto biscuit. Black tea is served good and hot in tulip-shaped glasses, and there's a decent range of coffees, from Turkish-style to a very palatable latte.

EDEBİYAT KIRAATHANESİ

Divan Yolu Cad 14 Ⓣ1 Sultanahmet
0212 526 1615. Daily 9am–10pm.
MAP P.34–35, POCKET MAP G11

Elegant period tearooms right next to the Sultanahmet tram stop, with a superb range of Turkish desserts, coffees from Turkish (₺5) to latte (₺7), and glasses of tea (₺2). It's run by the Turkish Society for Literature, so expect cultured Turks at the next table.

ÇİĞDEM PATISSERIE

TARİHİ SULTANAHMET KÖFTECİSİ

Divan Yolu Cad 4 Ⓣ1 Sultanahmet
0212 511 3960. Daily 11am–11pm.
MAP P.34–35, POCKET MAP G11

If you don't like grilled meatballs don't even consider this place. If you do, it is an İstanbul institution and one of the few places in tourist-orientated Sultanahmet to attract large numbers of Turkish diners. The owners are proud of the myriad Turkish celebrities who have eaten here, their photos and letters of thanks adorning the walls. What you get is firm *köfte* (meatballs) accompanied by a white bean salad, spicy tomato sauce, pickled peppers and crusty bread (₺4) – best chased down with the salty yoghurt drink *ayran*. Unlicensed.

THE PUDDING SHOP

Divan Yolu Cad 6 Ⓣ1 Sultanahmet
0212 522 2970. Daily 7am–11pm.
MAP P.34–35, POCKET MAP G11

The service is canteen style, the queues can be long and the food OK rather than exceptional, but this bustling café played a signature role in the hippy-era as "the" hang out for travellers heading to India. The same owners still run it today, and continue serving the *sütlaç* (rice pudding) from which its unofficial name derives (it's more properly the *Lale Restaurant*). It also does a wide range of traditional savoury dishes, with mains such as *köfte* (meatballs), kebabs and stews from ₺10 – and is licensed.

Restaurants

ALBURA KATHİSMA

Akbıyık Cad 26 Ⓣ1 Sultanahmet
☎ 0212 517 9031. Daily 10am–11pm.
MAP P.34–35, POCKET MAP H12

One of the best options on this bustling hotel-, restaurant- and bar-lined street, with an attractive bare-brick interior and tables outside. Service is good by Turkish standards and the wine (go for a recognized brand like Angora) reasonably priced. *Meze* include *mücver*, courgette fritters, here served in garlicky yoghurt. Traditional Anatolian dishes are the real pull, though, usually lamb or chicken based – try the lamb casserole with figs and almonds. Mains around ₺25. Licensed.

AMEDROS

Hoca Rüstem Paşa Sok 7 Ⓣ1 Sultanahmet
☎ 0212 522 8356. Daily 11am–1am.
MAP P.34–35, POCKET MAP G11

Tucked-away up a pedestrian alleyway off Divan Yolu, this professionally run place successfully combines local and international cuisine. The subtly lit interior is effortlessly stylish, all bare-boards and neutral walls, though in summer the most popular tables are those out on the alleyway. The mixed-*meze* plate is very popular, with seven types of Turkish starter. Mains (₺20 and up) include traditional dishes such as Ottoman chicken, served in a sweet-sour sauce with rice. Licensed. Reservations advised.

BALIKÇI SABAHATTİN

Seyit Hasan Kuyu Sok 1 Ⓣ1 Sultanahmet or Ⓑ1 Cankurtaran ☎ 0212 458 1824.
Daily 11am–1am. MAP P.34–35, POCKET MAP J12

BALIKÇI SABAHATTIN

Unpromisingly located – or set in a charmingly dilapidated area of town down by the defunct railway line – whatever your view it can't be denied that this is the only Sultanahmet-area restaurant to draw monied locals from elsewhere in the city. The attraction here is freshly caught and cooked fish – from bluefish to sea bass, swordfish to red mullet – enjoyed in winter in an atmospheric old wooden house or, in summer, on tables set out front on a vine-shaded cobbled area. It's expensive, with mains ₺30–70, but you are paying to eat alongside İstanbul's elite. Licensed. Reservations advised.

DOY DOY

Sifa Hama Sok 13 Ⓣ1 Sultanahmet
☎ 0212 517 1588. Daily 8am–11pm.
MAP P.34–35, POCKET MAP G12

This four-storey restaurant serves local workers and the more impecunious visitor, concentrating on hearty portions of Turkish standards. There's *pide* (Turkish pizza, big ovals of semi-leavened *pide* bread topped by cheese or meat), plenty of kebabs, classic soups such as *mercimek çorbası* (lentil soup) and, definitely best at lunchtime, *sulu yemek* (various stews served-up from steamtrays). Mains from ₺11. Unlicensed.

DUBB

Incili Çavuş Sok Ⓣ1 Sultanahmet ⓣ0212 513 7308. Daily noon–midnight. MAP P.34–35, POCKET MAP H11

Indian restaurants are as rare as hens' teeth in İstanbul, so to find one so good in Sultanahmet is quite something. There a few tables set out on the quiet street, otherwise dining is in a series of small rooms spread over four floors or, with fantastic views, a roof terrace. Tandoori dishes are the speciality, though there are thalis and fish dishes. Licensed. Reservations advised.

GİRİTLİ

GİRİTLİ

Kerestici Hakkı Sok Ⓣ1 Sultanahmet or Ⓑ1 Cankurtaran ⓣ0212 458 2270. Daily noon–midnight. MAP P.34–35, POCKET MAP H9

The main reason to come here, and it's a worthy one, is to enjoy a full-blown set menu for ₺125 which includes all (local) alcoholic drinks, over twenty mini-*meze*, three hot starters, a grilled fish main and fruit to follow. The food, based on traditional Cretan recipes, is very good quality and the dining room is in a period wooden house, with a shady garden just across the street for al fresco summer eating. This is a good place to try *rakı*, the traditional aniseed spirit, a wonderful accompaniment to fish. Reservations advised.

KHORASANİ

Ticarethane Sok 39/41 Ⓣ1 Sultanahmet ⓣ0212 519 5959. Daily noon–1am. MAP P.34–35, POCKET MAP G11

Especially for visitors reluctant to stray far from the heart of the old city, *Khorasani* makes a great place to try the distinctive cuisine of southeast Turkey – generally hotter, sourer and spicier than standard Turkish fare. Typical is *muhamara* (Arabic), a spicy dip blended together from bread, olive oil, walnuts and hot pepper, delicious with the unleavened bread *lavaş*. The kebabs, grilled barbecue-style over charcoal, are excellent – try the pistachio-studded version for ₺34. There are outside tables on the pedestrianized street, and an elegant split-level interior. Licensed. Reservations advised.

MATBAH

Caferiye Sok 6/1 Ⓣ1 Sultanahmet ⓣ0212 514 6151. Daily 11am–midnight. MAP P.34–35, POCKET MAP H11

This concept restaurant, attached to the *Ottoman Imperial Hotel*, bases all its dishes on those once prepared in the kitchens of the Topkapı Palace. Ottoman cuisine, much richer than standard contemporary Turkish cooking, used fruit in many recipes. Try *kavun dolması*, melon stuffed with lamb and pilaf rice, or *mahmudiye*, tender cinnamon-flavoured chicken served with almonds and apricots. White-clothed tables are laid out on a plant-decked terrace overlooking the leaded domes of the Cafer Ağa Theological School. Mains around ₺40. Licensed. Reservations advised.

Bars

ARCADIA BLUE TERRACE

Dr Imran Oktem Cad 1 Ⓣ1 Sultanahmet
Ⓣ 0212 516 6118. Daily 10am-midnight.
MAP P.34–35, POCKET MAP G11

Opened in 2013 after a long period of restoration, this hotel roof bar gives one of the best vantage points in the city. To the southeast the Sea of Marmara glimmers behind the Hippodrome and Blue Mosque, straight ahead the Haghia Sophia and grounds of the Topkapı Palace are backed by distant Asia, to the northeast stretches the thin ribbon of the Bosphorus. It all looks particularly appealing, conveniently enough for those in need of a drink at the end of a day's exploration, as the sun goes down. A 50cl beer is ₺18.

COZY PUB

Divan Yolu Cad 66 Ⓣ1 Sultanahmet
Ⓣ 0212 520 0990. Daily 10am–2am.
MAP P.34–35, POCKET MAP G11

Probably the most atmospheric bar in Sultanahmet, with a pub-like dark wood interior and plenty of tables in the narrow alley disgorging onto Divan Yolu. The beers are a tad more expensive than usual but worth it for the ambience. It also does quite reasonable international/Turkish food, including usual suspects like pasta, burgers and salads.

JUST BAR

Akbıyık Cad 26 Ⓣ 0532 387 5729. Daily 10am–2pm. MAP P.34–35, POCKET MAP H12

This lively bar is very popular with guests from the myriad hotels and hostels in this popular neighbourhood. There's a small seating area fronting the busy street, perfect for people-watching on warm evenings, inside the tables are cleared to make a small dance floor on weekend nights. Beers ₺10.

PIERRE LOTİ ROOF-BAR

Piyer Loti Cad 5 Ⓣ1 Sultanahmet
Ⓣ 0212 518 5700. Daily 11am–midnight.
MAP P.34–35, POCKET MAP G8

Hotel bars seldom drip character and this place, though smart, is no exception. But the vistas over İstanbul's exotic skyline are fabulous – best enjoyed at sunset. It's quite dear, but your drink comes accompanied by a bowl of quality *çerez* (salted Turkish nibbles that usually include roasted chickpeas, peanuts, almonds and pistachios).

PIERRE LOTI ROOF-BAR

Topkapı Palace to the Golden Horn

Superbly located on the first of the old city's seven hills, right at the snout of the peninsula pointing up the continent-dividing Bosphorus strait, the Topkapı Palace was the nerve centre of the powerful Ottoman Empire. This sprawling, walled compound encompasses not only the courtyards and pavilions of the palace itself but also İstanbul's excellent Archeology Museum, an important Byzantine church and Gülhane Park, the only major green and open space in the congested old city. Following the busy tramline downhill to the northwest, you come to the more workaday business district of Sirkeci, best known to visitors for its late nineteenth-century station, once the easternmost terminus of the famous Orient Express. Beyond it, fronting the ferry-filled waters of the Golden Horn, is mega-bustling Eminönü, with its fragrant, Ottoman-era Spice Bazaar.

SCULPTURE, ARCHEOLOGY MUSEUM

ARCHEOLOGY MUSEUM
ARKEOLOJİ MÜZESİ

Osman Hamdi Bey Yokuşu Ⓣ1 Gülhane
Ⓣ0212 520 7740, Ⓦistanbularkeoloji.gov.tr.
Tues–Sun: April–Oct 9am–7pm; Nov–March 9am–5pm. ₺15, audio-guides ₺10.
MAP P.52–53, POCKET MAP H7

Reached either from the first court of the Topkapı Palace or via the main entrance to Gülhane Park, this fascinating but often overlooked museum comprises three separate sections, each housed in a historic building. The first, on your left as you enter, is the small **Museum of the Ancient Orient**, built in 1883. Pick of the exhibits is a clay tablet inscribed in cuneiform, copied from a silver original, marking a treaty signed between the Hittites and Egyptians after a major battle in 1269 BC. The world's first known peace treaty, a copy is housed in the UN headquarters in New York. The blue and yellow glazed bricks decorated with animals in raised relief, dating to the reign of Nebuchadnezzar (604–562 BC), once formed a frieze lining the processional way to Babylon's Ishtar Gate. The monumental Neoclassical-style building on the right as you head into the grounds was built by French architect Vallaury in 1891. This is the main building of the **Archeology Museum** complex, and contains a stunning range of artefacts ranging from the Paleolithic to the Ottoman periods. Unmissable, on the ground floor, are the **Sidon Sarcophagi**, discovered in what is today Lebanon in the late nineteenth century. The relief-carving on the surfaces of the Alexander, Lycian and Mourning Women sarcophagi is quite superb. Also on the ground floor is a comprehensive display of marble statuary from the Archaic to Roman periods. Upstairs the excellent **İstanbul through the Ages** exhibition is a compulsory introduction to the city's complex history, and includes oddities like a bronze snake-head from the Serpentine Column in the Hippodrome (see p.42) and a section of the chain stretched across the Golden Horn in Byzantine times to prevent enemy shipping entering. Also worth seeking out are the **Byzantine collection** in the semi-basement and the **Anatolia and Troy through the Ages** exhibition on the second floor. Opposite the main building is the third museum in the complex, the **Museum of Turkish Ceramics**. Built in the fifteenth century as part of the Topkapı Palace complex and known as the Çinili Köşk or Tiled Pavilion, it houses a vibrant display of Turkish tiles and other ceramic ware.

HAGHIA EIRENE
AYA İRENİ

Wed-Mon 9am-4pm. ₺20. MAP P.52–53, POCKET MAP H7

The predominantly brick-built Haghia Eirene or "Church of the Holy Peace", is tucked away in the northwest corner of the first court of the Topkapı Palace. One of the earliest churches in Constantinople, it burned down in the same 532 riot that destroyed the second incarnation of the Haghia Sophia (see p.36) and was rebuilt in its current form soon after. It is rectangular in shape and topped by a relatively small dome surmounted on a drum. Inside, the most prominent features are the simple black on gold mosaic cross in the apse and, below it, a curved seating area for the clergy, the synthronon.

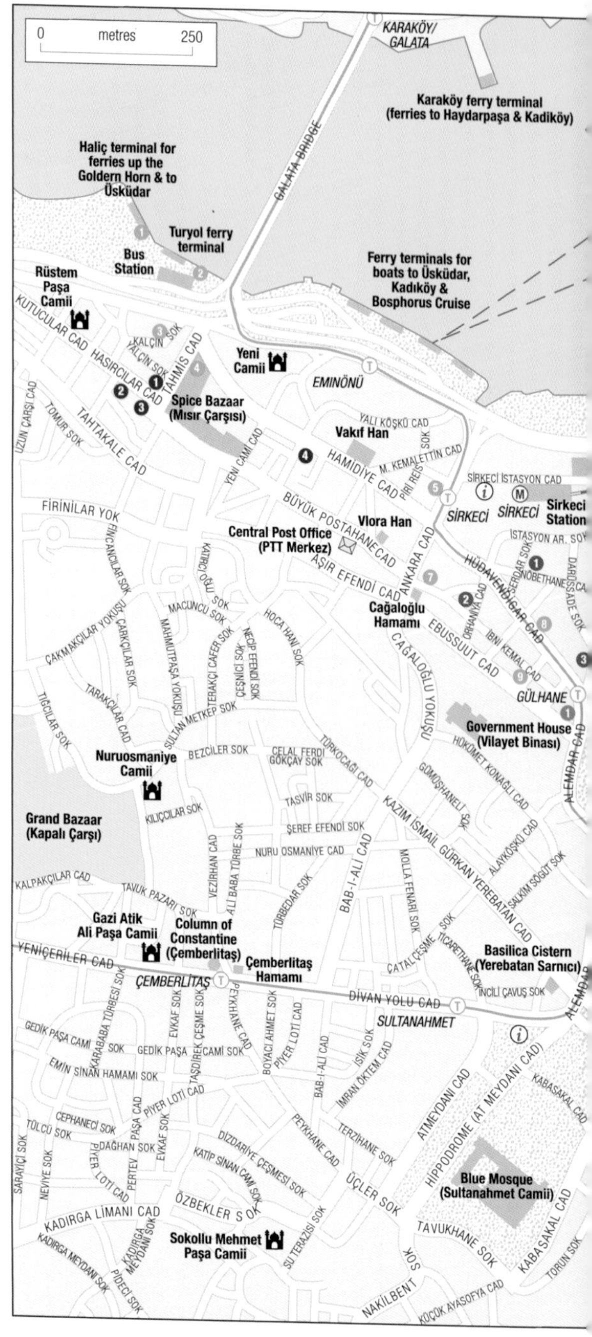
0 metres 250
KARAKÖY/ GALATA
Karaköy ferry terminal (ferries to Haydarpaşa & Kadiköy)
Haliç terminal for ferries up the Goldern Horn & to Üsküdar
GALATA BRIDGE
Turyol ferry terminal
Bus Station
Rüstem Paşa Camii
Ferry terminals for boats to Üsküdar, Kadıköy & Bosphorus Cruise
KUTUCULAR CAD
KALÇIN SOK
YALÇIN SOK
HASIRCILAR CAD
TAHMIS CAD
Yeni Camii
EMINÖNÜ
Spice Bazaar (Mısır Çarşısı)
UZUN ÇARŞI CAD
TOMUR SOK
TAHTAKALE CAD
YENI CAMI CAD
YALI KÖŞKÜ CAD
Vakıf Han
HAMIDIYE CAD
M. KEMALETTIN CAD
PIRI REIS
SIRKECI İSTASYON CAD
SIRKECI
Sirkeci Station
FIRINILAR YOK
BÜYÜK POSTAHANE CAD
Vlora Han
Central Post Office (PTT Merkez)
AŞIR EFENDI CAD
ANKARA CAD
İSTASYON AR. SOK
HÜDAVENDIGAR CAD
NÖBETHANE
SERDAR SOK
FINCANCILAR SOK
KATIRCI OĞLU SOK
MACUNCU SOK
HOCA HANI SOK
Cağaloğlu Hamamı
EBUSSUUT CAD
ORHANIYE CAD
IBNI KEMAL CAD
ÇAKMAKÇILAR YOKUŞU
ÇARKÇILAR SOK
MAHMUTPAŞA YOKUŞU
TERAKÇI CAFER SOK
ÇEŞNICI SOK
NECIP EFENDI SOK
CAĞALOĞLU YOKUŞU
GÜLHANE
TIĞCILAR SOK
TARAKÇILAR CAD
SULTAN METKEP SOK
Government House (Vilayet Binası)
HÜKÜMET KONAĞLI CAD
ALEMDAR CAD
Nuruosmaniye Camii
BEZCILER SOK
CELAL FERDI GÖKÇAY SOK
TÜRKOCAĞI CAD
GÜMÜŞHANELI SOK
TASVIR SOK
KAZIM ISMAIL GÜRKAN YEREBATAN CAD
Grand Bazaar (Kapalı Çarşı)
KILIÇCILAR SOK
ŞEREF EFENDI SOK
NURU OSMANIYE CAD
VEZIRHAN CAD
ALI BABA TÜRBE SOK
BAB-I-ALI CAD
MOLLA FENARI SOK
ALAYKÖŞKÜ CAD
SALKIM SÖĞÜT SOK
KALPAKÇILAR CAD
TAVUK PAZARI SOK
TÜRBEDAR SOK
Gazi Atik Ali Paşa Camii
Column of Constantine (Çemberlitaş)
Çemberlitaş Hamamı
ÇATALÇEŞME SOK
TICARETHANE SOK
Basilica Cistern (Yerebatan Sarnıcı)
YENIÇERILER CAD
ÇEMBERLITAŞ
INCILI ÇAVUŞ SOK
DIVAN YOLU CAD
SULTANAHMET
KARABABA TÜRBESI SOK
EVKAF SOK
TAŞDIREK ÇEŞME SOK
PEYKHANE CAD
BOYACI AHMET SOK
PIYER LOTI CAD
GEDIK PAŞA CAMI SOK
GEDIK PAŞA
CAMI SOK
IŞIK SOK
IMRAN ÖKTEM CAD
ATMEYDANI CAD
HIPPODROME (AT MEYDANI CAD)
KABASAKAL CAD
EMIN SINAN HAMAMI SOK
CEPHANECI SOK
TÜLCÜ SOK
PAŞA CAD
DAĞHAN SOK
DIZDARIYE ÇEŞMESI SOK
KATIP SINAN CAMI SOK
TERZIHANE SOK
SARAYIÇI SOK
NEVIYE SOK
PERTEV
PIYER LOTI CAD
ÜÇLER SOK
Blue Mosque (Sultanahmet Camii)
KADIRGA LIMANI CAD
ÖZBEKLER SOK
SU TERAZISI SOK
TAVUKHANE SOK
KADIRGA MEYDANI SOK
Sokollu Mehmet Paşa Camii
PIDECI SOK
NAKILBENT SOK
KÜÇÜK AYASOFYA CAD
TORUN SOK

Topkapı Palace to the Golden Horn

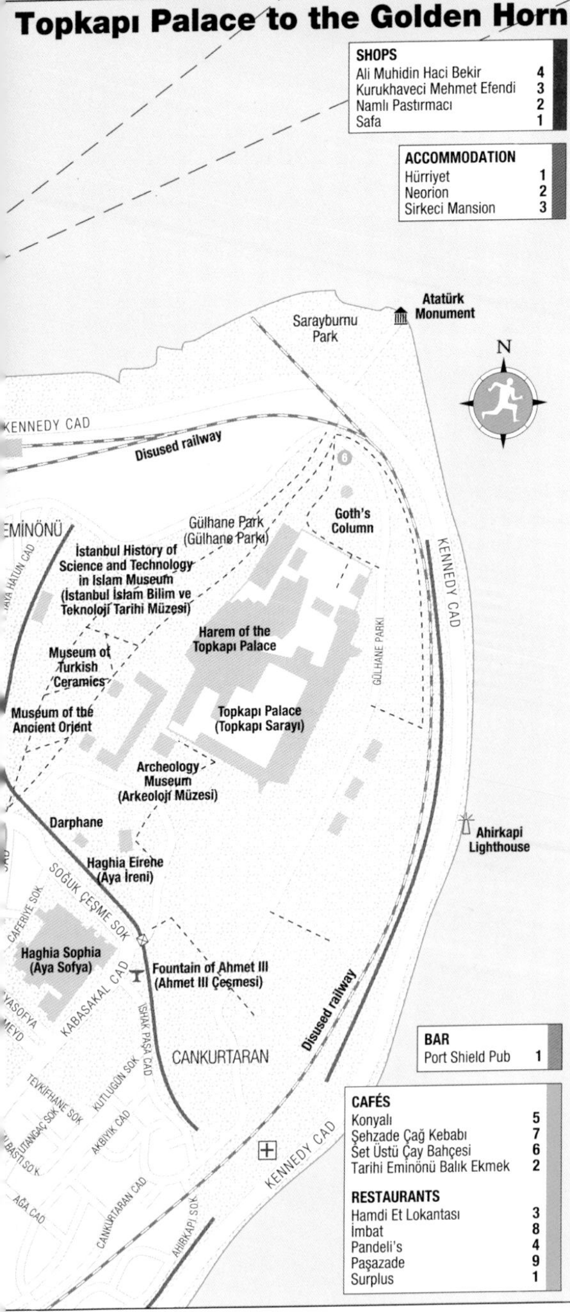

TOPKAPI PALACE
TOPKAPI SARAYI

Topkapı Sarayı Müzesi Ⓣ1 Sultanahmet ⓣ0212 512 0480, Ⓦtopkapisarayi.gov.tr. Daily except Tues: April–Oct 9am–7pm; Nov–March 9am–5pm. ₺30, audio-guides ₺10. MAP P.52–53, POCKET MAP J7

Completed in 1465, this palace complex, a collection of buildings ranged around four large courtyards, was the administrative and political heart of the Ottoman Empire until 1853, when the sultan decamped to the European-style Dolmabahçe Palace across the Golden Horn. Along with neighbours the Haghia Sophia and Blue Mosque, it's the most visited sight in İstanbul. Enter the **first court** (free admission) by the Bab-ı-Hümayün, a gateway piercing the defensive wall which separated the palace from the city. This area was home to the bakeries and imperial mint. The ticket office for the remainder of the courts is in the wall to the right of the Bab-ı Selam or **Gate of Salutations**, with its fairy-tale-like conical turrets. Inside the gate are a couple of models of the palace complex, useful for orientation. The **second court** is flanked to the right by the kitchens, to the left are the Privy Stables and the Divan. The latter, beautifully decorated in sixteenth-century Ottoman style, was the council chamber where the chief officials (viziers) met to discuss matters of state, secretly watched from a grilled window in the wall behind by the sultan. Next door, the inner treasury is now the **Armoury Museum**. Court ceremonies were presided over, and military campaigns launched, by the sultan seated in his throne in front of the Bab-üs Saadet or **Gate of**

Topkapı Palace

1 Ortakapı or Middle Gate
2 Kitchens and Cooks' Quarters
3 Stables and Harness Rooms
4 Barrack of the Halberdiers of the Long Tresses
5 Hall of the Divan
6 Offices of the Divan
7 Inner Treasury
8 Gate of Felicity (Bab-üs Saadet)
9 Throne Room
10 Library of Sultanahmet III
11 Rooms of the Relics of the Prophet
12 Imperial Treasury (Pavilion of Mehmet II)
13 Hall of the Expeditionary Force
14 Circumcision Köşkü
15 Baghdad Köşkü
16 Revan Köşkü
17 Tulip Gardens of Ahmet III
18 Mustafa Paşa Köşkü
19 Mecidiye Köşkü
20 Entry to the Harem (Carriage Gate)
21 Aviary Gate (Kuşhane Kapisi)
22 Valide Sultan's Court
23 Valide Sultan's Dining Room
24 Valide Sultan's Bedroom
25 Golden Road
26 Ahmet III Dining Room

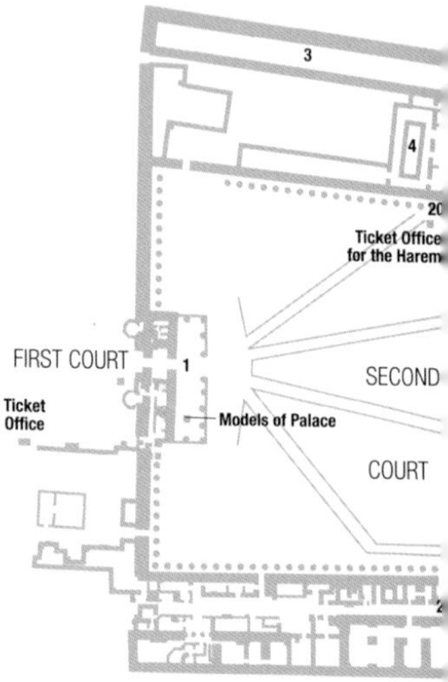

Felicity. Beyond this, the **third court** was the nerve centre of the Ottoman-era palace as it contained both the Palace School, which trained the empire's officials, as well as the **Throne Room** where decisions taken in the Divan were sealed by the sultan. Behind the Throne Room is the pretty **Library of Sultanahmet III**. The **Rooms of the Relics of the Prophet** in the northwest corner of the court contain the mantle and standard of the Prophet Mohammed, among many other holy relics, while **the Imperial Treasury** to the right is now home to treasures amassed by the sultans over the centuries, including the famed Topkapı Dagger and Spoonmaker's Diamond. The **Hall of the Expeditionary Force**, in the same row as the treasury, contains some splendid costumes worn by various sultans. The fourth court was devoted to leisure, comprising a series of **pavilions** set in pretty gardens, including the Baghdad, Revan and Circumcision pavilions. A fourth, the Mecidiye, houses the expensive *Konyalı cafe & Restaurant*, with its fine views across the Bosphorus to Asia.

CIRCUMCISION ROOM, TOPKAPI PALACE

HAREM OF THE TOPKAPI PALACE

Topkapı Palace, second court
Ⓣ1 Sultanahmet. Daily except Tues: April–Oct 9am–5pm; Nov–March 9am–4pm. ₺15. MAP P.52–53, POCKET MAP H6

Owing to its location within the grounds of the Topkapı Palace's second court, you can't visit the **women's quarters** or Harem (literally meaning "forbidden" in Arabic) without first paying to enter the palace itself. The Harem was a suite of rooms within the palace complex, over four hundred of them, where the sultan's wives, female slaves (concubines) and children resided. It also contained the quarters of the Black Eunuchs who guarded them, and the private quarters of the sultan. Largely constructed during the reign of Murat III in the late sixteenth century, the Harem is thus a century or so more recent than the Topkapı Palace. The ticket office is by the distinctive Divan Tower, entry through the **Carriage Gate**, so called because this is where the concubines mounted carriages for trips out. Leading right through the maze-like complex, from its entrance in the second court to its exit in the third, is a cobbled path known as the Golden Way, purportedly named after a new sultan's habit of throwing gold coins to his concubines. The first important suite of rooms are those of the **Valide Sultan** (the sultan's mother), ranged around a spacious courtyard. North of here are the apartments and reception rooms of the sultan himself. Largest of these is the **Imperial Hall**, lush with Baroque gilt and İznik tiles, where the sultan entertained visitors. More beautiful though is **Murat III's Salon**, designed by Sinan in 1578 and boasting a stunning bronze fireplace and walls gleaming with finest-period İznik tiles. The small, domed **Library of Ahmet I** (1608–09) is exquisite, as is the **dining room of Ahmet III**, probably so called because of the bowls of fruit painted on the wood-panelled walls. The notorious Cage, where the sultan's brothers were confined to avoid squabbles between potential successors to the throne, were probably located in rooms on the first floor, closed to visitors. Exit the complex through the **Aviary Gate**.

GÜLHANE PARK
GÜLHANE PARKI

Alemdar Cad Ⓣ1 Gülhane. MAP P.52–53, POCKET MAP H6, H7, J6, J7

Once the extended gardens of the Topkapı Palace, today Gülhane Park makes a great place to escape the tourist bustle of the big-hitter sights on the crown of the hill above. A few pieces of distinctly average play equipment for young kids aside, there's little to do except unwind, though it's worth strolling down to the **Goth's Column** in the northeast of the park, not far from the tip of the peninsula at Saray Burnu (Palace Point). Built to commemorate a third- or fourth-century victory over said Goths, it is over 18m high and

GÜLHANE PARK

İznik tiles

Both the Topkapı Palace and its Harem gleam with them, as does the Rüstem Paşa Camii, the Sokullu Mehmet Paşa Camii and scores of Ottoman-era buildings across the city. The Blue Mosque even derives its "English" name from the predominantly blue İznik tiles sheathing its interior. Production began in İznik (ancient Nicea) on the south shores of the Sea of Marmara in the fifteenth century and soon these tiles, inspired by Persian designs and made mostly from quartz rather than clay, became all the rage. So much so that by the sixteenth century there were over three hundred kilns churning out top-quality tiles (and other ceramics) often decorated with blue stylized flowers or geometric shapes on a white ground, enlivened by splashes of vivid red. Quality and output peaked in the late sixteenth and early seventeenth centuries. After a long period of decline, studio-potters based in İznik have revived the art.

topped by a large, intricately carved Corinthian capital. Nearby is *Set Üstü Çay Bahçesi* (see p.64), a decent tea garden with great views up the Bosphorus and across to Asia.

İSTANBUL HISTORY OF SCIENCE AND TECHNOLOGY IN ISLAM MUSEUM *İSTANBUL İSLAM BİLİM VE TEKNOLOJİ TARİHİ MÜZESİ*

Gülhane Parkı Ⓣ1 Gülhane. Daily except Tues 9am–5pm. ₺10. MAP P.52–53, POCKET MAP H6

Showcasing the invaluable contribution made to civilization by scientists and inventors from the Islamic world between the eighth and sixteenth centuries, this fine museum is housed in what were the imperial stables, built into the inside of the walls encircling Gülhane Park. If you're looking for genuine artefacts, be prepared to be disappointed, as all the exhibits are meticulous models made at Johann Wolfgang von Goethe University, Frankfurt. The replicas are extremely impressive, however, and are beautifully displayed artworks in their own right, not least an elephant-shaped water clock based on a twelfth-century original and a planetarium based on an idea by tenth-century astronomer as-Siğzi.

ISTANBUL HISTORY OF SCIENCE AND TECHNOLOGY IN ISLAM MUSEUM

CAĞALOĞLU HAMAMI

Kazım İsmail Gürkan Cad 34 Ⓣ1 Sultanahmet Ⓣ 0212 52 2424, Ⓦ cagalogluhamami.com.tr. Daily: men 8am–10pm; women 8am–8.30pm. Baths from ₺30. MAP P.52–53, POCKET MAP G6

Some 400m north of Divan Yolu, these Turkish baths are probably the most famous in the city, not least because *Indiana Jones and the Temple of Doom* included a scene shot in this *hamam*, and luminaries as varied as Florence Nightingale and John Travolta are reputed to have bathed here. Built in 1741 during the reign of Sultan Mahmut I in Ottoman Baroque style, profits were used to fund the sultan's library in the Aya Sofya Camii. In an era when only the very richest citizens had private baths, baths such as these were essential for both cleanliness and hygiene and not, as they are today, merely an (admittedly thoroughly pleasurable) afterthought to a day's sightseeing. Bathers begin in the *camekan*, the largest room in the bath-house, surmounted by a large dome, where there are changing rooms and areas to relax with tea or other refreshments. Beyond the small *soğukluk* or cold room is the main event, the *hararet* or steam room, presided over by a large dome supported by a circle of columns, which diffuses soft light through the tiny, round glass windows studding it. The bath-house comprises two sections, with separate entrances and bathing rooms for men and women.

CAĞALOĞLU HAMAMI

ALEMDAR STREET
ALEMDAR CADDESİ

Ⓣ1 Gülhane. MAP P.52–53, POCKET MAP H7

The lower part of this street, from where it curves around past the main entrance to Gülhane Park, has a few points of interest up and down it when crossing. The first, actually just above the park entrance, is the **Zeynep Sultan Camii**. At first sight this attractive building looks very much like a Byzantine church, with its contrasting bands of brick and pale-coloured stone and scallop-edged dome. It is in fact a mosque, built in 1769 by Zeynep, daughter of Sultan Ahmet III. Not far below it is a small, domed and extremely pretty **marble kiosk** (*büfe* in Turkish) selling cigarettes, gum, tissues and the like. In the Ottoman period this was a *sebil*, from which free water was handed out to passers-by. These *sebil*s were dotted throughout the city, donated by wealthy citizens who hoped to secure their place in paradise through their good deeds. A short way down the street is a grand gateway on the left, notable for its sinuous, Baroque-style overhanging roof – the **Bab-ı Ali** – remodelled in 1843. From the mid-eighteenth century

SIRKECI STATION

onwards, this gate led to the personal quarters and offices of the grand vizier, the chief official of the Ottoman Empire, where most state business was handled – an institution which became known to the West as the Sublime Porte. Opposite is the **Alay Köşk**, built into the line of walls now surrounding the park but which were originally the outer fortifications of the Topkapı Palace, built in 1465 by Mehmet the Conqueror. Beautifully restored in 2011, this polygonal structure allowed suspicious sultans to observe the comings and goings of the Sublime Porte opposite. The more trusting used it to review the great processions held in the city, such as that of the Guilds, involving virtually every tradesman in the city and held every fifty years or so. Deli İbrahim, or İbrahim the Mad (1640–48), is reputed to have shot passers-by with a crossbow from this eyrie. Access is from inside the park, with a sloping ramp allowing the sultan to enter without dismounting.

SİRKECİ STATION

Ankara Cad Ⓣ1 Sirkeci. MAP P.52–53, POCKET MAP G6

The eastern terminus of the fabled Orient Express, which first pulled-up here in 1888 after its 2900km journey from Paris via Vienna, Sirkeci station has withstood the vicissitudes of time remarkably well. Intact are its clock towers, Moorish arches and Parisian-style domed roof, a surprisingly successful architectural hotchpotch of Neoclassical and Islamic architecture, designed by the Prussian architect August Jachmund. Many distinguished visitors once arrived at Sirkeci station from Europe, including King Boris III of Bulgaria and Agatha Christie, the latter immortalizing the service in *Murder on the Orient Express*. Today, the station serves neither kings nor famous authors, or indeed overground trains. But inside this iconic station building is the Sirkeci stop on the Marmaray metro line (see p.156) which connects Europe to Asia via the Bosphorus tunnel. There's also a small museum (Tues-Sun 9am-5pm; free) for rail buffs (see p.156).

CENTRAL SİRKECİ

Sirkeci Merkez Ⓣ1 Sirkeci. MAP P.52–53, POCKET MAP G6

The heart of this bustling commercial district, centred on two major streets, Büyük Postane Caddesi and Hamidiye Caddesi, offers some early twentieth-century delights. Built in 1909 and easiest to find is the monumental **PTT Merkez** or **Central Post Office** on Büyük Postane Caddesi. It was designed by Paris-trained Turk Vedat Tak, an exponent of the First National Architectural Movement, which sought to blend Ottoman and western styles to produce original buildings representative of the rapidly modernizing empire. With its imposing stone facade combining Ottoman elements such as İznik tiles with Neoclassical Corinthian pilasters, it certainly succeeds. The inside of the building, with its glazed roof and period fittings, is worth a look even if you're not buying stamps. Diagonally opposite the PTT Merkez is an overtly European-style import, the **Vlora Han**, today a run-down office-block which nonetheless still impresses with its curved facade, panels of stylized roses in raised-relief plasterwork and whiplash wrought-iron balcony rails. Far more austere is the **Vakıf Han** on Hamidiye Caddesi. Built as a seven-storey office block to a design by another principal exponent of the First National Architectural Movement, Kemaleddin Bey, its severe stone facade, leavened by Ottoman-style domed turrets, conceals a steel skeleton.

SPICE BAZAAR

SPICE BAZAAR *MISIR ÇARŞISI*

Cami Meydanı Ⓣ1 Eminönü. Mon–Sat 9am–7pm. MAP P.52–53, POCKET MAP F6

Close to the waterfront in Eminönü, more or less opposite the Galata Bridge, the Spice Bazaar (*Mısır Çarşısı*) was built as part of the Yeni Camii complex, the revenues raised from it used to fund the running of the mosque and its associated philanthropic institutions. The L-shaped building is typically Ottoman in style, with 88 vaulted chambers and more rooms above, usually entered by a monumental gateway at the northeast corner. The origins of its name are uncertain. *Mısır* in Turkish can mean either corn or Egypt, and it's possible this name derives either from the fact that in the Byzantine period the area was the centre of corn trading or that many of the spices imported into İstanbul came from Egypt. Today, the bazaar still sells myriad spices, usually attractively piled in mounds of contrasting colours (and smells) outside the hole-in-the-wall cells inside, alongside other tempting goodies like Turkish delight and pistachio nuts. Prices are high, however, as this is the most popular market in the city after the Grand Bazaar so look, as the locals do, in the surrounding streets for cheaper buys.

AROUND THE SPICE BAZAAR

Ⓣ1 Eminönü MAP P.52–53, POCKET MAP F6

Keen shoppers should peruse **Tahmis Caddesi**, a row of stalls lining the western wall of the bazaar selling a huge variety of traditional Turkish cheeses, olives, nuts and spices as well as cured meats. There's more of the same on narrow **Hasırcılar Caddesi** (Street of the Strawmakers) running northwest of the bazaar. On the corner of Tahmis and Hasırcılar *caddesi*s is the ever-busy coffee emporium *Kurukhaveci Mehmet Efendi* (see p.63), in one of İstanbul's few Art Deco buildings.

On the east side of the Spice Bazaar is a fascinating market, the **garden and pet bazaar**, which sells everything from caged goldfinches to chicks dyed the colours of one of the city's big football teams (buy a yellow chick and a red one for Galatasaray, a yellow and a blue for Fenerbahçe). You might even spot a leech or two wriggling in a jar.

YENİ CAMİ

Yeni Cami Cad Ⓣ1 Eminönü. MAP P.52–53, POCKET MAP G6

The domes and minarets of the "New Mosque" soon become a familiar landmark to visitors heading up or across the Bosphorus, or trundling over the Galata Bridge to Galata/Beyoğlu on the north side of the Golden Horn, and the steps outside it are invariably busy, not least with purveyors of seed to feed the thousands of pigeons that flock into the square in front of it. This was the last of the imperial mosques to be built in the city, hence its name, and although construction began in 1597, it wasn't completed until 1663. Like its predecessors, it was part of a complex to provide for the needs of the local community, comprising a hospital, soup kitchen, baths and fountains and, of course, the Spice Bazaar. Designed by an apprentice of the Ottoman Empire's master architect Sinan, the mosque follows convention, with the faithful first entering a large courtyard centred on a ritual ablutions fountain and surrounded on three sides by porticoes. The prayer hall, fronted by a raised platform covered by a portico for late comers or when the interior is packed, is cruciform in plan, the central dome flanked by four semi-domes.

YENİ CAMİ

GALATA BRIDGE

Eminönü Ⓣ1 Eminönü or Karaköy. MAP P.52–53, POCKET MAP F5

The entire Eminönü waterfront heaves with humanity; kindly souls feeding pigeons in the square, the faithful heading to prayers in the Yeni Cami, commuters rushing to catch a ferry home to Asia having elbowed their way to the best buys in the packed, narrow alleys around the Spice Bazaar, vendors flogging knock-off wares in one of the underpasses and hungry visitors munching on cut-price fish sandwiches on the quay. So it's little surprise that the **Galata Bridge**, while far from being the most elegant or historic bridge in the world, is one of its busiest and most vibrant, accommodating as it does the overspill from the congested waterfront area. The lower deck is lined with cafés and restaurants, while the upper deck teems with anglers and itinerants peddling fake Adidas socks and gimcrack watches, shouting to be heard above the roar of trucks and rumble of the tram. The first bridge, built of wood in 1845, was some 500m long and symbolically linked the Muslim-dominated old city with the Christianized European quarters of Galata and Pera (Beyoğlu). Today's steel version dates back to the 1980s, and the central section can be hoisted to allow big ships access to the Golden Horn.

GALATA BRIDGE

RÜSTEM PAŞA CAMİİ

Hasırcılar Çarşısı Ⓣ1 Eminönü. MAP P.52–53, POCKET MAP F5

Dating back to 1561, internally this is one of the most attractive mosques in the whole of İstanbul. Another Sinan masterpiece, it is cleverly constructed on a raised terrace above the level of the alleys below. Built for Rüstem Paşa, the grand vizier of Süleyman the Magnificent in 1561, the mosque is reached by steps leading through a passageway to the terrace, which is dominated by an unusual double portico. The entrance for visitors is through a side-door to the left of the building. Essentially a simple dome supported by four large piers, its real wonder is the finest-period İznik tiles covering virtually every available surface. As usual, predominantly blue on a white ground, many of these tiles are embellished by the addition of vivid red, slightly raised-relief details. As this colour was very tricky for the craftsman to achieve, they represent the high-point of İznik tile production.

Shops

ALİ MUHİDİN HACI BEKİR

Hamidiye Cad 83 Ⓣ1 Eminönü. Mon–Sat 9am–7pm, Sun 9am–9pm. MAP P.52–53, POCKET MAP G6

This is not the cheapest place to buy traditional *lokum* (Turkish delight) but it is one of the best. Established way back in 1717, this charming shop stocks twenty-plus flavours of the sticky stuff, all colourfully displayed in a shop interior lined with old-fashioned wood shelves and glass-fronted cabinets. There's much more than *lokum* here too, including traditional boiled sweets, hazlenut-paste goodies and sugared almonds.

KURUKHAVECİ MEHMET EFENDİ

Tahmis Sok 66 Ⓣ1 Eminönü. Mon–Sat 9am–7pm. MAP P.52–53, POCKET MAP F5

An İstanbul institution, this is the place to come if you want to buy coffee roasted and ground the way it should be to make both genuine Turkish and filter coffee. The queues of locals from across the city attest to its quality. This Art Deco period gem of a shop also sells *sahlep*, a powdered-orchid-root-based beverage popular in İstanbul's cold winters.

NAMLI PASTIRMACI

Hasırcılar Cad 14 Ⓣ1 Eminönü. Mon–Sat 8.30am–8pm. MAP P.52–53, POCKET MAP F5

One of the best delicatessens in the city, established in 1929, it sells a very wide range of cheeeses from across the country (and some imported), a cornucopia of cured meats, including garlicky *pastırma* (a form of pastrami) and *sucuk* (a spicy-sausage ring traditionally sliced and cooked up with eggs), as well as more prosaic items like olives, olive oil and pickles.

KURUKHAVECİ MEHMET EFENDİ

SAFA

Hasırcılar Cad 10 Ⓣ1 Eminönü. Daily 9am–7pm. MAP P.52–53, POCKET MAP F5

Not so famous as *Karaköy Güllüoğlu* across the Golden Horn and consequently considerably cheaper, this is a great place to stock up on walnut-filled *baklava* or *fıstık sarması*, rolls of paper-thin filo pastry wrapped around a delicious pistachio filling. They also do more inexpensive favourites such as *tulumba*, a kind of corrugated donut roll soaked in syrup.

Cafés

KONYALI

Ankara Cad 5 Ⓣ1 Sirkeci ☎ 0212 527 1935. Mon–Sat 7am–8pm. MAP P.52–53, POCKET MAP G6

Opposite the entrance to Sirkeci station, this traditional *pastahane* has been supplying breakfasts, lunches and on-the-way-home snacks to local office-workers and traders for decades. The tea comes in tulip-shaped glasses and there's a wide range of bread-based delights to choose from, such as bagel-like sesame-seed-studded *simit* and lasagne-like *su böreği* (₺6 a portion), layers of boiled pastry filled with goat's cheese and parsley. Attached is the sister *Konyalı Lokantası*, a traditional Turkish restaurant dating back to 1897.

ŞEHZADE ÇAĞ KEBABI

Hocapaşa Sok 3/A Ⓣ1 Sirkeci ⓣ 0212 520 3361. Mon–Sat 11.30am–8pm. MAP P.52–53, POCKET MAP G6

An ideal lunch-time stop-off if you want to try an authentic kebab, Çağ Kebabı originates in the high steppe lands of Eastern Anatolia. Cooked on a horizontal spit, the tender slices of grilled meat are served as either a portion or in a dürüm (wrap) for ₺14.

SET ÜSTÜ ÇAY BAHÇESİ

Gülhane Parkı Ⓣ1 Gülhane ⓣ 0212 513 9610. Daily 9am–10pm. MAP P.52–53, POCKET MAP J6

This open-air café is rarely visited by tourists as it is hidden away in the northeast corner of Gülhane Park, near the Goth's Column. This is a shame as the tea here, brought to the table samovar-style, is delicious and the views across to Asia and up the Bosphorus lovely. It also does basic food including *köfte* (grilled meatballs) and toasted sandwiches (₺6).

TARİHİ EMİNÖNÜ BALIK EKMEK

Turyol İskele Yanı Ⓣ1 Eminönü. Daily 9am–10pm. MAP P.52–53, POCKET MAP F5

Set up right on the quay front just to the left of the entrance to the Galata Bridge, this simple café has combined tradition – it began across the Bosphorus in Asia in 1948 – with twenty-first-century business savvy, relocating to its present location in 2007 to take advantage of the huge numbers of visitors milling around the Eminönü waterfront. Enjoy a cheap fish sandwich served by staff in faux-Ottoman brocade-decorated attire.

TARİHİ EMİNÖNÜ BALIK EKMEK

Restaurants

HAMDİ ET LOKANTASI

Kalçın Sok 17 Ⓣ1 Eminönü ⓣ 0212 528 0390. Daily 11am–midnight. MAP P.52–53, POCKET MAP F5

Set back from the Eminönü waterfront, this traditional restaurant specializing in southeast Turkish food serves up some of the best kebabs (over twenty varieties of them) and accompaniments in the central part of the old city, and has quality *baklava* for dessert. Tables on the upper floors of this five-storey establishment have good views across the Galata Bridge and Golden Horn. It's expensive by kebab-joint standards (mains ₺23 and up) and some diners have reported off-hand service. Licensed.

İMBAT

Hudavendigar Cad 34 Ⓣ1 Gülhane ⓣ 0212 520 7161. Daily noon–1am. MAP P.52–53, POCKET MAP G6

Perched on the flower-pot-bedecked rooftop of the *Orient Express Hotel* and with lovely views across to the Haghia Sophia and Topkapı Palace, this well-regarded restaurant specializes in Aegean Turkish dishes, served up in a thoroughly professional manner. Meat and fish mains are invariably livened-up with aromatic herbs – try the *çökterme kebabı*, leg of lamb roasted with thyme and accompanied by a smoky aubergine mash and goat's cheese sauce. Licensed.

PANDELİ'S

Mısır Çarşısı 1, Eminönü Meydanı Ⓣ1 Eminönü Ⓣ 0212 527 3909. Mon–Sat 11.30am–7.30pm. MAP P.52–53, POCKET MAP F6

Tucked away on the upper floor of the Spice Bazaar above the main, Golden Horn-facing entrance, this period restaurant has been going for over seventy years. The food mixes average Turkish with traditional "specials" such as the sea bass cooked in paper (₺40) and is generally overpriced. But the blue and white İznik tiles sheathing the walls and the domed ceiling give it real atmosphere. Licensed.

PAŞAZADE

Sirkeci İbn-i Kemal Cad 13 Ⓣ1 Gülhane Ⓣ 0212 513 3757. Daily noon–1am. MAP P.52–53, POCKET MAP G17

A bewildering number of restaurants have opened up in the once quiet(ish) alleys here. *Paşazade* was one of the first and best, offering Ottoman-style Turkish dishes at moderate prices (mains from ₺20) in a ground-floor restaurant that spills out onto the street in summer. Service is good and alcohol a sensible price.

SURPLUS

Zindan Han, Ragıp Gümüş Pala Cad 54 Ⓣ1 Eminönü Ⓣ 0212 520 1002, Ⓦ surplus.com.tr. Daily noon–11pm. MAP P.52–53, POCKET MAP F5

Sophisticated eating places are very rare in the old city, so the

PANDELIS

opening of *Surplus* in 2014 was a real boon to the culinary scene. Set on the top floor of a prominent jewellery han overlooking the Galata Bridge, the views are superb – as is the food – Ottoman classics given a very contemporary twist. There's a good Turkish wine menu and mains from ₺45-66.

Bar

PORT SHIELD PUB

Ebussud Cad 2 Ⓣ1 Gülhane Ⓣ 0212 527 0931. Daily 10am–2am. MAP P.52–53, POCKET MAP H10

Perennially popular sports bar handily located opposite the Gülhane tramstop, this well-run establishment does its best to re-create the atmosphere of an English pub. Flyers advertising the upcoming sports events being shown on the big screens are plastered to the outside walls – everything from English football matches through rugby to cricket and American football. It also has a typical pub-grub menu.

Grand Bazaar District

This sprawling area of the old city contains one of İstanbul's best-known and most-visited buildings, the ever-busy Grand Bazaar, reputedly the largest covered historic bazaar in the world – and fifteenth-century forerunner of today's shopping mall. Its real jewel, however, stands in imposing grandeur on top of the third hill of the old city – the Süleymaniye, a mosque complex of near architectural perfection. Viewing the silhouette of its cascading domes and bristling minarets from across the Golden Horn at sunset is stunning, an intimate walk around its hallowed grounds moving. North and west of the Grand Bazaar a rather grittier area, merging into the business district of Aksaray, is embellished by some important Ottoman mosques, along with a few Byzantine-era gems, all the more enjoyable to explore as so few visitors make the effort to get off the beaten track.

SÜLEYMANIYE MOSQUE COMPLEX SÜLEYMANİYE KÜLLİYESİ

Prof Siddik Sami Onar Cad, Vefa Ⓣ1 Beyazıt or Laleli/Üniversite Ⓜ2 Vezneciler. MAP P.68–69, POCKET MAP E6

Northwest of the Grand Bazaar, the Süleymaniye Külliyesi (mosque complex) is best reached by walking up from the Laleli/Üniversite tramstop, first along Büyük Resit Paşa Caddesi, then onto 10 Mart Şehit and Süleymaniye *caddesi*s. En route you'll pass the **Kalenderhane Camii**, a distinctive brick-built mosque once the thirteenth-century Byzantine Church of Kyriotissa, and under an arch of the fourth-century Aqueduct of Valens (see p.74). At the top is **Tırayakı Çarşısı**, "market of the addicts", a street in front of the mosque named after the opium addicts who puffed away their lives here. You are now in the **Süleymaniye Mosque Complex,** a group of buildings with the mosque at its heart, arguably the pinnacle of achievement of the architect Sinan, and worthy legacy of the

SÜLEYMANIYE KÜLLIYESI

sultan who founded it, Süleyman the Magnificent. Begun in 1550 on a tricky hill-top site, it took seven years to complete. Entering the **Süleymaniye Camii** by the side door, it's hard not to be impressed by the sheer sense of space the architect has achieved by cleverly hiding the piers supporting the massive dome (53m high by 26.5m in diameter) in the colonnaded supporting walls, adding half domes to the west and east and piercing the arched tympanum walls on the other two sides with rows of windows. It may be virtually the same plan as the Haghia Sophia, which was clearly its inspiration, but Sinan makes it his own achievement, especially as the interior is so gloriously austere. İznik tiles are used with great restraint, the marble-clad prayer-niche (*mihrab*) and pulpit (*mimber*) are simple in design and the painted arabesque panels on the plasterwork muted in colour.

Outside, in the southeastern grounds of the mosque are the *türbes* or **tombs** of Süleyman the Magnificent and his wife Haseki Hürrem or Roxelana (daily 7am–8pm; free). Süleyman's is an octagonal marble drum with a domed roof; inside is the centotaph of the greatest Ottoman sultan.

SÜLEYMANIYE CAMII INTERIOR

Ranged in an L-shape around the southwest and northwest sides of the mosque are medreses, a hospital, the soup kitchen, today the *Darüzziyafe* restaurant (see p.78), and a caravansaray for travellers – all once integral parts of this great philanthropic complex. The baths built as part of the complex are excellent and open to mixed bathing (**Süleymaniye Hamamı**, Mimar Sinan Cad 20 T 0212 519 5569, W suleymaniyehamami.com; daily 10am–midnight; bath and scrub packages €35).

The genius of Sinan

By far the most brilliant and prolific Ottoman architect, Sinan was a Christian by birth. Swept up in the annual *devişirme*, a levy of Christian youth taken into the sultan's service and compelled to convert to Islam, he was trained at the Topkapı Palace. In 1536, Sinan became imperial architect and is responsible for some 81 mosques, 50 theological schools, 32 palaces and numerous other structures, from bridges to hospitals – 321 in total. A devout Muslim and simple family man, he lived on site with his family while the Süleymaniye complex was under construction. He was buried here, aged 97, in a tomb, fittingly, he designed himself.

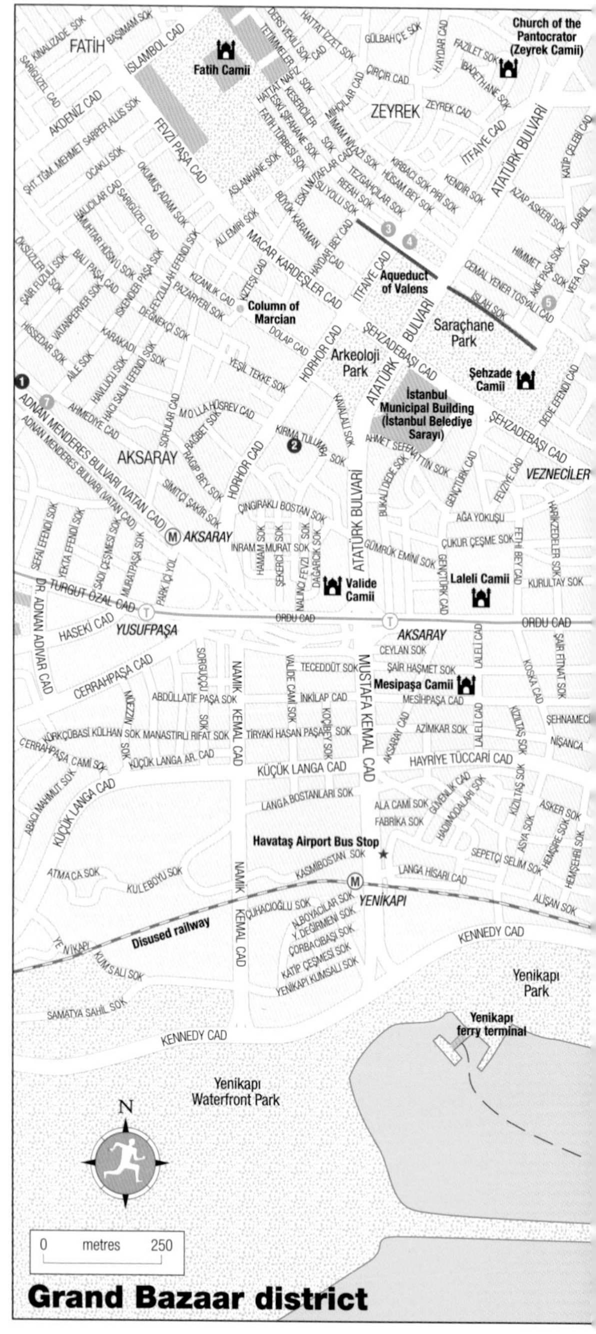
Grand Bazaar district
FATİH
Fatih Camii
Church of the Pantocrator (Zeyrek Camii)
ZEYREK
Aqueduct of Valens
Column of Marcian
Saraçhane Park
Arkeoloji Park
Şehzade Camii
İstanbul Municipal Building (İstanbul Belediye Sarayı)
AKSARAY
VEZNECİLER
Valide Camii
Laleli Camii
YUSUFPAŞA
Mesipaşa Camii
Havataş Airport Bus Stop
YENİKAPI
Disused railway
Yenikapı Park
Yenikapı ferry terminal
Yenikapı Waterfront Park
ATATÜRK BULVARI
ADNAN MENDERES BULVARI (VATAN CAD)
TURGUT ÖZAL CAD
ORDU CAD
KENNEDY CAD
MUSTAFA KEMAL CAD
NAMIK KEMAL CAD
KÜÇÜK LANGA CAD
ŞEHZADEBAŞI CAD
MACAR KARDEŞLER CAD
FEVZİ PAŞA CAD
N
0 metres 250

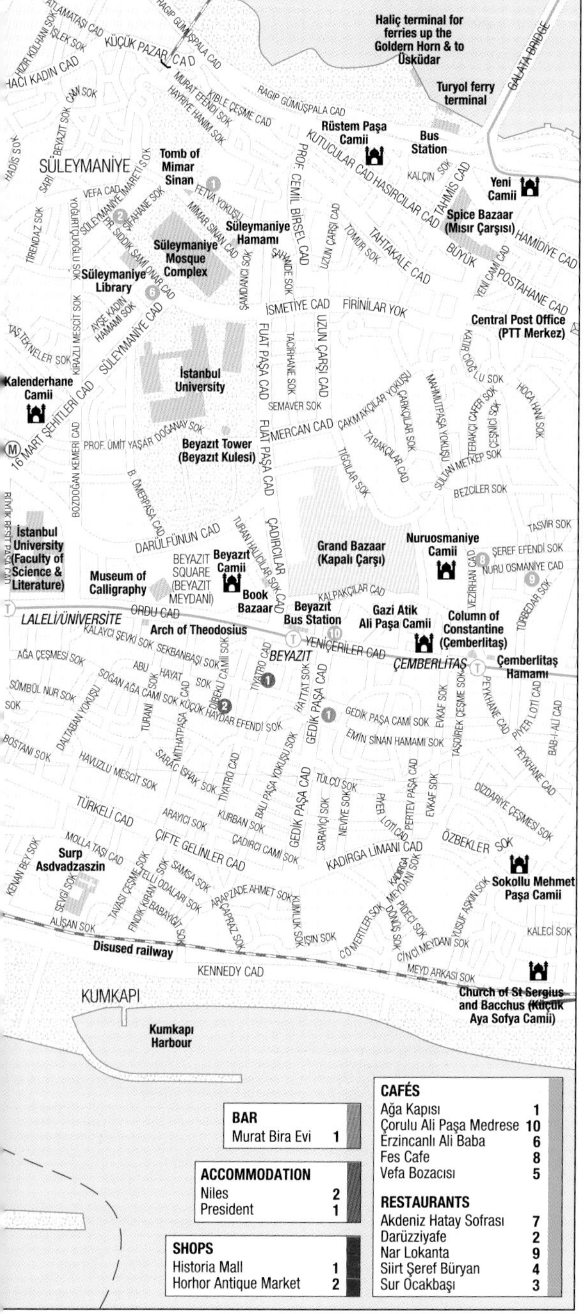
Haliç terminal for ferries up the Goldern Horn & to Üsküdar
Turyol ferry terminal
GALATA BRIDGE
Rüstem Paşa Camii
Bus Station
Yeni Camii
Spice Bazaar (Mısır Çarşısı)
SÜLEYMANİYE
Tomb of Mimar Sinan
Süleymaniye Hamamı
Süleymaniye Mosque Complex
Süleymaniye Library
Central Post Office (PTT Merkez)
Kalenderhane Camii
İstanbul University
Beyazıt Tower (Beyazıt Kulesi)
İstanbul University (Faculty of Science & Literature)
Museum of Calligraphy
BEYAZIT SQUARE (BEYAZIT MEYDANI)
Beyazıt Camii
Book Bazaar
Grand Bazaar (Kapalı Çarşı)
Nuruosmaniye Camii
Beyazıt Bus Station
Gazi Atik Ali Paşa Camii
Column of Constantine (Çemberlitaş)
Çemberlitaş Hamamı
LALELİ/ÜNİVERSİTE
Arch of Theodosius
BEYAZIT
ÇEMBERLİTAŞ
Surp Asdvadzaszin
Sokollu Mehmet Paşa Camii
Disused railway
KENNEDY CAD
KUMKAPI
Kumkapı Harbour
Church of St Sergius and Bacchus (Küçük Aya Sofya Camii)
BAR
Murat Bira Evi 1
ACCOMMODATION
Niles 2
President 1
SHOPS
Historia Mall 1
Horhor Antique Market 2
CAFÉS
Ağa Kapısı 1
Çorulu Ali Paşa Medrese 10
Erzincanlı Ali Baba 6
Fes Cafe 8
Vefa Bozacısı 5
RESTAURANTS
Akdeniz Hatay Sofrası 7
Darüzziyafe 2
Nar Lokanta 9
Siirt Şeref Büryan 4
Sur Ocakbaşı 3

GRAND BAZAAR
KAPALI ÇARŞI

Beyazıt Ⓣ1 Beyazıt or Çemberlitaş. Mon–Sat 9am–7pm. MAP P.68–69, POCKET MAP F7

Known in Turkish as the Kapalı Çarşı or Covered Bazaar, this great shopping complex was originally built not long after the Ottoman Turkish conquest of the city in 1453, on the site of a Byzantine precursor. Like all bazaars in the Ottoman Empire, it was an open area in the beginning, centred on the *bedesten*, a lockable, covered (usually domed) building where valuable goods were stored. The commercial hub of the Grand Bazaar comprised two *bedesten*, the İç Bedesten, today containing jewellery and other shops, and the Sandal Bedesteni, not built until the sixteenth century, which was used for storing precious fabrics.

GRAND BAZAAR

Needless to say, it's a magnet for visitors, though plenty of locals still use it as well. If you're unused to Middle-Eastern ways it can be a little intimidating, not only because of the importuning of a few of the owners of its 4000 or so shops, but also owing to the maze-like meanderings of the **66 vaulted streets** (the

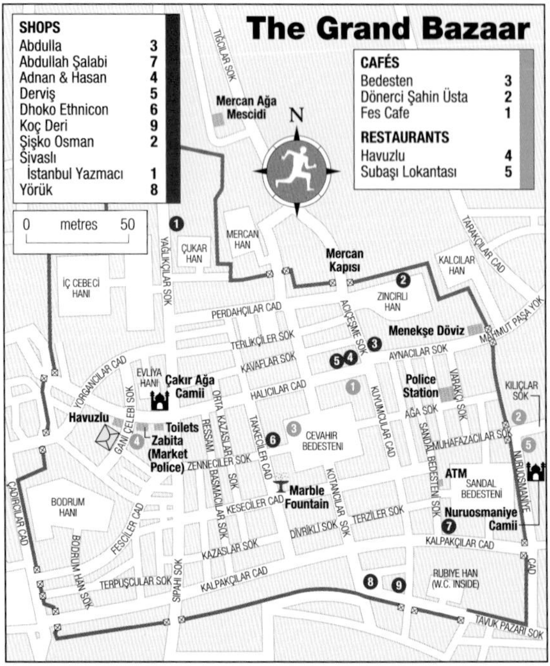

The Grand Bazaar

SHOPS	
Abdulla	3
Abdullah Şalabi	7
Adnan & Hasan	4
Derviş	5
Dhoko Ethnicon	6
Koç Deri	9
Şişko Osman	2
Sivaslı İstanbul Yazmacı	1
Yörük	8

CAFÉS	
Bedesten	3
Dönerci Şahin Üsta	2
Fes Cafe	1

RESTAURANTS	
Havuzlu	4
Subaşı Lokantası	5

name-plaques of which are often hidden beneath displays) and the sheer crush of people at busy times. It's also easy to exit by the "wrong" one of the twenty gates puncturing its walls and end up, disorientated, in an unfamiliar labyinth of alleyways – some of which are still lined by workshops producing goods for the bazaar. In addition to shops, there's a plethora of **cafés and restaurants**, a mosque, moneychangers and banks and, essential given the annual turnover in gold here – over 18 billion pounds in 2012 – market police known as *zabita*. Fortunately, the variety of goods on display, from exquisite gold and silver jewellery, antique carpets and flat-weave rugs (kilims) to fake designer clothes and accessories and gaudy belly-dancer outfits, keeps most people entertained, the majority of shop owners pleasant and friendly, and some of the eating places more than reasonable.

BOOK BAZAAR *SAHAFLAR ÇARŞISI*

Sahaflar Çarşısı Sok Ⓣ1 Beyazıt. Daily 8am–7pm. MAP P.68–69, POCKET MAP E7

Reachable either from the southwest corner of the Grand Bazaar or from Beyazıt Square, this famous booksellers' market dates back to the Byzantine period. No longer the best place to hunt for secondhand or antiquarian rarities, it concentrates on academic tomes for students from nearby İstanbul University, but has a fair smattering of decent books in English on İstanbul.

NURUOSMANİYE CAMİİ

Vezirhan Cad Ⓣ1 Çemberlitaş. MAP P.68–69, POCKET MAP F7

More or less opposite the Çarşı Kapısı gate on the east side of the Grand Bazaar, this attractive building, built between 1748 and 1755, was the first of the city's mosques to be influenced by the Baroque style. The prayer hall is little more than an impressively high central dome supported by four great bricked-in arches filled by windows, which flood the interior with light and make its name, the "Sacred Light of Osman", particularly apt. Flanked by twin cylindrical minarets, the mosque has a rare grace, especially as it is fronted by an elegant semicircular, rather than the usual square, courtyard. Due to its proximity to the Grand Bazaar, it is invariably very busy, especially at Friday midday prayers, and its pleasant courtyard, shaded by spreading plane trees, offers a peaceful respite to busy shoppers and workers.

NURUOSMANIYE CAMII

COLUMN OF CONSTANTINE ÇEMBERLİTAŞ

Yeniçeriler Cad Ⓣ1 Çemberlitaş. MAP P.68–69, POCKET MAP F8

Among all the domed Ottoman buildings hereabouts, this is a reminder of an earlier, Byzantine past, when this 35m-high column presided over the great oval Forum of Constantine. Erected by Constantine to commemorate the inauguration of his new city in 330, it was surmounted by a massive statue of the emperor himself, dressed as Apollo, which was toppled by a storm in 1106. Its Turkish name Çemberlitaş, or "hooped stone", refers to the reinforcing iron rings clamped around the joints of its ten porphyry drums following an earthquake in 416. It is sometimes called the "burnt column" after it was scorched by a great fire in 1179.

ÇEMBERLİTAŞ HAMAMI

Vezirhan Cad 8 Ⓣ1 Çemberlitaş ❶ 0212 522 7974, Ⓦ cemberlitashamami.com.tr. Daily 6am–midnight. Baths from ₺39. MAP P.68–69, POCKET MAP F8

Opposite the Column of Constantine, this historic bath-house is one of the three most popular in the old city and well used to foreign visitors. It was founded in the sixteenth century by Nur Banu Valide Sultan. An Italian by birth, she had been seized from the Greek island of Paros and brought to İstanbul to be a concubine in the Harem. Eventually she ended up as consort to Selim II (1566–74) and mother to Sultan Murat III (1574–95). It follows the usual pattern of the city's Ottoman *hamams* and certainly makes an atmospheric and very conveniently located introduction to the Turkish bath ritual.

GAZİ ATİK ALİ PAŞA CAMİİ

Yeniçeriler Cad Ⓣ1 Çemberlitaş. MAP P.68–69, POCKET MAP F8

Often overlooked in favour of more imposing rivals such as the Blue and Süleymaniye mosques, the Gazi Atik Ali Paşa Camii, located a short way west along the tramline from the Column of Constantine, is important, as it is one of İstanbul's oldest mosques. Constructed in 1496 by a eunuch who became grand vizier and whose name the mosque bears, it consists of a 12m-diameter dome seated on the walls of the main body of the prayer hall, extended by a semi-dome covering another section of the mosque containing the Mecca-facing *mihrab*.

ÇEMBERLİTAŞ HAMAMI

BEYAZIT SQUARE
BEYAZIT MEYDANI

Ordu Cad Ⓣ1 Beyazıt. MAP P.68–69, POCKET MAP E7

Flanked to the west by the Grand Bazaar, to the south by traffic-filled Ordu Caddesi and to the north by the grounds of İstanbul University, this large square is one of the few (relatively speaking in this congested city) oases of peace in central İstanbul. The imperial mosque that gives the square its name, the **Beyazıt Camii**, was completed in 1506, making it the second oldest imperial mosque in the city. It's splendidly austere in style, with the usual colonnades ranged around three sides of the courtyard, supported by pillars of fine marble and centred on a pretty, octagonal ablutions fountain. The prayer hall of the mosque is exactly the same dimensions as the courtyard, making for a pleasing symmetry, and the central dome is abutted to west and east by semi-domes, giving it the same spacious feel as the Haghia Sophia and Süleymaniye Camii. Walking northwest across the pigeon-filled square, you soon come to the massive, ornamental gate of İstanbul University, one of the most prestigious in Turkey. Visible beyond it, in the grounds, is a striking white tower, the **Beyazıt Tower** (Beyazıt Kulesi in Turkish), erected in 1828, which once served as a fire watchtower. The **Museum of Calligraphy**, housed in an Ottoman-era medrese in the northwest corner of the square, has been closed for many years. On the south side of the tramline and busy main road from the southwest corner of the square is a tangle of fallen columns, relief-carved with striking tear-drop motifs. This is all that remains of the once-monumental **Arch of Theodosius**, a triumphal arch that spanned the main road into the city centre, and marking the western entrance to what was once the largest forum or public space in Constantinople, the Forum of Theodosius I (379–395).

UNIVERSITY GATES, BEYAZIT SQUARE

LALELİ CAMİİ

Ordu Cad Ⓣ1 Aksaray. MAP P.68–69, POCKET MAP D7

It's worth continuing west from Beyazıt Square down traffic-clogged Ordu Caddesi to see the attractively ornate Laleli Camii, a mosque built in the Ottoman Baroque style between 1759 and 1763, during the reign of Mustafa II. As an imperial mosque, it used to be surrounded by a number of other buildings which served the surrounding community. The most obvious survivor of these is the attractive *sebil* or street fountain, which once dispensed water to the local populace. The mosque's graceful Baroque curves are best viewed from the exterior, but step inside to admire the plethora of columns supporting the main dome and galleries.

ŞEHZADE CAMİİ

Şehzadebaşı Cad Ⓣ1 Laleli/Üniversite Ⓜ2 Vezneciler. MAP P.68–69, POCKET MAP D6

This, the Mosque of the Prince, is named in honour of Prince Mehmet, eldest son of Süleyman the Magnificent, who died in 1543 at the tender age of 21. It's another work of Sinan, and although most experts do not rate it as among his best, for the average visitor it is one of the most attractive – at least when viewed from the outside. Completed in 1548, the interior is very plain, with a central dome supported by four piers flanked by four semi-domes, giving it a trefoil plan. Outside, the courtyard is very satisfying aesthetically, with the porticoes surrounding all four sides roofed with a total of 16 small domes. But it's the twin minarets that really catch the eye, with their ribbing and low-relief-carved geometric patterns.

İSTANBUL MUNICIPALITY BUILDING *İSTANBUL BELEDİYE SARAYI*

Şehzadebaşı Cad Ⓣ1 Laleli/Üniversite. MAP P.68–69, POCKET MAP D7

Important as the first International Modern building in the old city, the design for this 1950s classic was by architect Nevzat Erol. Comprising a typical modernist-style eight-storey office block with a grid facade raised on columns, it is fronted by a meeting hall-cum-reception area surmounted by an unusual cross-arched roof. It may be at odds with its ancient surroundings, but it is certainly striking.

AQUEDUCT OF VALENS

Atatürk Bulvarı Ⓣ1 Aksaray Ⓜ2 Vezneciler. MAP P.68–69, POCKET MAP C6–D6

Spanning traffic-clogged Atatürk Bulvarı in two-tiered, 18.5m-high splendour, this aqueduct was in use from its construction around 375 under Emperor Valens through to the nineteenth century. Water was brought from various sources outside the city, piped under the land walls and all the way to the fourth hill, where a major valley between it and the third hill (where the Süleymaniye mosque complex now stands) meant a raised aqueduct was needed – the splendid construction you see today. From a storage reservoir near Beyazıt Square the water was distributed throughout the city. It's possible to follow its ever-decreasing height west from Atatürk Bulvarı to near the **Kalenderhane Camii** (see p.66), perhaps pausing for unusual refreshments at the wonderful *Vefa Bozacısı* (see p.78) en route.

AQUEDUCT OF VALENS

Shops: Grand Bazaar

ABDULLA

Halıcılar Cad 53 Ⓣ1 Beyazıt or Çemberlitaş ☎0212 527 3684. Mon–Sat 9am–7pm. MAP P.70, POCKET MAP F7

The fixed prices make this a popular bet with visitors, drawn in by the elegant displays of scarves, pastel-coloured cotton bath wraps, plump traditional towels, mohair rugs and all manner of handmade olive-oil soaps.

ABDULLAH ŞALABİ

Cevahir Bedesteni 143–151 Ⓣ1 Beyazıt or Çemberlitaş ☎0212 520 2250. Mon–Sat 9am–7pm. MAP P.70, POCKET MAP F7

Great little antiques stall established in 1880, stocking a wide range of curios and presided over by knowledge-able English-speaker Pol Şalabi. One speciality is icons.

ADNAN & HASAN

Halıcılar Cad 89–92 Ⓣ1 Beyazıt or Çemberlitaş ☎0212 527 9887. Mon–Sat 9am–7pm. MAP P.70, POCKET MAP F7

Long-established carpet and kilim purveyor stocking everything from very expensive Hereke carpets to moderately priced Anatolian and Caucasian kilims.

ADNAN & HASAN

DERVİŞ

Keseciler Cad 51 Ⓣ1 Beyazıt or Çemberlitaş ☎0212 528 7883. Mon–Sat 9am–7pm. MAP P.70, POCKET MAP F7

Choose from a well-displayed array of silk scarves, cotton bath towels and robes, pashmina scarves, natural soaps and, more unusually, antique kaftans from Central Asia.

DHOKO-ETHNİCON

Takkeciler Sok 52-60 Ⓣ1 Beyazıt or Çemberlitaş ☎0212 527 6841. Mon–Sat 9am–7pm. MAP P.70, POCKET MAP F7

The concept is contemporary ethnic, hence the beautiful range of flat-weave kilims with strikingly modern geometric designs which often look far better at home than more traditional rugs.

Grand Bazaar shopping tips

Few goods bear price labels in the Grand Bazaar, so for most things you'll have to haggle. Before beginning negotiations for a particular item, ask the price of identical or similar items at other stores to give a ball-park figure. Then offer considerably less than the trader is asking (he'll likely be asking far more than he will accept). Walking away is a tactic that sometimes produces results but remember that once you've begun to bargain seriously it is rude not to pursue the process to the end – and to not buy once you've agreed a price is very bad form. The price of gold and silver jewellery fluctuates on a daily basis with prices for items based on the going rate – the jeweller should base his asking price on the weight of the piece you are interested in.

KOÇ DERİ

Kürküçüler Cad 22/46 Ⓣ1 Beyazıt or Çemberlitaş ⓣ 0212 527 5533. Mon–Sat 9am–7pm. MAP P.70, POCKET MAP F7

Leather goods are as traditionally Turkish in origin as carpets and İznik pottery, and this place sells some of the best-quality jackets, bags and other accessories in the city.

ŞİŞKO OSMAN

Zincirli Han Ⓣ1 Beyazıt or Çemberlitaş ⓣ 0212 528 3548. Mon–Sat 9am–7pm. MAP P.70, POCKET MAP F7

A rambling store presided over by the knowledgeable and voluble Şişko (Fat) Osman, stocking all manner of antique carpets and kilims. Come here for apple tea and an entertaining soft-sell.

SIVASLI İSTANBUL YAZMACI

Yağlıkcılar Cad Ⓣ1 Beyazıt or Çemberlitaş ⓣ 0212 526 7748. Mon–Sat 9am–7pm. MAP P.70, POCKET MAP F7

This textile cornucopia, sometimes known as Necdet Danış, that has been knocking-out quality *peştemals* (Turkish bath towels), tablecloths and scarves, as well as bolts of stunning fabrics, for over 40 years. Well regarded by thrifty locals for quality goods at fair prices.

ŞİŞKO OSMAN

YÖRÜK

Kürküçüler Cad Ⓣ1 Beyazıt or Çemberlitaş ⓣ 0212 527 3211. Mon–Sat 9am–7pm. MAP P.70, POCKET MAP F7

Traders from the central Anatolian city of Kayseri are known for their business acumen – this reliable store, run by Kayseri-born Ersoy, sells everything from cheap, chemically dyed kilims to genuine vintage rugs coloured with natural dyes.

Shops: Aksaray

HISTORIA MALL

Adnan Menderes Bulvarı. Buses #38, #39, #55EB ⓣ 0212 532 0202. Daily 10am–10pm. MAP P.68–69, POCKET MAP B6

Handily located next to the excellent *Akdeniz Hatay Sofrası* restaurant (see p.78), this mall is tricky to reach (best bet from Sultanahmet is the T1 tram to the Aksaray stop followed by a fifteen-minute walk). Spread over four floors are international favourites such as Levi and Converse along with good Turkish fashion outlets like *Mavi* (jeans etc) and *Derimod* (leather). One floor is taken up by a food court.

HORHOR ANTIQUE MARKET

Yorum Kırık Tulumba Sok 13/22 Ⓣ1 Aksaray ⓣ 0212 525 9977. Daily 10am–8pm. MAP P.68–69, POCKET MAP C7

Out-of-the-way location but easy enough to reach from the Aksaray T1 tramstop, this massive antiques centre has all manner of wares displayed on five floors, much of it stuff imported from Europe in the nineteenth and early twentieth centuries. You'll have to hunt and haggle hard for a real bargain though.

Cafés

AĞA KAPISI

Nazir Hizmet Efendi Sok 11 Ⓣ1 Laleli/Üniversite Ⓜ2 Vezneciler ⓣ 0212 519 5176. Daily 8am–midnight. MAP P.68–69, POCKET MAP E6

If you're visiting the Süleymaniye complex, don't miss this great café hidden on an alley below Sinan's tomb. The views of the Golden Horn and Galata Bridge are as unexpected as they are superb. Try an Ottoman fruit sherbert, Turkish coffee or *gözleme* (₺6), a paratha-like bread-round stuffed with cheese or potato, or even a puff on a *nargile* on the upper floor – all usually in the company of students from the university.

BEDESTEN

Cevahir Bedesteni 143–151 Ⓣ1 Çemberlitaş ⓣ 0212 520 2250. Mon–Sat 8.30am–6.30pm. MAP P.70, POCKET MAP F7

Tucked away in the Cevahir Bedesteni in the heart of the Grand Bazaar, this well-run and stylish place makes a great spot to rest-up between shopping bouts. Well-priced food is a mix of Turkish (try the yoghurt-drenched Turkish ravioli, *mantı*, for ₺17) and international (brownies and cheesecake) and the coffee is good. The decor is special too, dominated by two giant *alem*, the brass crescent and star finials that adorn mosque domes and minarets.

ÇORULU ALI PAŞA MEDRESE

Ali Baba Türbe Sok Medrese, Yeniçeriler Cad 36–38 Ⓣ1 Beyazit ⓣ 0212 528 3785. Daily 7am–midnight. MAP P.68–69, POCKET MAP F7

Housed in the three-hundred-year-old Çorulu Ali Paşa Medrese, the Erenler Çay Bahçesi is a great place to stop for a bargain-priced traditional Turkish *çay* (tea) sipped from a tiny, tulip-shaped glass, or to toke on a *nargile* (water pipe).

AĞA KAPISI

DÖNERCİ ŞAHİN ÜSTA

Nuruosmaniye Kılıçlar Sok 7 Ⓣ1 Çemberlitaş ⓣ 0212 526 5297. Mon–Sat 10am–3pm. MAP P.70, POCKET MAP F7

Most visitors pass this hole in the wall, stand-up *döner* kebab joint thinking it's just another cheap place dishing up bland, pre-prepared *döner*s brought in from outside. It isn't, as the queues of loyal regulars attest. Enjoy tender lamb painstakingly layered on the vertical spit each morning, grilled to perfection then sliced onto a small *pide* bread and served with juicy tomatoes and sumac-smothered onion – ₺8.

ERZİNCANLI ALİ BABA

Sidik Sami Onar Cad 11 Ⓣ1 Laleli/Üniversite ⓣ 0212 513 6219. Daily 9am–7pm. MAP P.68–69, POCKET MAP E6

Overlooking the fabulous Süleymaniye mosque and with tables out on the "market of the addicts", this is an ideal lunch stop – especially if you like the beans (*kuru fasulye*) which have made it famous. Tender, buttery, dripping with tomato sauce and topped by a spicy pepper, a bowl of these cheap (₺6) and delicious pulses is a delight. They also do a decent range of other traditional Turkish dishes.

FES CAFE

FES CAFE

Ali Baba Türbe Sok 25/7A, off Nuruosmaniye Cad Ⓣ1 Çemberlitaş ⓣ0212 526 3071.Daily 8am–9pm. MAP P.68–69, POCKET MAP F7

Just outside the Grand Bazaar and with a smaller branch inside on Halıcılar Cad 62, this contemporary take on a traditional Turkish café serves-up good sandwiches and cakes to a mainly middle-class Turkish clientele. Also does very decent coffee.

VEFA BOZACISI

Katip Çeşebi Cad 104/1 Ⓣ1 Laleli/Üniversite Ⓜ2 Vezneciler ⓣ0212 519 4922. Daily 8am–9pm. MAP P.68–69, POCKET MAP D6

Whether you like the traditional speciality *boza*, a viscous fermented millet drink topped by connoisseurs with roasted chickpeas (bought from a shop across the road), is almost beside the point, as the ambience of the delightful interior is what counts. Caught in an early twentieth-century time-warp, it's all dark-wood shelves and cut-glass mirrors. Slightly sweet and fizzy, *boza* (₺3 a glass) is delicious – Atatürk himself thought so and the glass he drank from in the 1930s is proudly on display on one wall. You can also stock-up on chunky souvenir bottles of *nar suyu* (pomegranate syrup) and *üzüm sirkesi* (grape vinegar).

Restaurants

AKDENİZ HATAY SOFRASI

Ahmediye Cad 44/A. Buses #38, #55/EB ⓣ0212 531 3333. Mon–Sat 9am–midnight, Sun 8am–1pm. MAP P.68–69, POCKET MAP B6

Unpromisingly located place specializing in the Arab-influenced food of the Syrian-border province of Hatay, this is nonetheless one of the city's best restaurants. There's an extensive range of *meze* ranging from *zahter*, a thyme-based salad, to hummus topped by *pastırma* (pastrami) or pine nuts, and spectacular mains like *tuzda tavuk*, a whole chicken stuffed with fragrant pilaf rice, oven-roasted in a thick salt coating and brought to the table flaming. Just as ostentatiously delicious are the metre-long kebabs. Unlicensed.

DARÜZZİYAFE

Sifahane Sok 6 Ⓣ1 Laleli/Üniversite M2 Vezneciler ⓣ0212 511 8414. Daily noon–11pm. MAP P.68–69, POCKET MAP E6

Located in the former *imaret* (soup kitchen) of the Süleymaniye complex, you couldn't ask for more atmospheric surroundings to sample reasonably priced Ottoman favourites such as *hünkar beğendi* and contemporary Turkish dishes. Drawbacks are that it is group-orientated and unlicensed. Mains from ₺17.

HAVUZLU

Gani Çelebi Sok 3 Ⓣ1 Çemberlitaş ⓣ0212 520 2250. Mon–Sat 10am–5pm. MAP P.70, POCKET MAP F7

Brisk-bordering-brusque service is the order of the day in this Grand Bazaar institution, appreciated by locals for its good-quality kebabs (from ₺12) and hearty stews and by visitors for the atmospheric dining room beneath a four-hundred-year-old vaulted ceiling. Choose from over twenty varieties of *sulu yemek* (stew-type dishes) laid out in a giant steamtray and changing daily, with desserts including *sutlaç* (oven-baked rice pudding) and *kabak tatlısı* (candied pumpkin). Unlicensed.

NAR LOKANTA

Armaggan, Nuruosmaniye Cad 65 Ⓣ1 Çemberlitaş Ⓣ 0212 522 2800, Ⓦ narlokantasi.com. Mon–Sat 8:30am–10pm. MAP P.68–69, POCKET MAP G7

Located on the fifth floor of a well-known store, this is the first venture of NAR Gourmet, a brand highly-regarded for high quality, organic local produce. There's much on offer here that you'll find hard to track down elsewhere and the quality of the food compensates for the high prices. Best value is the lunchtime buffet of cold meze starters. Main courses ₺16-60.

SİİRT ŞEREF BÜRYAN

İtfaiye Cad 4. Bus #38 Ⓣ 0212 635 8085. Daily 11am–11pm. MAP P.68–69, POCKET MAP E6

Nestling in the shadow of the Aqueduct of Valens, this is the place to try the eastern Turkish speciality *büryan*, lamb cooked slowly in a clay *tandır* oven or, even better, *perde pilaf* (₺10), a delicious rice dish flavoured with almonds, shredded chicken, raisins and spices. Most of the food shops on the fascinating street on which it stands are run by Kurds from the southeast of Turkey and stock all manner of cheeses, spices and other goodies. Unlicensed.

DARÜZZİYAFE

SUBAŞI LOKANTASI

Nuruosmaniye Cad 48, Çarşı Kapı Ⓣ1 Çemberlitaş Ⓣ 0212 522 4762. Mon–Sat 9am–6pm. MAP P.70, POCKET MAP F7

Packed with traders from the Grand Bazaar at lunchtimes, this spit-and-sawdust *lokanta* (traditional Turkish restaurant) dishes up cheap and cheerful stews (from ₺10) from huge steamtrays as well as *köfte* and kebabs. It's conveniently located right outside the main, Çarşı, gate to the bazaar. Unlicensed.

SUR OCAKBAŞI

İtfaye Cad 27, Fatih Bus #38 Ⓣ 0212 533 8088, Ⓦ surocakbası.com. Daily 10am–midnight. MAP P.68–69, POCKET MAP C6

Fronting a lively pedestrianised square, this down to earth ocakbaşı is noted for its *saç tava*, a rich fried meat and vegetable stew usually eaten with copious chunks of *pide* flatbread, as well a startling array of kebabs, spicy lahmacun and even the stuffed intestine speciality bumbar. TV chef and food personality Anthony Bourdain was brought here when he visited the city.

Bar

MURAT BİRA EVİ

Gedikpaşa Cad 77/A Ⓣ1 Beyazit Ⓣ 0212 517 8228. Daily 8am–2am. MAP P.68–69, POCKET MAP F8

There are not a lot of places to drink around here, so this workers' den is a godsend if you're not fussy – with cheap beer, salted snacks and even *hamsi* (anchovies) and *midye* (stuffed mussels). Unsuitable for unaccompanied women.

Northwest quarter and the land walls

Compelling yet seldom visited, the northwest quarter stands astride the fourth, fifth and sixth hills of the old city. Best explored on foot, its narrow streets, the most evocative running steeply down to the shores of the Golden Horn beneath strings of washing hung between once grand nineteenth-century apartments, are the beat of skullcapped conservative Muslim men and veiled women. Yet working churches survive, including the spiritual centre of the Orthodox Christian world, the Fener Greek Patriarchate, as well as Byzantine treasures like St Saviour in Chora, today the Kariye Museum, with its stunning mosaics and frescoes. The quarter is bounded to the northwest by the remarkably intact fifth-century land walls of Theodosius which, if followed south, run through yet more atmospheric districts dotted with interesting sights, finally ending by the coruscating waters of the Sea of Marmara.

KARIYE MUSEUM
KARİYE MÜZESİ

Kariye Camii Sok Ⓜ1 Ulubatlı/Topkapı, buses #28, #36/V, #37/Y, #38, #38/E, #55/EB, #87 ☎0212 631 9241. Daily except Wed: April–Oct 9am–7pm; Nov–March 9am–4.30pm. ₺15, audio-guide ₺10. MAP P.82, POCKET MAP A2

Out by the land walls of Theodosius, some 5km from the centre of the old city, the Byzantine **Church of St Saviour in Chora** was converted into a mosque, the Kariye Camii, after the Ottoman conquest. Today, as the **Kariye Museum**, it is the one absolute must-see historic site beyond Sultanahmet and its environs. Possibly dating back to the fourth century, it originally lay beyond the walls of Constantinople – hence "Chora", Greek for "in the country" – but the pretty brick-built building you see today dates largely from an eleventh-century rebuild followed, in the early fourteenth century, by a remodelling by prominent Byzantine statesman and scholar, **Theodore Metochites**. Crucially, the wealthy Metochites added the twin narthexes (entrance

MOSAIC, KARIYE MUSEUM

FRESCOES, KARIYE MUSEUM

vestibules) and the funerary chapel (parecclesion) to the church, home to the bulk of the mosaics and frescoes which make it so stunning.

You enter the church via a door in the north wall, but to get your bearings, head straight for the outer narthex. The door in the external wall here is today's exit, but was originally the main entrance to the church. Above this door the *Virgin and Angels* mosaic shows Mary with an infant Christ in a medallion on her chest, flanked by two angels. Opposite, above the door to the inner narthex, another panel shows *Christ Pantocrator* or Christ the all-powerful. Running around the entire outer narthex and part of the parecclesion is a narrative sequence of twelve semicircular mosaic panels known as the *Infancy of Christ*, telling the story of Jesus from his birth to his entry into Jerusalem. The second narrative sequence, *Christ's Ministry*, some fifteen scenes spread over the vaults of the roof, begins in the outer narthex before spilling over into part of the inner narthex. Look out for Christ healing a leper covered in almost comic-book-like spots, and the *Miracle at Cana*. On the north wall of the inner narthex, a third wonderful sequence begins, the *Life of the Virgin Mary*, taken from the apocryphal Gospel of St James, which can be traced around the inner narthex from Joachim praying in the wilderness to the miraculous pregnancy of Mary. The twin domes of the inner narthex are filled with the *Genealogy of Christ*, while above the door to the nave, an accomplished mosaic panel shows a wonderfully turbanned Theodore Metochites presenting a model of his church to Christ, flanked by two more mosaics depicting St Peter and St Paul. The nave is notable for its fine marble panels and mosaic of the *Dormition of the Virgin*, but don't leave without admiring the frescoes in the funerary chapel. Pick of these is the *Resurrection*, with Christ smashing down the doors of hell and rescuing Adam and Eve from their tombs, a painting every bit as brilliantly vibrant as those of the (unknown) artist's Renaissance contemporary, Giotto.

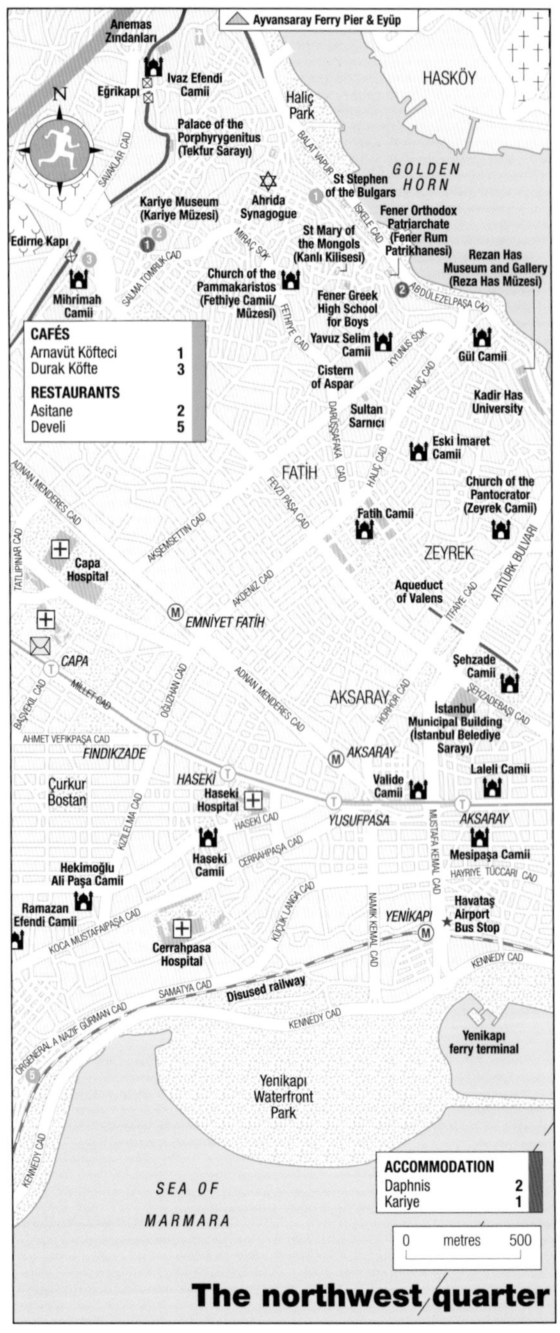

Ayvansaray Ferry Pier & Eyüp
Anemas Zındanları
Ivaz Efendi Camii
Eğrikapı
HASKÖY
Haliç Park
Palace of the Porphyrygenitus (Tekfur Sarayı)
SAVAKLAR CAD
BALAT VAPUR
GOLDEN HORN
St Stephen of the Bulgars
Kariye Museum (Kariye Müzesi)
Ahrida Synagogue
ISKELE CAD
Fener Orthodox Patriarchate (Fener Rum Patrikhanesi)
Edirne Kapı
MIRAÇ SOK
St Mary of the Mongols (Kanlı Kilisesi)
SALMA TOMRUK CAD
Church of the Pammakaristos (Fethiye Camii/ Müzesi)
Rezan Has Museum and Gallery (Reza Has Müzesi)
ABDÜLEZELPAŞA CAD
Mihrimah Camii
Fener Greek High School for Boys
FETHIYE CAD
Yavuz Selim Camii
KYUNUS SOK
Gül Camii
CAFÉS
Arnavüt Köfteci 1
Durak Köfte 3
RESTAURANTS
Asitane 2
Develi 5
Cistern of Aspar
HALIÇ CAD
Sultan Sarnıcı
DARÜŞŞAFAKA CAD
Kadir Has University
Eski İmaret Camii
FATİH
HALIÇ CAD
ADNAN MENDERES CAD
FEVZI PAŞA CAD
Church of the Pantocrator (Zeyrek Camii)
Fatih Camii
AKŞEMSETTIN CAD
TATLIPINAR CAD
Capa Hospital
ZEYREK
ATATÜRK BULVARI
AKDENIZ CAD
Aqueduct of Valens
ITFAIYE CAD
EMNİYET FATİH
ÇAPA
Şehzade Camii
OĞUZHAN CAD
ADNAN MENDERES CAD
AKSARAY
HORHOR CAD
ŞEHZADEBAŞI CAD
MILLET CAD
BAŞVEKIL CAD
İstanbul Municipal Building (İstanbul Belediye Sarayı)
AHMET VEFIKPAŞA CAD
FINDIKZADE
AKSARAY
Çurkur Bostan
HASEKİ
Haseki Hospital
Valide Camii
Laleli Camii
KIZILELMA CAD
HASEKI CAD
YUSUFPASA
AKSARAY
MUSTAFA KEMAL CAD
Haseki Camii
CERRAHPAŞA CAD
Mesipaşa Camii
HAYRIYE TÜCCARI CAD
Hekimoğlu Ali Paşa Camii
KÜÇÜK LANGA CAD
Ramazan Efendi Camii
NAMIK KEMAL CAD
YENİKAPI
Havataş Airport Bus Stop
KOCA MUSTAFAPAŞA CAD
Cerrahpasa Hospital
KENNEDY CAD
SAMATYA CAD
Disused railway
ORGENERAL A NAZIF GÜRMAN CAD
KENNEDY CAD
Yenikapı ferry terminal
Yenikapı Waterfront Park
KENNEDY CAD
ACCOMMODATION
Daphnis 2
Kariye 1
SEA OF MARMARA
0 metres 500
The northwest quarter

REZAN HAS MUSEUM & GALLERY *REZAN HAS MÜZESİ*

Kadir Has Üniversitesi. Bus #99 Ⓜ2 Haliç Ⓣ 0212 533 6532, Ⓦ rhm.org.tr. Daily 9am–6pm. ₺3. MAP P.82, POCKET MAP D4

Close to the waterfront beyond busy Atatürk/Unkapanı Bridge, this museum-cum-exhibition-space is housed in Kadir Has University, once a nineteenth-century tobacco factory. A must-see for archeology buffs, a series of cases exhibit exquisite finds from the Neolithic period through to the Selçuk Turkish era, atmospherically set out in a Byzantine cistern in the bowels of the university. The artefacts are mainly Anatolian and superb examples of their type – from Urartian metalwork to Hellenistic-era surgical equipment, seal stones to Roman figurines. The adjoining gallery hosts a mixed bag of exhibitions.

CHURCH OF THE PANTOCRATOR *ZEYREK CAMİİ*

İbadethane Sok, İtfaiye Cad. Buses #28, #28/T. MAP P.82, POCKET MAP D5

Converted into a mosque after the Ottoman conquest, this fine late-Byzantine building stands on a hilltop above Atatürk Bulvarı. Built in 1136, it comprised two churches linked by a chapel. The interior retains some fine marble panels and opus sectile flooring of differently coloured marble pieces. A short walk southwest is the Kadınlar Pazarı (Women's Bazaar), home to a plethora of food shops run mainly by Kurds.

FENER GREEK HIGH SCHOOL FOR BOYS

Sancaktar Yokuşu Sok 36, Fener Bus #99. MAP P.82, POCKET MAP B3

This imposing Victorian-Gothic building, built with bricks imported from France in 1883, is an unmissable sight on the slopes of the old city's fifth hill. There has been a school here since Byzantine times but today it's hard not to view it without thinking about the precipitous decline of the Greek minority in the city since its construction. Then there were over 400,000 Greeks in a city with a population of around one million. Today, there are just 2,000 or so in a metropolis of seventeen million; in 2014, less than 60 pupils attended this cavernous school.

FATİH CAMİİ

İslambol Cad. Buses #28,#28/T, #36/V, #37/Y, #38/E. MAP P.82, POCKET MAP C5

Northwest along the line of the aqueduct is the monumental and newly restored Fatih Camii (Mosque of the Conqueror). This impressive structure was İstanbul's first purpose-built (as opposed to a converted church) mosque. Finished in 1470, it was largely rebuilt after an earthquake in 1776. At the centre of the usual complex, this is the heart of the old city's most conservative district and bearded men in skullcaps are a common sight, as are chador-clad women. On Wednesdays the streets roundabout are home to İstanbul's most vibrant street market, the **Çarşamba Pazarı**.

FATİH CAMİİ INTERIOR

CHURCH OF THE PAMMAKARISTOS

YAVUZ SELİM CAMİİ

Yavuz Selim Cad. Buses #28, #28/T, #36/V, #37/Y, #38/E. MAP P.82, POCKET MAP C3

This austerely beautiful mosque lies northwest of the Fatih Camii, on the fifth hill. Its shallow single dome spans the prayer hall with sublime simplicity and İznik tiles are used with great restraint. Almost as impressive as the mosque are the splendid views from the attractive grounds, down over the Golden Horn and beyond. Behind the mosque the **tomb of Selim the Grim** (daily except Tues 9am–4.30pm; ₺1) is worth a look, as he was arguably the most successful Ottoman sultan, adding parts of Persia plus Syria, Palestine, Arabia and Egypt to the empire. He was known as "the Grim" for his habit of chopping off the heads of unsatisfactory grand viziers on a regular basis. The tomb retains a couple of superb tile panels.

The large, square hollow as you approach Yavuz Selim Camii used to function as the early Byzantine **Cistern of Aspar**, an open cistern once the largest of its kind in the city. Its brick-built retaining walls are still partially visible. Also nearby, down narrow Ali Naki Sokak, is the **Sultan Sarnıcı**. This beautiful, covered **Byzantine cistern** is some 29m by 19m and has a brick-vaulted ceiling supported by a series of marble pillars each topped by a richly-sculpted Corinthian capital. The cistern, now completely dry, functions as an atmospheric venue for wedding receptions and the like, so has no set opening times; if open, entry is free.

CHURCH OF THE PAMMAKARISTOS *FETHİYE CAMİİ/MÜZESİ*

Fethiye Cad. Bus #28. Daily except Wed 9am–4.30pm. ₺5. MAP P.82, POCKET MAP B3

Overshadowed by the nearby Kariye Museum (see p.80), the **mosaics** in the funerary chapel of **the former Church of the Pammakaristos** are one of the "hidden" treasures of the city. The church was converted into a mosque in 1573 and still functions as one today, but the former funerary chapel containing the mosaics has been turned into the **Fethiye Museum**. The typically brick-built domed building of the Byzantine church dates back to the twelfth century, while the chapel containing the mosaics was added in 1310. Well signed, the superbly preserved and vibrant mosaics include Christ Pantocrator in the dome, surrounded by the twelve Prophets, and a baptism scene showing Christ and John the Baptist. Between 1456 and 1587, this church was the Greek Orthodox Patriarchate.

CHURCH OF ST MARY OF THE MONGOLS *KANLI KİLİSE*

Tevkii Cafer Mektebi Sok. Bus #99. MAP P.82, POCKET MAP C3

Reached either from the fifth hill above or the shores of the

Golden Horn in Fener below, the unusual thirteenth-century Church of St Mary of the Mongols, in the shadow of the massive Fener Greek High School for Boys, is well worth a look. It's the only church in the city where Orthodox services have been carried out from the Byzantine period to the present day, but entry is dependent on the caretaker being at home.

FENER ORTHODOX PATRIARCHATE *FENER RUM PATRİKHANESİ*

Mursel Paşa Cad. Bus #99 ☎ 0212 525 2117. Daily 9am–5pm. Free. MAP P.82, POCKET MAP C3

On level ground close to the Golden Horn waterfront and stretches of the Byzantine sea walls that once ringed the peninsula and joined up with the land walls (see p.87), the Greek Orthodox Patriarchate remains, at least in theory, the spiritual centre of Orthodox Christians worldwide. The **Church of St George** at the heart of the complex, built in 1720, has a barrel-vaulted ceiling, an excess of gilt but one particularly fine portable mosaic icon of the Virgin Mary.

ST STEPHEN OF THE BULGARS

Murel Paşa Cad 85–88. Bus #99. Daily 8am–5pm. Free. MAP P.82, POCKET MAP C2

Stranded in a traffic island very close to the waterfront, this church was entirely constructed from prefabricated cast-iron panels in Vienna in the late nineteenth century and floated down the Danube into the Black Sea and thence on to İstanbul. With its golden domes, it's very attractive, especially when viewed from the Haliç ferry, but was undergoing restoration at the time of writing.

AHRIDA SYNAGOGUE

Kürkçüçeşme Sok. Bus #99 ☎ 0212 243 5166. Contact the Chief Rabbinate at least one day before to arrange a visit. Free. MAP P.82, POCKET MAP B2

Hidden away in the backstreets of the atmospheric district of Balat, once home to a sizeable Jewish community, this originally fifteenth-century synagogue was rebuilt in Baroque style in 1694. The Jews have long since moved to other parts of the city or emigrated to Israel, but it receives a fair number of visitors despite the problems of having to arrange a visit in advance.

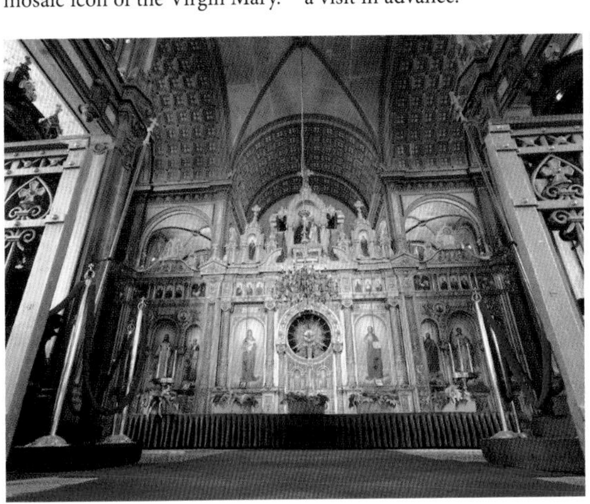

ST STEPHEN OF THE BULGARS

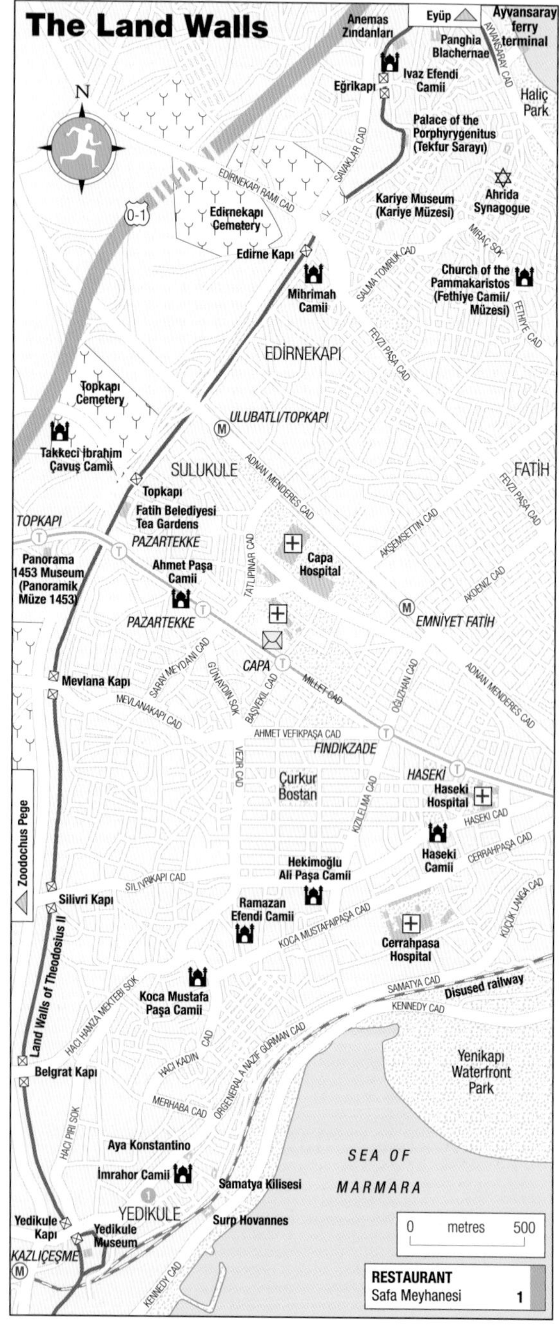
The Land Walls
N
Anemas Zindanları
Eyüp
Ayvansaray ferry terminal
Panghia Blachernae
AYVANSARAY CAD
Ivaz Efendi Camii
Eğrikapı
Haliç Park
Palace of the Porphyrygenitus (Tekfur Sarayı)
SAVAKLAR CAD
EDIRNEKAPI RAMI CAD
Kariye Museum (Kariye Müzesi)
Ahrida Synagogue
O-1
Edirnekapı Cemetery
MIRAÇ SOK
Edirne Kapı
SALMA TOMRUK CAD
Church of the Pammakaristos (Fethiye Camii/ Müzesi)
Mihrimah Camii
FETHIYE CAD
FEVZI PAŞA CAD
EDİRNEKAPI
Topkapı Cemetery
ULUBATLI/TOPKAPI
Takkeci İbrahim Çavuş Camii
SULUKULE
ADNAN MENDERES CAD
FATİH
FEVZI PAŞA CAD
Topkapı
Fatih Belediyesi Tea Gardens
TOPKAPI
PAZARTEKKE
AKŞEMSETTIN CAD
TATLIPINAR CAD
Capa Hospital
Panorama 1453 Museum (Panoramik Müze 1453)
Ahmet Paşa Camii
AKDENIZ CAD
PAZARTEKKE
EMNİYET FATİH
SARAY MEYDANI CAD
GÜNAYDIN SOK
CAPA
BAŞVEKIL CAD
MILLET CAD
OĞUZHAN CAD
ADNAN MENDERES CAD
Mevlana Kapı
MEVLANAKAPI CAD
AHMET VEFIKPAŞA CAD
FINDIKZADE
VEZIR CAD
Çurkur Bostan
KIZILELMA CAD
HASEKİ
Haseki Hospital
HASEKI CAD
Haseki Camii
CERRAHPAŞA CAD
Zoodochus Pege
Hekimoğlu Ali Paşa Camii
SILIVRIKAPI CAD
KÜÇÜK LANGA CAD
Silivri Kapı
Ramazan Efendi Camii
KOCA MUSTAFAPAŞA CAD
Cerrahpasa Hospital
Land Walls of Theodosius II
SAMATYA CAD
Disused railway
KENNEDY CAD
Koca Mustafa Paşa Camii
HACI HAMZA MEKTEBI SOK
ORGENERAL A NAZIF GÜRMAN CAD
HACI KADIN CAD
Yenikapı Waterfront Park
Belgrat Kapı
MERHABA CAD
HACI PIRI SOK
Aya Konstantino
SEA OF MARMARA
İmrahor Camii
Samatya Kilisesi
1
YEDIKULE
Surp Hovannes
Yedikule Kapı
Yedikule Museum
0 metres 500
KAZLIÇEŞME
KENNEDY CAD
RESTAURANT
Safa Meyhanesi 1

Land walls of Theodosius

This superb feat of Byzantine engineering stretches some 6.5km, from the Sea of Marmara to the Golden Horn, thus cutting off the peninsula on which the city was built from the rest of Europe – and kept foes as formidable as **Atilla the Hun** and the Arab armies of Islam at walls-width for a thousand years. Constructed as a single wall in 413 under Theodosius II, following a disastrous earthquake in 447 the defences were rebuilt in triplicate. The inner wall of the defences was now 5m thick and 12m high, strengthened by 96 towers; the outer wall 2m by 8.5m, again fortified by towers spaced between those on the main wall behind; in front lay a 20m-wide moat. **Walking** the line of the walls today is an adventure, with opportunities to mount the battlements and visit a number of other sights en route. Avoid leaving late in the day as the wall runs through poor neighbourhoods, and petty theft is not unknown around dusk and after dark.

To get to the south end of the walls at Yedikule, take the #80 bus from Eminönü or the #80/T from Taksim. Much easier is to take the Marmaray metro from Sirkeci to the Kazlıçeşme stop, just outside the walls near Yedikule. From the north end of the walls, the Haliç ferry runs down the Golden Horn from Ayvansaray to Eminönü, or take the #99 bus to the same destination.

YEDİKULE MUSEUM

Kale Meydanı Cad. Ⓑ1 train, buses #80, #80/T. Tues–Sun 9am–6pm. ₺10. MAP P.86

Wall-walking enthusiasts should start where the wall began, at the **Marble Tower** on the south side of traffic-filled Kennedy Caddesi. A short walk north on the outside of the walls is **Yedikule Gate** (Yedikule Kapı). Enter here as access to Yedikule Museum is on the inside of the walls. Essentially a fortress added to the line of the Byzantine walls by Mehmet the Conqueror in 1457–58, it consists of three large towers linked by a curtain wall and connected to a section of the land walls which boasts four towers of its own. This gives rise to the fortification's Turkish name Yedikule, "The Seven Towers". Yedikule was, ironically given its appearance, never used as a fort. Two of its towers left of the entrance were in Ottoman times a prison and treasury, and the section of land walls incorporates the earlier, famous **Golden Gate**. This triple-arched structure, now bricked up, was a triumphal arch erected under Theodosius I in 390 over one of the main roads leading into Constantinople.

BELGRAT KAPI

Bus #93/T. MAP P.86

From **Yedikule Kapı**, it's possible to follow the outside of the partially restored walls northwards. The moat is now used for market gardens, but there are well-preserved sections of outer and inner wall. The next gate, **Belgrat (Belgrade) Kapı**, was originally a military gate that included portals through the inner and outer walls but did not have – as the public gates had – a bridge across the moat.

ZOODOCHUS PEGE
BALIKLI KİLİSE

Seyit Nizam Cad 3. Bus #93/T. Daily 8.30am–4.30pm. Free.

Following the walls north you reach **Silivri Kapı**, known as Pege in Byzantine times because of the nearby shrine of **Zoodochus Pege**. Cross the busy six-lane highway paralleling the walls and follow a road 500m west through mixed Muslim and Christian cemeteries to a pretty nineteenth-century Greek church, built over a much earlier Byzantine structure. It's famed for the fish living in its *ayazma*, a sacred underground spring.

PANORAMA 1453 MUSEUM
PANORAMİK MÜZE 1453

Topkapı Kültür Parkı Ⓜ1 Topkapı Ⓣ0212 415 1453, Ⓦpanoramikmuze.com. Daily 9am–6.30pm. ₺10, audio-guide ₺5. MAP P.86

North of Silivri Kapı is Mevlana Kapı. Northwest of this gate, across the six-lane highway in an area of urban park stranded in a major junction, is the Panorama 1453 Museum. Turks outnumber foreigners here, no doubt because the museum glorifies the iconic conquest of what was then Christian Constantinople by the Muslim, Ottoman Turks on 29 May 1453. Downstairs a circular viewing gallery runs beneath a large dome on which is cleverly painted – in an eye-boggling 360-degree panorama – the army of the young Sultan Mehmet I besieging the walls of Constantinople. Flaming balls of Greek fire, the Byzantines' "secret" weapon, pour down on the hapless attackers, who hold the green flag of Islam aloft in defiance, and the mighty walls crack and crumble under the assault of the Orban, a monster cannon some 27 feet long and with a bore wide enough to allow a man to crawl inside. The impressive scene, reputed to contain over 10,000 figures,

PANORAMA 1453 MUSEUM

is enhanced by a realistic battlefield tableau ringing the viewing gallery.

THE WALLS – TOPKAPI TO EDİRNE KAPI

Back across the busy thoroughfare from the Panorama 1453 Museum and on the north side of Millet Caddesi, which runs either side of the T1 tramline, is the Topkapı or **Gate of the Cannonball**, named after the Orban cannon that pulverized the land walls with shot weighing up to half a tonne. Continuing north you have to negotiate traffic-choked Adnan Menderes (Vatan) Caddesi – preferably by the underpass that also leads to the M1 Ulubatlı/Topkapı stop. Between here and Edirne Kapı is a pronounced dip, the valley of the Lycus river, a weak point because the walls along the valley floor were lower than the besiegers' weaponry. This is where the Turks finally and decisively pierced the walls and poured into the city. The walls now run through Sulukule, a neighbourhood home to a **gypsy community** for centuries. Many of the traditional wood houses they inhabited have been controversially (UNESCO was outraged) bulldozed by the municipality, with posh villas in walled compounds put in their place.

MİHRİMAH CAMİİ

Edirnekapı. Buses #28, #36/V, #37/Y, #38, #38/E, #55/EB. MAP P.86

Majestically located on the summit of the sixth of the old city's seven hills, this recently restored mosque is one of architect Sinan's (see p.67) earlier masterpieces. It was commissioned by Rüstem Paşa, grand vizier to Süleyman the Magnificent, and his wife Mihrimah, the sultan's favourite

MIHRIMAH CAMII

daughter. Access is via steps on the north side of the mosque. The beautiful prayer hall is incredibly light and airy due to the three rows of windows puncturing each of the four filled arches supporting the 20m-diameter dome. Just beyond the Mihrimah Camii is **Edirne Kapı** which bears, on the outside, a modern plaque in Turkish proclaiming it the entry point of the victorious Sultan Mehmet II on 29 May 1453.

PALACE OF THE PORPHYROGENITUS *TEKFUR SARAYI*

Edirnekapı, Şişhane Cad. Buses #28, #36/V, #37/Y, #38, #38/E, #55/EB. MAP P.86, POCKET MAP A2

The walls dip down towards the Golden Horn past Edirne Kapı. Built into the line, well-preserved here, is the **Tekfur Saray** or **Palace of the Porphyrogenitus**. Until 2014 a mere shell, this former annexe of the Blachernae Palace is being controversially rebuilt as a congress and exhibition centre. The palace marks the start of a change in the walls, now a single, thicker line bulging out to the west and running down the steep hill towards the Golden Horn, built in the seventh century.

EYÜP

EYÜP CAMİİ

Cami Kebir Sok. Buses #99, #39, or Haliç ferry.

A short walk north of the land walls is the district of Eyüp, named after Eyüp Ensari, standard bearer of the Prophet Mohammed, who died and was buried here during the first Arab siege of Constantinople (674–78). At the heart of the area the mosque bearing the standard-bearer's name, and his tomb, stand opposite each other across a courtyard – usually thronged with pilgrims. The mosque dates back to 1458 but was rebuilt in Baroque style in 1800 following an earthquake. The tomb (Tues–Sun 9.30am–4.30pm; free) itself is covered in an eclectic mix of fine tiles. This is a sacred spot for Muslims – arguably the third most important Islamic pilgrimage site after Mecca and Jerusalem – and the whole area very conservative, so make sure you are modestly attired and women should cover their heads in both mosque and tomb.

TOMB OF SOKULLU MEHMET PAŞA

Cami Kebir Cad. Buses #99, #39, or Haliç ferry. Tues–Sun 9.30am–4.30pm.

A short way south of Eyüp Camii is a fine tomb, one of the many dotted around here. It houses the remains of Sokullu Mehmet Paşa, a Bosnian who became one of the empire's greatest grand viziers under Süleyman the Magnificent. The work of the leading architect of the day, Sinan, it was completed in 1574. It's a beautiful work of art, a severe octagonal structure topped by a dome and embellished with some lovely stained glass. The other buildings ranged around it are part of the tomb complex and include a library, medrese, Koran school and the tombs of the Grand Vizier's family.

EYÜP CEMETERY

Gümüssuyu Karyağdı Sok. Buses #99, #39, or Haliç ferry.

On the prominent hill north of the mosque and tombs is a Muslim cemetery, thick with cypress trees standing sentinel over Ottoman-era, and much more recent and decidedly less ornate, tombstones. At the top is a very popular tea garden, the *Pierre Lotte Café* (daily 8am–midnight), named after the French Romantic novelist who frequented the area in the late nineteenth century. A cable car links the banks of the Golden Horn, some 400m north of the Eyüp ferry quay, to the hilltop café (daily 8am–midnight ₺3).

Cafés

ARNAVÜT KÖFTECİ

Mursel Paşa Cad 149. Bus #99. Daily 4.30am–6.30pm. MAP P.82, POCKET MAP B2

A cult institution on the banks of the Golden Horn, specializing in cheap (₺9), tender grilled Albanian-style meatballs (*köfte*). The attractive European-style building dates back to the nineteenth century when this was a really cosmopolitan neighbourhood, the eclectic slew of formica-topped tables only to the 1950s – just a few years after the place first opened its doors in 1947.

DURAK KÖFTE

Mihrimah Sultan Camii Altı 361. Bus #28, #36/V, #37/Y, #38, #38/E, #55/EB ⓣ 0212 587 9868. Daily 10am–6.30pm. MAP P.82

Meatballs are a staple Turkish fast food and this place does a fine line in Macedonian-style *köfte* along with a range of other good-value workers' favourites such as *kuru fasulye* or haricot beans in tomato sauce. Set right beneath the lovely Mihrimah mosque with a few outside tables.

Restaurants

ASİTANE

Kariye Hotel, Kariye Camii Sok 18 Ⓣ1 Topkapı/Ulubatlı or buses #28, #36/V, #37/Y, #38, #38/E, #55/EB ⓣ 0212 534 8414. Daily 11.30am–11pm. MAP P.82, POCKET MAP A2

Well worth splashing out on, this lovely restaurant in the chestnut-tree-shaded courtyard of the *Kariye Hotel* (see p.145) was one of the first places in the city to revive Ottoman-style cuisine, bringing new/old flavours to foreigners and locals alike. Try the *hünkar beğendi* (literally "the sultan liked it"), an Ottoman classic done to perfection here. Mains around ₺35. Licensed.

DEVELİ

Gumuş Yüzük Sok 7 Ⓑ1 Kocamustafapaşa ⓣ 0212 529 0833. Daily noon–midnight. MAP P.82

Founded in 1912 by émigrés from the south of the country, and it is still sizzling-out some of the tenderest, tastiest meat (kebabs from ₺22) in the city. Overlooking an atmospheric little square, the top-floor terrace has great views over the Sea of Marmara. The *meze* and *baklava* are just as good as the wide range of kebabs. Licensed.

SAFA MEYHANESİ

İlyasbey Cad 12, Yedikule Marmaray Ⓜ Kalıçeşme, ⓣ 0212 585 5594, ⓦ safameyhanesi.com. Daily noon–midnight. MAP P.86

This delightful old school *meyhane* looks like the stage set for a 1940s movie, with its wooden walls, high ceiling and glittering chandelier, shelves of *rakı* bottles and the original posters advertising this potent aniseed spirit. It's a little out of the way and has no live music so it appeals to İstanbul intellectuals and academics out for an evening. *Meze*s are reasonable at between ₺7-13, fish of the day is priced by the kilo.

ASITANE

Galata and the waterfront districts

Dominated by the landmark Galata Tower, which takes its name from the vibrant district at its feet, Galata's cobbled alleys tumble down to the busy north shore of the Golden Horn. An autonomous Genoese colony in the late Byzantine era, home to thriving Jewish, Moorish, Armenian and Greek communities since the Ottoman conquest, it has always been different from the conservative, mainly Muslim old city. Over the last decade it has blossomed from a run-down port area to a bohemian quarter of trendy shops, artists' studios, musicians' workshops, street art, hip bars and clubs. The city's best contemporary art gallery, İstanbul Modern, lies just along the waterfront, a quaint nineteenth-century underground funicular continues to toil up the hill and dervishes still whirl at the Galata Mevlevi Lodge.

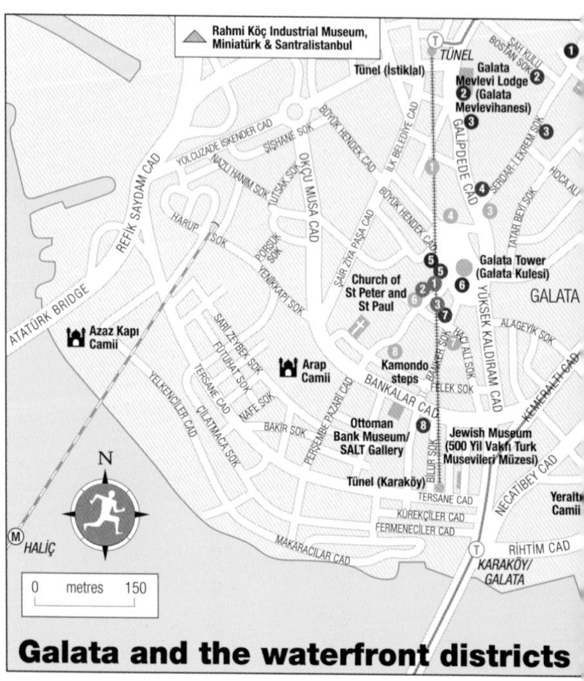

GALATA TOWER
GALATA KULESİ

Galata Meydanı ☎ 0212 293 8180, 🌐 galatatower.net. Daily 9am–8pm. €6.5.
MAP P.92–93, POCKET MAP A15

Best reached by walking down Galip Dede Caddesi from İstiklal Tünel station, this soaring, 61m-high medieval tower, capped by a distinctive conical roof, was known as the Tower of Christ when it was built by the Genoese in 1349. Originally part of the fortification wall constructed to protect the Genoese mercantile colony established within it, it was turned into a jail in the fifteenth century. In the seventeenth century, it was used, successfully according to famous Ottoman traveller Evliya Çelebi, by pioneers experimenting in manned flight. From the eighteenth century, its purpose was more prosaic and pragmatic, as a watchtower for the then all too common fires. It is by far the biggest attraction in Galata, with long queues sometimes snaking around the square – particularly for the ever-popular sunset viewing period. The lookout gallery, reached today by a lift, is often crowded, but the views are worth it, with a foreground of the ferry-filled Golden Horn and manic Eminönü waterfront backed by the serene, mosque-lined skyline of the old city, all stately domes and elegant minarets. The tower is home to an expensive café and touristy oriental floor-shows take place most evenings after 8pm.

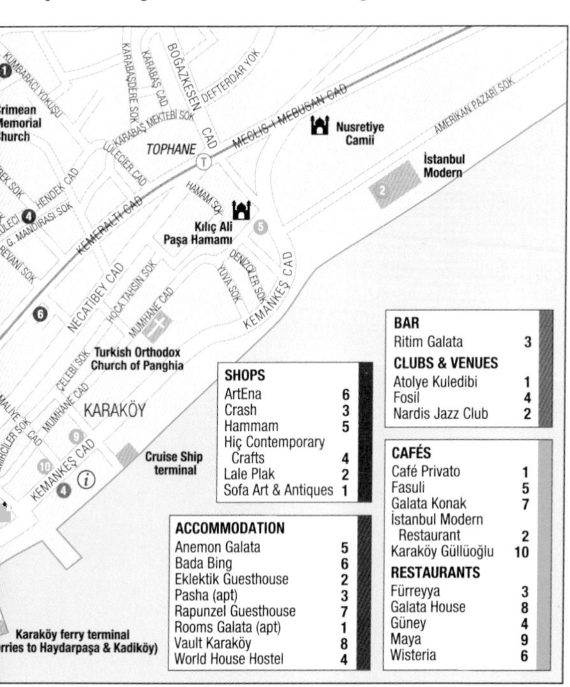

GALATA MEVLEVI LODGE *GALATA MEVLEVİHANESİ*

Galipdede Cad ⓣ 0212 678 0618, ⓦ rumimevlevi.com. Daily except Tues 9:30am–5pm. ₺10. MAP P.92–93, POCKET MAP A14

This former lodge or monastery (*tekke*) of the Mevlevi Sufi order was home to one of Islam's mystical sects, the Mevlevis. The order was founded in the thirteenth century by Mevlana who, tired of the constraints of mainstream Sunni Islam, took his followers down the path of love and acceptance. Mevlana's disciples, or dervishes, are best known in the West for their hypnotic rotating dance, hence "whirling dervish". This ritual dance, along with prayer, meditation, contemplation and music, enabled adherents to achieve mystical union with God. The Mevlevis, along with all sufi orders, were deemed reactionaries by Atatürk and, in 1923, banned. The order went "underground" for decades but today is semi-officially tolerated. The lodge, built in the fifteenth century but much remodelled, is now a fascinating museum. Exhibits in the downstairs rooms, reached via a peaceful courtyard/garden area, are arranged clockwise. Here, you can see the traditional instruments that provided the musical accompaniment to the dances, dervish costumes, begging bowls, kitchen utensils and a host of other interesting items. Upstairs is the *semahane*, where the dervishes whirled, a beautifully decorated, high-ceilinged octagonal room where dervish shows for visitors are held most Sundays between April and September at 5pm, twice monthly the rest of the year (₺40).

OTTOMAN BANK MUSEUM/ SALT GALLERY

Bankalar Cad 35 ⓣ 0212 334 2200, ⓦ obmuze.com. Tues–Sat noon–8pm, Sun 10.30am–6pm. Free. MAP P.92–93, POCKET MAP A15

Aptly situated on the "Street of Banks" and today owned by one of Turkey's leading banks, Garanti, this grandiose building was once the headquarters of the Ottoman Imperial Bank. The French architect behind this typically nineteenth-century European-style building was Vallaury, who also designed the Archeology Museum (see p.51) and Pera Palace Hotel (see p.147). Its cavernous interior has been cleverly modernized for Garanti Bank's **SALT contemporary arts project** and hosts a variety of temporary exhibitions. If the current exhibitions are not to your

GALATA MEVLEVI LODGE

Getting to, and around, Galata

Most people coming to Galata from the old city take the T1 tram to the Karaköy stop and walk up into the compact, hillside neighbourhood to see the sights, shop, eat or go to a club. Alternatively take the nearby late nineteenth-century underground funicular, Tünel (see p.155) to its top, İstiklal station, and walk down. Coming from Taksim Square, the antique tram (see p.155) running down pedestrianized İstiklal Caddesi will save you 1.5km of walking. Coming in from the northern suburbs and Taksim, the M2 metro to Şişhane is useful. All sights and listings in Galata and its immediate environs are best approached in this way, unless otherwise stated, and thence on foot.

taste, it's worth perusing the permanent **Ottoman Bank Museum** on the ground floor. The bank served Galata's mainly non-Muslim, Greek, Armenian and Jewish inhabitants.

AROUND BANKALAR CADDESİ

MAP P.92–93, POCKET MAP A15

The whole of Bankalar Caddesi is lined with fine, European-style nineteenth- and early twentieth-century buildings. Just west of the Ottoman Bank Museum, the **Kamondo steps**, sinuously curved, Art Nouveau-style twin staircases, were commissioned by the wealthy Jewish Kamondo family in 1860. They achieved iconic status in the 1960s when they were photographed by Henri-Cartier Bresson, a friend of equally accomplished İstanbul-Armenian photographer and local resident Ara Güler. Just off Bankalar Caddesi on Galata Kulesi Sokak, the **Church of St Peter and St Paul** dates back to the fifteenth century and still holds Mass every Sunday. Running parallel to Bankalar Caddesi is Galata Mahkamesi Caddesi, where you'll find the **Arap Camii**. Built as a Genoese church, it was converted into a mosque for the Moorish community in the sixteenth century.

JEWISH MUSEUM
500 YIL VAKFI TÜRK MUSEVİLERİ MÜZESİ

Perçemli Sok ⓣ 0212 292 6363, ⓦ muze500.com. Mon–Thurs 10am–4pm, Fri & Sun 10am–2pm. ₺10. MAP P.92–93, POCKET MAP A16

Housed in the former Zulfaris Synagogue, rebuilt in 1904 on the site of the seventeenth-century original, and opened to celebrate the five hundredth anniversary of the arrival of the Jews expelled from Spain, this small museum is hidden up a side street right of the Karaköy Tünel entrance. Inside are the usual menorahs, scrolls, costumes and other ethnographic materials – but the black-and-white photographs are evocative and the display boards give a good introduction to the complex history of the Jews in Turkey.

THE KAMONDO STEPS

ISTANBUL MODERN

İSTANBUL MODERN

Meclis-i-Mebusan Cad Ⓣ1 Tophane Ⓣ 0212 334 7300, Ⓦ istanbulmodern.org. Tues–Sun 10am–6pm, Thurs 10am–8pm. ₺17. MAP P.92–93, POCKET MAP D14

The city's answer to London's Tate Modern might not be quite so large or cutting edge but succeeds in bringing **contemporary art** to the heart of this thriving metropolis. The setting, in a converted Bosphorus-front warehouse well-east of Galata proper, is superb, with grand views across the water to the Topkapı Palace and the old city. The permanent exhibition upstairs outlines the development of Turkish art from the early nineteenth century through to the 1950s and beyond, which you can take a break from on the waterfront veranda of the more than acceptable, if pricey, café-restaurant (see p.99), or in the decent gift-shop. The temporary exhibitions, held in a suitably large, blank space downstairs are the real pull, though, so check the website for what's on. There's also an art-house cinema here – again check the website for details – free for museum visitors or ₺8 cinema-only. While you're out here, it's worth having a look at a couple of fine mosques, both recently restored. Just north of İstanbul Modern is the **Nusretiye Camii**, a Baroque-style mosque built in the 1820s, the work of Armenian architect Balian. The older **Kılıç Ali Paşa Camii**, a couple of minutes' stroll southeast of the art gallery, was built in 1580 for the Ottoman admiral after whom it is named, by the ubiquitous architect Sinan.

KILIÇ ALİ PAŞA HAMAMI

Kılıç Ali Paşa Hamamı Hamam Sok 1 Ⓣ1 Tophane Ⓣ 0212 393 8010 Ⓦ kilicalipasahamami.com. Daily 8am–4pm (women); 4:30pm–midnight (men). ₺130 including scrub and massage. MAP P.92–93, POCKET MAP C14

Attached to the sixteenth century Kılıç Ali Paşa mosque, on the north side of Galata bridge, this superb Turkish bath-house opened in 2013 after a seven year restoration process. Like the mosque, it's the work of Sinan and is a quite beautiful example of an Ottoman-era *hamam* (bath-house), with the brickwork of the domed changing room lovingly exposed, light streaming in through small, star-shaped windows in the dome surmounting the bathing areas.

RAHMI M. KOÇ INDUSTRIAL MUSEUM

Hasköy Cad 27. Buses #47, #47E, #54/HT or Haliç ferry to Hasköy pier ⓣ 0212 369 6000, ⓦ rmk-museum.org.tr. April–Sept Tues–Fri 10am–5pm, Sat & Sun 10am–8pm; Oct–March 10am–6pm. ₺12.5.

The first and best of three worthwhile and, certainly for İstanbul, unusual sights dotted along the north bank of the Golden Horn. Long a ship-building area, part of the museum is appropriately housed in what was, in the eighteenth century, a foundry for ships' chains and anchors. Today, it is home to everything from penny farthings to Royal Enfield motorcycles, Trabants to Rolls Royces and a working tram to a model railway. Other highlights include a working ship's bridge, complete with echo sounder and alarm, and a street of period shops and houses. It's the largest collection of industrial-era artefacts in Turkey, the vision of a member of one of Turkey's wealthiest families, and contains a couple of upmarket café-restaurants.

MINIATÜRK

MİNİATÜRK

İmrahor Cad. Buses #47, #47E or #54/HT or Haliç ferry to Sütlüce and walk ⓣ 0212 222 2882, ⓦ miniaturk.com.tr. Daily 8.30am–5.30pm. ₺10.

Northwest of the Rahmi M. Koç Industrial Museum, just beyond the massive Haliç bridge, this attraction is a great hit with the locals, displaying a hundred 1:25 scale models of Turkey's most important sights. The majority are buildings, though a couple of geological wonders, Cappadocia's famed fairy chimneys and Pamukkale's travertine terraces, have snuck-in. The models are arranged around a near-2km-long signed route in a walled enclosure near the banks of the Golden Horn. If you're pressed for time to see the real thing, here are İstanbul's very own Süleymaniye Mosque, Dolmabahçe Palace and Haghia Sophia – there's even the 1970s Bosphorus Bridge and Atatürk airport.

SANTRALİSTANBUL ENERGY MUSEUM

Kazımkarabekir Cad 2. Free shuttle bus from Taksim Square, buses #54/HT, #99 or Haliç ferry to Eyüp pier and walk ⓣ 0212 311 7878, ⓦ santralistanbul.org. Tues–Fri 10am–5pm, Sat & Sun 10am–8pm. ₺10 combined entry.

The furthest of the three Golden Horn attractions from the city centre and right at the head of the inlet, the Energy Museum is housed in a converted power station that began life in 1914 and was for many years the city's sole electricity producer. The Energy Museum has carefully preserved the plant's control room, where a massive bank of dials, switches and gauges helped workers keep control of the giant Siemens engines. Thrown in for good measure is some far more cutting-edge technical wizardry, including a thermal-imaging screen.

Shops

ARTENA

Camekan Sok 1. Daily 10am–8pm. MAP P.92–93, POCKET MAP A15

Established in 2004, this designer boutique stocks a range of handcrafted jewellery, home-spun hats and bags, plus a range of ethnic artefacts collected from Anatolian villages and traditional jewellery from southeast Turkey. You'll likely be offered tea or coffee as you browse.

CRASH

Galipdede Cad 55. Mon–Sat 10am–9pm. MAP P.92–93, POCKET MAP B14

The Galata neo-bohemian's outlet of choice, this small store stocks a range of carefully chosen (to be slightly alt and cool) end-of-line jeans, shorts, tees, hoodies, dresses and the like – and knocks them out at fair prices.

HAMMAM

Kule Çıkmazı. Daily 11am–7pm. MAP P.92–93, POCKET MAP A15

A wide range of Turkish bath accessories is on offer here, from quality cotton *peştemal* wraps to fancy soap bowls, as well as handmade soaps and lotions – all presented with panache.

HİÇ CONTEMPORARY CRAFTS

Lüleci Hendek Sok 35, Karaköy ⓣ 0212 251 9973, ⓦ hiccrafts.com. Mon–Sat 11am–7pm. MAP P.92–93, POCKET MAP B14

This small shop specialises in tasteful furniture and accessories by local designers. Most items have an ethnic feel about them, though they are very contemporary in style. Look out also for the fine ikat and suzani fabrics from Central Asia.

LALE PLAK

Galipdede Cad 1. Daily 9am–7pm. MAP P.92–93, POCKET MAP A14

HİÇ CONTEMPORARY CRAFTS

In a great location where Galipdede Caddesi joins throbbing İstiklal Caddesi, *Lale Plak* is İstanbul music-buffs' store of choice. Established over fifty years ago, leafing through the racks of jazz and rock vinyl classics is a retro delight, but there's plenty of Turkish and Western music on CD too.

SOFA ART AND ANTIQUES

Serdar-ı Ekrem Sok 47, Galata ⓣ 0212 292 3977, ⓦ kashifsofa.com. Mon–Sat 9am–7pm. MAP P.92–93, POCKET MAP B14

Established back in 1976 by husband and wife team Kaşif and Dilek, *Sofa* is situated on very fashionable Serdar-I Ekrem street, near the Galata Tower. It is a reputable place to hunt down antiques and vintage items both from Europe and Ottoman Turkey, including calligraphy, tiles, miniatures and textiles. There's another branch in the Grand Bazaar.

Cafés

CAFÉ PRIVATO

Tımarcı Sok 3B, Galata ⓣ 0212 293 2055, ⓦ privatocafe.com. Daily 9am–midnight. MAP P.92–93, POCKET MAP A14

This cosy café is well-known for its superb fixed menu breakfast spread (¨30). Sit down to enjoy a mouth-watering array of dishes that include homemade organic jams, Georgian pancakes (the owner is of Georgian origin), several different cheeses, dressed olives and much more. One breakfast is generally enough for two people, and there are lots of other options for later in the day.

FASULİ

İskele Cad 10–12 Ⓣ1 Tophane ⓘ0212 243 6580. Daily 7am–11pm. MAP P.92–93, POCKET MAP B5

White beans in tomato sauce (*kuru fasulye*) are a standard Turkish dish. Here they are an art form. The tender, melt-in-your-mouth beans are grown in the foothills of the Pontic Alps, high above the owners' native Trabzon on the Black Sea, then smothered in a butter-rich tomato sauce. They make for a bargain (₺8) lunchtime treat, but there's much else to choose from besides. The restaurant, housed in an attractive period building, has a pleasant roof terrace. Unlicensed.

GALATA KONAK

Haci Ali Sok 2 ⓘ0212 252 5346. Daily 9am–11pm. MAP P.92–93, POCKET MAP A15

Really two places in one, the ground-floor patisserie is great for a range of quality Turkish and European-style cakes and desserts. Upstairs, reached by the antiquated lift original to this turn-of-the-nineteenth-century building, is a popular roof-terrace restaurant with a range of local and international dishes ranging from *menemen*, a scrambled egg, onion and pepper delight, to pasta dishes (₺9 and ₺15 and up respectively). It's especially packed for Sunday brunch. Great views but unlicensed.

İSTANBUL MODERN RESTAURANT

Medis-i-Mebusan Cad, Antrepo 4 Ⓣ1 Tophane ⓘ0212 292 2612. Daily 10am–midnight. MAP P.92–93, POCKET MAP D14

Part of the trendy gallery and very popular with the city's middle-classes, this is a great place for a latte on the waterfront terrace or a more substantial meal chosen from a Turkish and international menu. A bit pricey for what it is (mains ₺30 and up), but worth it for the relaxed ambience and the fact it's licensed.

KARAKÖY GÜLLÜOĞLU

Rihtim Cad 17 ⓘ0212 293 0910. Daily 10am–midnight. MAP P.92–93, POCKET MAP B15

This cavernous place is certainly not the cheapest in the city for *baklava* and other Turkish nut and pastry concoctions, but it's arguably the best. Rich, buttery and with a dry texture (cheaper places often skimp on the nuts and overdo the syrup), it's invariably packed with locals tucking into walnut- or pistachio-rich *baklava*, often accompanied by a splodge of chewy (it contains gum mastic) Maraş ice cream. Unlicensed.

KARAKÖY GÜLLÜOĞLU

Restaurants

FÜRREYYA

Serdar-ı Ekrem Sok 2B, Galata ⓣ 0212 252 4853, ⓦ furreyyagalata.com. Daily noon–11pm. MAP P.92–93, POCKET MAP B14

This small, cosy yet stylish fish restaurant serves up excellent seafood at very reasonable prices. Try the fish wrap (₺10), shrimp casserole (₺22) or fishcakes with basil sauce (₺19). There's a decent selection of wines, too.

GALATA HOUSE

Galata Kulesi Sok 61 ⓣ 0212 245 1861. Daily 3pm–midnight. MAP P.92–93, POCKET MAP A15

Intimate, fifty-seater restaurant (booking advised) atmospherically housed in the old British Prison just down from the Galata Tower – ask owners Mete and Nadire to point out some of the graffiti left by former inmates and give you a run-down of the whole history of this fascinating little quarter. Georgian-influenced cuisine is a real draw here – try the savoury stuffed dumplings. Nice garden out back, too. Mains ₺25 and up. Licensed.

GÜNEY

GÜNEY

Kuledibi Sah Kapısı 6 ⓣ 0212 249 0393. Mon–Sat 7am–10pm. MAP P.92–93, POCKET MAP A14

Not so long ago, this was a traditional *lokanta* dishing up hearty stews to hungry, cost-conscious artisans. The gentrification/bohemianization of the quarter has seen off most of the workers but the food is just as substantial (stew-type dishes chosen from a steamtray, *pide* – Turkish pizza – and kebabs). The location, right on the square below the tower, is appealing and good value with mains from ₺14. Unlicensed.

MAYA

Kermankeş Cad 35/A ⓣ 0212 252 6884. Tues–Sat noon–11pm, Mon noon–5pm. MAP P.92–93, POCKET MAP C15

Returning from New York's French Culinary Institute brimming with ideas and know-how, owner Didem has opened a deservedly popular place knocking-out traditional Turkish fare given a thoroughly modern twist. Both lunch and evening menus change on a daily basis and all ingredients are lovingly sourced – for example, the olive oil from Marmaris, pomegranate syrup from Antakya and bread from Bolu. Stylish interior and good location near the waterfront in Karaköy. Licensed.

WİSTERİA

Galata Kulesi Sok 20 ⓣ 0212 252 7218. Tues–Sun 8am–2am. MAP P.92–93, POCKET MAP A15

Definitely a place to highlight Galata's rapid morph from urban bohemia to upmarket metropolitanism, the cuisine is good-quality Mediterranean/Italian, though the real draw is the ambience, with tasteful decor and a large, pretty courtyard with nightly piano recitals.

Bar

RİTİM GALATA

Galata Kulesi Sok 3/C ⓣ 0212 292 4926. Daily 11am–2am. MAP P.92–93, POCKET MAP A15

Halfway between the Galata Tower and *Nardis Jazz Club*, this laidback little bar combines a stylish exposed-brick and mezzanine-floor split interior with mellow sounds from the DJ and a decent Turkish/international menu. There are a few tables out on the cobbled street for hot evenings – and the inevitable smokers.

RİTİM GALATA

Clubs & venues

ATOLYE KULEDİBİ

Galata Kulesi Sok 4 ⓣ 0212 243 7656, ⓦ atolyekuledibi.com. Mon, Tues & Thurs noon–midnight, Wed, Fri & Sat noon–4am. MAP P.92–93, POCKET MAP A15

Bohemian venue run by a co-operative of local artists, musicians, academics, journalists and the like, it's good for cocktails and Italian/ Mexican dishes. There's live music most nights – especially jazz and blues – most reliably on Fridays and Saturdays. In the day, there are often workshops and discussions in a variety of disciplines, with herb teas and fresh juices the order of the day.

FOSİL

Kemankeş Cad 34C, 3rd Floor, Karaköy ⓣ 0507 812 8531, ⓦ fosil.com.tr. Sun–Tue noon–midnight, Wed–Sat noon–4am. MAP P.92–93, POCKET MAP B15

Nowhere is more indicative of this once gritty neighbourhood's transformation from dockland grit to urban hip than this über-cool bar/club, with its interior of exposed piping, bricks and bare bulbs. The narrow entrance way leaves you unprepared for the great Bosphorus views once inside. Very busy Friday and Saturday nights despite small beers at ₺14.

NARDİS JAZZ CLUB

Kuledibi Sok 14 ⓣ 0212 244 6327, ⓦ nardisjazz.com. Sets start Mon–Thurs 9.30pm, Fri & Sat 11.30pm. Admission ₺30–50. MAP P.92–93, POCKET MAP A15

The most accessible and intimate jazz club in the city, with the usual roster of (very talented) Turkish jazz performers leavened by international artists. Admission prices are quite reasonable considering the trendy location and it attracts fans of all ages. Atmospheric bare-brick interior and a bar-grub-type menu.

Beyoğlu and Taksim

Draped across the hilltop above Galata is Beyoğlu, the frenetic entertainment quarter of the metropolis. Heart of the action is one-and-a-half-kilometre-long İstiklal Caddesi (Independence Street), running from the upper Tünel station north to bland but impressively vast Taksim Square. From the seventeenth century onwards this became the European quarter of the city, home to the palatial residences of foreign merchants, ambassadors and members of the city's Greek and Armenian communities. Typically late nineteenth-century Neoclassical-, Art Nouveau- and Secessionist-style apartment blocks line streets punctuated by grand consular buildings, churches and period arcades. Beneath their grand facades, İstanbulites and foreign visitors shop, visit a gallery, take in a film, head up to a rooftop bar to watch the sun sink over the old city across the water and while away the night at a trendy club or live music venue.

İSTİKLAL CADDESİ: TÜNEL TO GALATASARAY MEYDANI

MAP P.104–105, POCKET MAP B13–D11

Leaving the upper İstiklal Tünel station and following the antique tramline round onto İstiklal Caddesi, the first sight of interest is the beautiful curvilinear Art Nouveau facade of the **Botter House**, built in 1901 by Italian architect D'Aronco for the Dutch tailor to Sultan Abdülhamit II. A little way beyond, best reached by heading down steep Kumbaracı Sokak, the pretty Anglican **Crimean Memorial Church** or Christchurch, was constructed in 1868 to commemorate those who fell in the Crimean War. The architect was G.E. Street, also responsible for the Royal Courts of Justice in London.

TRAM, İSTİKLAL CADDESİ

CRIMEAN MEMORIAL CHURCH

Attractively set in a green, walled compound, visitors are requested to leave a ₺10 donation, but it's not always open – try a Sunday morning service. Further up on the right, steps lead down to **St Mary Draperis** (Mon & Wed–Sat 10am–noon, Tues & Sun 2–6pm; Mass Mon–Fri 8am, Sun 9am), a Catholic church designed by Semprini in 1904 on the site of a 1678 original.

On the opposite side of the street, the defunct **Patisserie Markiz**, still advertised by gold-leaf lettering on the glass, has a stunning fin-de-siècle interior with a pair of faïence tile wall panels, *Le Printemps* and *L'Automne*, imported from France. It's now a fast-food café. The **Borusan Arts & Cultural Centre** (İstiklal Cad 213 ⓣ 0212 336 3280, ⓦ borusansanat.com) higher up on the right is home to one of Turkey's leading private orchestras and an art gallery. Continuing up İstiklal on the right is the impressive Dutch consulate, the **Palais de Hollande**, built in Neoclassical style in 1858. On the same side further up the **Merkez Han**, owned by Koç University, houses the Research Centre for Anatolian Studies, which has regular free exhibitions of an archeological and historical nature. More or less opposite is **SALT İstiklal** (ⓦ saltonline.org), a contemporary gallery established by Garanti Bank, and partner to the one in Galata (see p.94). Back on the right, set back from the road, is the very attractive **St Anthoine** (daily 8am–7pm; Mass Sun 10am), a Franciscan church with a red-brick Neogothic facade, built in 1913 on the site of a much earlier church.

Getting to, and around, İstiklal Caddesi (Beyoğlu)

You can reach İstiklal Caddesi from the old city on the T1 tram to Karaköy and then either walk up the hill or take the Tünel funicular (see p.155) to the southern end of the street. Alternatively, with the opening of the Haliç Bridge in 2013, you can now also use the M2 metro to Şishane or Tasksim. For the north Taksim end, it's possible to ride the T1 tram to Kabataş, then the F1 funicular to Taksim Square. Wherever you start, explorations are best done on foot, though judicious use of the antique tram that runs the whole length of the street, stopping at points en route (see p.155), is fun. From the northern suburbs, you can use the M2 metro to Taksim at the north end of İstiklal Caddesi, or Şişhane at the south end. Unless otherwise stated, these will be the best ways to visit the sights and venues in this chapter.

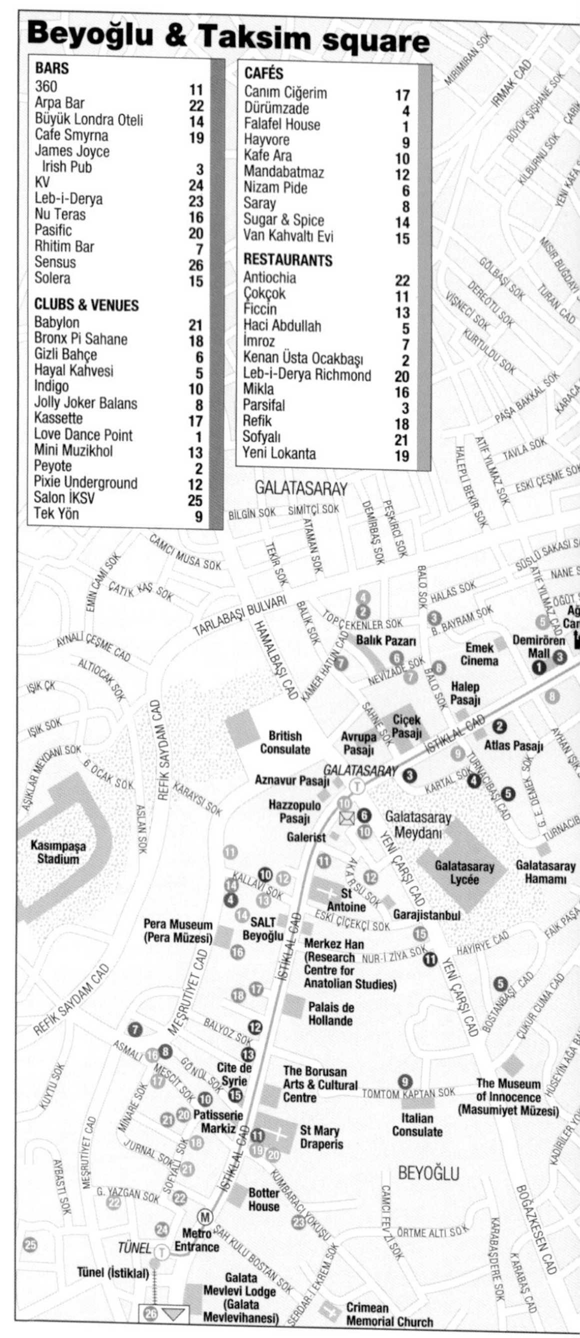
Beyoğlu & Taksim square
BARS
360 11
Arpa Bar 22
Büyük Londra Oteli 14
Cafe Smyrna 19
James Joyce Irish Pub 3
KV 24
Leb-i-Derya 23
Nu Teras 16
Pasific 20
Rhitim Bar 7
Sensus 26
Solera 15
CLUBS & VENUES
Babylon 21
Bronx Pi Sahane 18
Gizli Bahçe 6
Hayal Kahvesi 5
Indigo 10
Jolly Joker Balans 8
Kassette 17
Love Dance Point 1
Mini Muzikhol 13
Peyote 2
Pixie Underground 12
Salon İKSV 25
Tek Yön 9
CAFÉS
Canım Ciğerim 17
Dürümzade 4
Falafel House 1
Hayvore 9
Kafe Ara 10
Mandabatmaz 12
Nizam Pide 6
Saray 8
Sugar & Spice 14
Van Kahvaltı Evi 15
RESTAURANTS
Antiochia 22
Çokçok 11
Ficcin 13
Haci Abdullah 5
İmroz 7
Kenan Üsta Ocakbaşı 2
Leb-i-Derya Richmond 20
Mikla 16
Parsifal 3
Refik 18
Sofyalı 21
Yeni Lokanta 19
GALATASARAY
TARLABAŞI BULVARI
Balık Pazarı
Emek Cinema
Demirören Mall
Halep Pasajı
Çiçek Pasajı
British Consulate
Avrupa Pasajı
Atlas Pasajı
İSTİKLAL CAD
Aznavur Pasajı
Hazzopulo Pasajı
Galatasaray Meydanı
Galerist
Kasımpaşa Stadium
Galatasaray Lycée
Galatasaray Hamamı
St Antoine
Garajistanbul
Pera Museum (Pera Müzesi)
SALT Beyoğlu
Merkez Han (Research Centre for Anatolian Studies)
Palais de Hollande
Cite de Syrie
The Borusan Arts & Cultural Centre
The Museum of Innocence (Masumiyet Müzesi)
Italian Consulate
Patisserie Markiz
St Mary Draperis
BEYOĞLU
Botter House
Metro Entrance
TÜNEL
Tünel (İstiklal)
Galata Mevlevi Lodge (Galata Mevlevihanesi)
Crimean Memorial Church

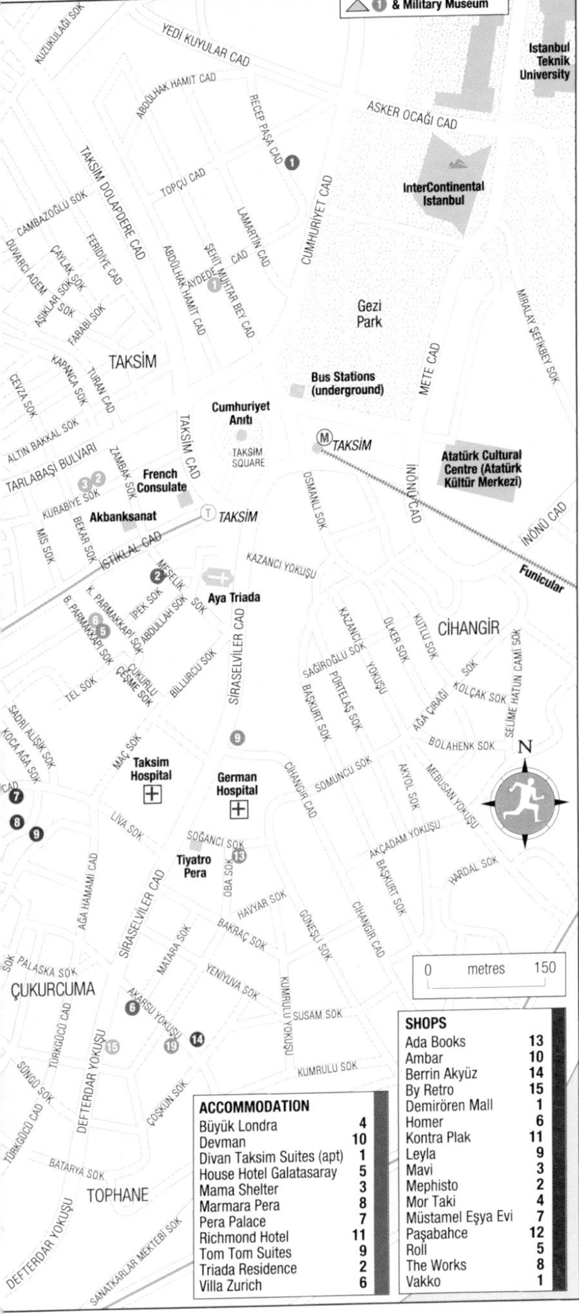
1 & Military Museum
Istanbul Teknik University
YEDİ KUYULAR CAD
ABDÜLHAK HAMİT CAD
RECEP PAŞA CAD
ASKER OCAĞI CAD
InterContinental Istanbul
CUMHURİYET CAD
TOPÇU CAD
TAKSİM DOLAPDERE CAD
LAMARTİN CAD
ŞEHİT MUHTAR BEY CAD
AYDEDE CAD
Gezi Park
MİRALAY ŞEFİKBEY SOK
METE CAD
TAKSİM
Bus Stations (underground)
Cumhuriyet Anıtı
TAKSİM SQUARE
TAKSİM CAD
TAKSİM
Atatürk Cultural Centre (Atatürk Kültür Merkezi)
TARLABAŞI BULVARI
French Consulate
OSMANLI SOK
İNÖNÜ CAD
Akbanksanat
TAKSİM
İSTİKLAL CAD
KAZANCI YOKUŞU
Funicular
Aya Triada
CİHANGİR
SIRASELVİLER CAD
BOLAHENK SOK
Taksim Hospital
German Hospital
CİHANGİR CAD
SOMUNCU SOK
AKÇADAM YOKUŞU
MEBUSAN YOKUŞU
HARDAL SOK
Tiyatro Pera
SOĞANCI SOK
HAVYAR SOK
BAKRAÇ SOK
ÇUKURCUMA
AKARSU YOKUŞU
KUMRULU YOKUŞU
SUSAM SOK
KUMRULU SOK
DEFTERDAR YOKUŞU
TOPHANE
BATARYA SOK
0 metres 150
SHOPS
Ada Books 13
Ambar 10
Berrin Akyüz 14
By Retro 15
Demirören Mall 1
Homer 6
Kontra Plak 11
Leyla 9
Mavi 3
Mephisto 2
Mor Taki 4
Müstamel Eşya Evi 7
Paşabahce 12
Roll 5
The Works 8
Vakko 1
ACCOMMODATION
Büyük Londra 4
Devman 10
Divan Taksim Suites (apt) 1
House Hotel Galatasaray 5
Mama Shelter 3
Marmara Pera 8
Pera Palace 7
Richmond Hotel 11
Tom Tom Suites 9
Triada Residence 2
Villa Zurich 6

MEŞRUTİYET CADDESİ

MAP P.104–105, POCKET MAP A13–B12

Running parallel to İstiklal Caddesi to the west and easily reached by cutting through one of the alleys joining them, this busy street is home to yet more fine turn-of-the-nineteenth-century buildings as well as a smattering of rooftop bars and restaurants such as *Nu Teras* (see p.117), *Mikla* (see p.115), and the fin-de-siècle *Büyük Londra Hotel* (see p.146) and its wonderful period bar (see p.116). At the north end of the street, where it joins Hamalbaşı Caddesi, is the grandiose, Renaissance-style **British Consulate**, built in 1855. Architect Charles Barry was also responsible for London's Houses of Parliament, but unfortunately today his work is semi-obscured by massive compound walls built after a terrorist bomb attack in 2003.

PERA PALACE HOTEL

Meşrutiyet Cad 52 ⓣ 0212 377 4000, ⓦ perapalace.com. MAP P.104–105, POCKET MAP A13

The most famous building on Meşrutiyet Caddesi, this grand hotel was completed in 1892 to accommodate gentry arriving in "Stamboul" on the trans-European Orient Express (see p.152). The architect was the prolific Frenchman Alexander Vallaury, also responsible for the Neoclassical Archeology Museum across in the old city (see p.51) and the Ottoman Bank down in Galata (see p.94). After years of neglect, it has been restored to its former glory, a necessary process that has resulted in a loss of some of its former character and a steep rise in prices but nostalgia buffs will be tempted to take afternoon tea and cake in the elegant ground-floor **tea rooms** and conjure up the shenanigans of past guests. These have included Greto Garbo and Zsa Zsa Gabor, Ernest Hemingway, Alfred Hitchcock and Atatürk, the founder of the Turkish Republic (the room he regularly used, 401, is a museum). The notorious spy Mata Hari also stayed here and, last but not least, another regular, Agatha Christie, wrote *Murder on the Orient Express* in her favoured room, 411.

PERA PALACE HOTEL

PERA MUSEUM
PERA MÜZESİ

Meşrutiyet Cad 25 ⓣ 0212 334 900, ⓦ peramuzesi.org. Tues–Thurs & Sat 10am–7pm, Fri 10am–10pm, Sun noon–6pm. ₺10. MAP P.104–105, POCKET MAP A13

As much an art gallery as a museum, the Pera Museum is housed in a beautifully restored late nineteenth-century building that was originally the prestigious *Bristol Hotel* – once a rival to the nearby *Pera Palace* and *Büyük Londra* hotels. On the first floor is a permanent exhibition of Kütahya tiles, similar to the more famous İznik ware, alongside a collection of surprisingly interesting weights and

A passage to Europe

One of the delights of exploring İstiklal Caddesi and its offshoots is its nineteenth-century arcades. These attractive covered passages (*pasaj* in Turkish) are redolent of an era when Beyoğlu was Pera, İstiklal Caddesi the Grand Rue de Pera and the area home to a cosmopolitan mix of Armenians, Jews, Greeks and foreign residents. By far the best known and touristy is the **Cite de Pera**, more commonly known by its Turkish name **Çiçek Pasajı** (Flower Arcade), just north of Galatasaray Meydanı. Beautifully restored and today full of overpriced restaurants, its name derives from the White Russian émigrés who sold flowers here in the 1920s. The **Cite de Syrie** (**Suriye Pasajı** in Turkish), at the southern end of İstiklal Caddesi, was designed by a Greek architect in 1908 and has an ornate facade as well as housing the vintage clothing store By Retro (see p.110). Perhaps the most attractive of them all, however, is the **Passage d'Europe** (**Avrupa Pasajı**), which links Meşrutiyet Caddesi with Sahane Sok. Three storeys high, with a barrel-vaulted glazed roof and lined with Neoclassical statues, each of which represents a different craft, it's home today to some fine antique and souvenir shops. Other historic arcades include **Hazzopulo**, **Aznavur**, **Halep** (Aleppo) and **Atlas** *pasajıs*.

measures from across the ages. On the second floor are the works of Orientalist painters from the seventeenth to nineteenth centuries, the most striking (and valuable) of which is Osman Hamdi's *Tortoise Trainer*, brought back to its native land from abroad for a cool $3.5 million in 2004. Floors three, four and five are devoted to temporary exhibitions – often by well-known artists. There's also a decent café and shop.

NEVİZADE SOKAK

MAP P.104–105, POCKET MAP B11

This narrow pedestrian alley, running parallel to İstiklal Caddesi behind Çiçek Pasajı (see box above), is arguably the liveliest in the city. Lined by restaurants and bars, all with tables spilling out into the alleyway, it's worth fighting your way down just for the atmosphere or, better, to join the raucous diners in a traditional *meyhane* (tavern) such as *İmroz* (see p.114).

NEVİZADE SOKAK

GALATASARAY MEYDANI

MAP P.104–105, POCKET MAP B12

This small square about halfway along İstiklal Caddesi is a stop for the antique tram. It's named after prestigious **Galatasaray Lycee** on the south side of the square, a school dating back to 1481, though the current building was erected in 1908. Students here formed one of Turkey's leading football clubs, Galatasaray, in 1905, and there's a small **museum** to the club (Mon–Sat 9am–5pm) in the restored Neoclassical building opposite. Hidden away below the square to the southeast is über-cool **Garajistanbul** (Kaymakan Reşit Bey Sok 11, off Yeniçarşı Caddesi ⓣ 0212 244 4499, ⓦ garajistanbul.org), the city's leading avant-garde performing arts and music venue.

ÇUKURCUMA AND CİHANGİR

MAP P.104–105, POCKET MAP C13 & E11

The warren of streets south and east of the northern section of İstiklal Caddesi makeup the districts of Çukurcuma and Cihangir. The former is home to the fascinating Museum of Innocence and boasts a welter of bric-a-brac shops and vintage/alternative clothing outlets – especially on Turnacıbaşı Sokak. This steep, twisting street is also known for its famous Turkish baths, the **Galatasaray Hamamı** (Turnacı Başı Sok 24 ⓣ 0212 249 4342, ⓦ galatasarayhamami.com; daily: men 7am–10pm, women 8.30am–8pm; bath only ₺60) which date back to 1481. Cihangir is the aspiring urban bohemian's abode of choice in İstanbul, and has a number of trendy café-bars and shops.

THE MUSEUM OF INNOCENCE

THE MUSEUM OF INNOCENCE *MASUMİYET MÜZESİ*

Çukurcuma Cad 24 ⓣ 0212 252 9738, ⓦ masumiyetmuzesi.org. Tues, Wed, Thurs, Sat & Sun 10am–6pm, Fri 10am–9pm. ₺25.

MAP P.104–105, POCKET MAP C13

It's probably only worth coming here if you've read the eponymous book by Turkey's Nobel Prize-winning author, İstanbulite Orhan Pamuk. In the book, the obsessive upper-class Kemal collects everyday objects touched by his object of desire, an unsuitable young woman from an impoverished background. The objects are displayed as they were acquired, starting with over 4000 cigarette butts. The sequence finishes on the top floor with the bed where Kemal lays dying at the close of the novel.

İSTİKLAL CADDESİ: GALATASARAY MEYDAN TO TAKSİM

MAP P.104–105, POCKET MAP B12–D11

Although still lined by mainly grand nineteenth-century apartments blocks, İstiklal Caddesi becomes increasingly mainstream, period arcades apart (see box, p.107), as you approach Taksim Square. There are a number of **cinemas** here showing foreign films (see p.156) including the **Atlas** at

İstiklal Cad 129 and further up on the left, the multiplex **Cinemaximum Fitaş** at no. 24–26. Also on the left is the Demirören shopping mall (see p.110) and, not far beyond it, the whitewashed **Ağa Camii** (1596), the only mosque on the street. A little way past the Fitaş cinema is the **Akbanksanat** (İstiklal Cad 8/A ⓣ0212 252 3500, ⓦakbanksanat.com), a culture and arts centre with exhibitions, a dance studio, theatre, cinema and café. Opposite is **Aya Triada**, a monumental Greek Orthodox church built in 1880.

TAKSIM SQUARE
TAKSİM MEYDANI

MAP P.104–105, POCKET MAP D10

Massive Taksim Square has little to recommend it bar its role as transport hub, but it has come to symbolize the secular identity of the Turkish Republic. It has long been a focal point for protests and in 2013 an occupy Wall Street type demonstration, protesting the destruction of a green area of the square, Gezi Park, brought Taksim to TV screens worldwide. Taksim Square takes its name from a reservoir built in 1732 (*taksim* means distribution) to distribute water through the city. The main building of interest is the **Atatürk Cultural Centre** (Atatürk Kültür Merkezi), a concrete International Modern structure erected in 1956. It was once the major venue for the state opera, ballet and symphony companies, but it has been closed for years, its future uncertain.

MILITARY MUSEUM
ASKER MÜZESİ

Valikonağı Cad, Harbiye Ⓜ2 Osmanbey ⓣ0212 233 2720. Wed–Sun 9am–5pm. ₺4.

A fifteen-minute walk north of Taksim Square along busy Cumhüriyet Caddesi, this interesting museum traces the history of Turkish warfare and weaponry from the origins of the Turks in Central Asia through to the intervention of the Turkish Republic in Cyprus in 1974. Most exhibits are staidly displayed in dark-wood glass-fronted cabinets, but it's easy to while away an hour or two looking at everything from a huge section of the chain used to block the Golden Horn in the Byzantine era to heavy machine guns used in the Turkish defence of Gallipoli in 1915, and the embroidered tents used by campaigning sultans to a superb collection of Ottoman armour and weaponry. The **Mehter Band**, who accompanied the Ottoman war machine into battle from 1289 onwards, play rousing martial music on the first floor between 3 and 4pm each afternoon.

MILITARY MUSEUM

Shops

ADA BOOKS

İstiklal Cad 20. Mon–Fri 7am–10pm, Sat & Sun 9am–10pm. MAP P.104–105, POCKET MAP B13
Stocks a decent range of glossy titles on İstanbul and Turkey along with CDs, DVDs and magazines; always busy because of its well-regarded (licensed) café-restaurant.

AMBAR

Kallavi Sok 12, off İstiklal Cad. Mon–Sat 9am–7.30pm, Sun 12.30–7.30pm. MAP P.104–105, POCKET MAP B12
A family business concentratng on organic and whole-foods as well as natural soaps and lotions.

BERRİN AKYÜZ

Akarsu Yokuşu 22. Mon–Fri 10am–8pm, Sat & Sun 10am–5pm. MAP P.104–105, POCKET MAP D13
Situated in trendy Cihangir, this small boutique is a treasure-trove of one-off fashion and home accessory objects, from sheep-shaped knitted bags to cushion covers, felt jewellery and silk scarves.

BY RETRO

Suriye Pasajı, off İstiklal Cad. Daily 10am–10.30pm. MAP P.104–105, POCKET MAP B13
A veritable cornucopia hidden away in the basement of this historic arcade, owner Hakan trawls Europe for vintage and retro clothing and decorative household items such as old phones and radios.

DEMİRÖREN MALL

İstiklal Cad. Daily 10am–10pm. MAP P.104–105, POCKET MAP C11
With so many high-street stores and historic shopping passages it's hard to see why İstiklal Caddesi needed a mall, but if you're in search of Gap, Mothercare or even a Turkish fashion giant like Vakko (see p.111) this accessible location means you don't have to head into the suburbs to find them.

HOMER

Yeni Çarşı Cad 28. Mon–Sat 10am–7.30pm. MAP P.104–105, POCKET MAP B12
Great bookshop tucked away just off İstiklal Caddesi with a superb range of Turkey-related material – art, archeology, literature and politics as well as specialist books on many other subjects – it even has a good children's section.

KONTRA PLAK

Kontra Plak Yeni Çarşı Cad 60/A, Galatasary. T 0212 243 8680, W kontrarecords.com. Daily 9am–10pm. MAP P.104–105, POCKET MAP B12
This hip basement record store caters to cool young İstanbulites and the youthful ex-pats who have made this neighbourhood their own. Browse through an impressive range of records and CDs of all genres, from Turkey and beyond.

LEYLA

Altıpatlar Sok 6. Mon–Sat 10am–7pm. MAP P.104–105, POCKET MAP C12
Leyla Seyhanlı has put together a fine collection of vintage clothing here – from the nineteenth century to the 1960s, as well as cushion-covers, throws and the like.

MAVI

MAVİ

İstiklal Cad 195. Mon–Sat 10am–10pm, Sun 11am–10pm. MAP P.104–105, POCKET MAP B12

Mavi is well-known in Turkey for its quality denim goods and other clothing, and if you're after a non-crass souvenir T-shirt its ever-changing and witty range of İstanbul-inspired designs is worth checking out.

MEPHISTO

Istiklal Cad 197, Beyoğlu. T 0212 249 0687, W mephisto.com.tr. Daily 9am–midnight. MAP P.104–105, POCKET MAP C11

This modern book and music store stocks a good range of a Turkish music CDs and is popular with young İstanbulites who head to its pleasant café to escape the throngs on the main shopping street outside.

MOR TAKI

Turnacıbaşı Sok 10B, off İstiklal Cad. Mon–Sat 10am–7.30pm. MAP P.104–105, POCKET MAP C12

At the İstiklal Caddesi end of this trendy street this chic, hole-in-the-wall outlet is worth a look for its range of alternative, handmade jewellery.

MÜSTAMEL EŞYA EVİ

Turnacıbaşı Sok 38/1, off İstiklal Cad. Mon–Sat 9am–7pm. MAP P.104–105, POCKET MAP C12

Antique, bric-a-brac and retro shops abound on this street and those branching off it. This is one of the best laid out, and has interesting 1950s to 1980s items aimed at young expats and neo-bohemian locals who have made this quarter their own.

PAŞABAHCE

İstiklal Cad 314. Mon–Sat 10am–8pm, Sun 11am–7pm. MAP P.104–105, POCKET MAP B13

Store of choice for middle-class İstanbulites in search of home accessories such as tableware, ceramics and glassware – much of the latter still made in the company's factory in Beykoz.

MÜSTAMEL EŞYA EVİ

ROLL

Turnacıbaşı 38/1, off İstiklal Cad. Mon–Sat 10am–10pm, Sun noon–9.30pm. MAP P.104–105, POCKET MAP C12

In a grubby passage full of grungy alternative clothes stalls, this one stands out for its amusing line of T-shirts inspired by Turkey's recent past, from iconic Turkish comic book and film characters to the logos of so-bad-they're-good Turkish cars.

THE WORKS

Faik Paşa Sok 6. Mon–Sat 11am–6pm. MAP P.104–105, POCKET MAP C12

A muddle of retro delights awaits the visitor here, from tin toys to vintage Pepsi bottles and the chrome hood mascots of 1950s American cars. It supplied the nearby Museum of Innocence (see p.108) with some exhibits.

VAKKO

Demirören Mall, İstiklal Cad. Daily 10am–10pm. MAP P.104–105, POCKET MAP C11

For a Turkish take on mainstream fashion for both men and women Vakko is a reliable choice – the fact it's been in business over fifty years speaks volumes about the quality materials it uses, and the timeless designs it produces.

Cafés

CANIM CİĞERİM

Minare Sok 1 ⓣ 0212 252 6060. Daily 10am–midnight. MAP P.104–105, POCKET MAP A13

Just off lively Asmalımescit, "My Dearest Liver" specializes in skewers of small cubes of the tenderest liver imaginable, dished-up with salad and fresh flatbread (₺18). Non-offal-eaters may prefer the chicken or lamb options. Unlicensed.

DÜRÜMZADE

Kamer Hatun Cad 26/A ⓣ 0212 249 0147. Daily 8am–4am. MAP P.104–105, POCKET MAP B11

If you want to sit and linger forget this place. If you want to try a dürüm (wrap) filled with with the most succulent chargrilled meat for a bargain ₺5–₺10, then Dürümzade is for you. One of the secrets employed here is to get the very best, slightly chewy flatbread, rub it with a subtle blend of spices and toast it on the grill before adding the meat filling.

FALAFEL HOUSE

Şehit Muhtar Cad 19, off Taksim Square ⓣ 0212 253 7730. Daily 11am–1am. MAP P.104–105, POCKET MAP D10

Many Turkey first-timers assume Middle Eastern street food like *hummus* and falafel will be staples here too – they're not. That's why this cheap and cheerful Palestinian-run place is such a great find. The decor is greasy spoon, but there are a few tables out on the street for people-watching. Unlicensed.

HAYVORE

Turnacıbaşı Sok 4, off İstiklal Cad ⓣ 0212 293 8561. Daily 11am–10pm. MAP P.104–105, POCKET MAP C12

Pick from a wide range of steamtray dishes in this authentic, eastern Black Sea restaurant – there's the inevitable corn bread to mop up the juices from delectable chickpea or white bean stews (₺8), or accompany the excellent cabbage soup. Unlicensed.

KAFE ARA

Tosbağı Sok 8/A, off Yeniçarşı Cad ⓣ 0212 245 4105. Mon–Thurs 8am–11pm, Fri 8am–midnight, Sat & Sun 10am–11pm. MAP P.104–105, POCKET MAP B12

Owned by Turkey's leading photographer, Armenian-İstanbulite Ara Güler, this sophisticated café is adorned with marvellous black-and-white images of his city. Mix of Turkish and international dishes. Unlicensed.

NİZAM PİDE

MANDABATMAZ

Olivia Geçidi, off İstiklal Cad. Daily 9am–midnight. MAP P.104–105, POCKET MAP B12

Having been superseded by tea as the national drink. Turkish coffee is not always as great as it would like to be. This tiny coffee joint is an exception. For just ₺3 you can sip a rich, velvet brew as good as you'll find anywhere in the Middle East. It's been going since 1967 but has remained resolutely unchanged since, with customers sitting on low stools in the cramped interior or out in the alley.

NİZAM PİDE

Büyükparmakkapı Sok 13, off İstiklal Cad ⓣ 0212 249 7918. Open 24hr. MAP P.104–105, POCKET MAP C11

Pide is often described as Turkish pizza. It's actually rather different – essentially a large, oval semi-leavened flatbread baked in a wood oven with a varierty of toppings – standards are cheddar-like *kaşarlı* cheese, chopped-meat *kuşbaşı* or *beyaz peynirli* – goat's cheese and parsley. This is a great place to try it. ₺11 and up. Unlicensed.

SARAY

İstiklal Cad 107 ⓣ 0212 292 3434. Daily 6am–11pm. MAP P.104–105, POCKET MAP C11

This popular place, spread over several floors, does main meals but is best known for its splendid traditional desserts, from *tavuk göğüsü* (a milk pudding enhanced with semolina and chicken breast) to *fırın sutlaç* (oven-baked rice pudding). Unlicensed.

SUGAR & SPICE

Saka Salim Çıkmazı 3/A, off İstiklal Cad ⓣ 0212 245 0096. Sun–Thurs 10am–1pm, Fri & Sat 10am–2pm. MAP P.104–105, POCKET MAP B12

Long-established, low-key and far from overtly gay café on a peaceful, narrow alley, it attracts a mix of locals and foreign visitors who eschew the louder and more obvious venues. Unlicensed.

VAN KAHVALTI EVİ

Van Kahvaltı Evi Defterdar Yokuşu 52/A, Cihangir ⓣ 0212 293 6437. Daily 8am–7pm. MAP P.104–105, POCKET MAP D13

This all-day breakfast place brings the cuisine of far-flung Van, a predominantly Kurdish city in eastern Turkey, to İstanbul. As well as Turkish standards like dressed olives and assorted cheeses, you can try *kavut* (roasted wheat flour blended with honey and walnuts), *jajı* (yoghurt and cottage cheese), and clotted cream with honey. Extremely busy weekend mornings/lunchtimes.

Restaurants

ANTİOCHİA

General Yazgan Sok 3, Asmalımescit ⓣ 0212 292 1100. Mon–Sat 11am–midnight. MAP P.104–105, POCKET MAP A13

Owner Lale Balcı has written about the unique cuisine of her native Hatay, close to the Syria border, and she and her chefs certainly know how to prepare it. Kebabs (from ₺22) done Hatay-style are juicier and spicier than the standard issue but the real pull is the tasty *meze*, including the thyme salad *zahter* and spicy hot *muammara*, a walnut and hot pepper dip. Licensed.

ÇOKÇOK

Meşrutiyet Cad 51 ⓣ 0212 292 6496. Tues–Sun noon–midnight. MAP P.104–105, POCKET MAP B12

If you can't survive İstanbul without a Thai fix, this is a worthy option, with a Thai chef, the freshest ingredients and stylish surroundings. Best option is the lunchtime special, but the good choice of cocktails is a bonus for a "night-out" feast. Mains from ₺30.

HACİ ABDULLAH

FICCIN

Kallavi Sok 13, off İstiklal Cad ⓣ 0212 293 3786. Tues–Sat 8am–10pm. MAP P.104–105, POCKET MAP B12

Not the most sophisticated place in Beyoğlu but nicely located down a quiet alley with street tables and great value for Caucasus-style dishes such as the eponymous *ficcin*, a tasty meat-pie, rocket soup and the yoghurt-drenched Caucasian ravioli *Çerkez mantısı*. Mains from ₺10. Licensed.

HACİ ABDULLAH

Sakızağacı Cad 17, off İstiklal Cad ⓣ 0212 245 7501. Daily 11am–10pm. MAP P.104–105, POCKET MAP C11

A Beyoğlu institution that has been serving traditional Turkish fare (soups, steamtray dishes, grills, pies and desserts) since 1888. It's right by the Ağa Camii (see p.109) so there's no alcohol, and it does trade on its reputation, so it's not the cheapest; but the food is good quality and the period ambience suitably sedate. Mains around ₺25.

İMROZ

Nevizade Sok 24, off İstiklal Cad ⓣ 0212 249 9073. Daily 11am–2am. MAP P.104–105, POCKET MAP B11

This perennially popular *meyhane* has been in business since 1941 and makes the ideal choice for a *rakı*-and-fish-fuelled night out – eat, drink, talk (if you can make yourself heard over the other diners) and watch the constant procession of revellers parade by. Mains from ₺18.

KENAN ÜSTA OCAKBAŞI

Kurabiye Sok 18, off İstiklal Cad ⓣ 0212 293 5619. Daily 10am–2pm. MAP P.104–105, POCKET MAP D11

A real treat for the carnivore, the master-chef here has been grilling choice cuts of meat over charcoal for forty-plus years. The *meze* are all freshly prepared to order, the kebabs (around ₺25) or other meat served up with thin unleavened bread (*lavaş*) deftly wiped across the grill and smeared with oil and spices. There are tables out on the street and it's licensed.

LEB-İ-DERYA RICHMOND

İstiklal Cad 227 ⓣ 0212 243 4375. Mon–Thurs & Sun 11am–2am, Fri & Sat 11am–3am. MAP P.104–105, POCKET MAP B13

Located on the sixth floor of the *Richmond Hotel* (see p.147), come here for the amazing views across to the Bosphorus and beautifully prepared international and Turkish dishes, including pistachio-studded kebabs and grilled sea bass in a lemon tahini sauce. The decor is stylish, with the central bar making a bold statement all of its own and positively inviting a pre-meal cocktail.

MİKLA

Marmara Pera Hotel, Meşrutiyet Cad 167/185 ⓣ 0212 293 5656. Daily noon–2am. MAP P.104–105, POCKET MAP A13

Seventeen floors up on the roof of the towering *Marmara Pera Hotel* (see p.147) this restaurant has sensational views over the old city and Bosphorus as well as excellent food – Turkish/Mediterranean with a Scandinavian twist. The fixed menu is ₺140 and there's wine by the glass from ₺15. It's expensive but worth it for the ambience and views – dress up a bit for this one.

PARSİFAL

Kurabiye Sok 13, off İstiklal Cad ⓣ 0212 245 2588. Daily 11am–11pm. MAP P.104–105, POCKET MAP C11

Attractive bistro-style vegetarian place well-known for its tasty veggie burgers, salads, spinach pie and a host of other non-meat dishes. Also does a great range of desserts and benefits from a quiet location on this well-used but not jam-packed street. Licensed.

KENAN ÜSTA OCAKBAŞI

REFİK

Sofyalı Sok 10–12, off İstiklal Cad ⓣ 0212 245 7879. Mon–Sat noon–midnight, Sun 6pm–midnight. MAP P.104–105, POCKET MAP A13

A low-key place in a busy alley, this intellectual take on the *meyhane* has a good range of *meze* – including some Black Sea specialities – and the usual grilled fish and meat mains. The set menu is good value if you're in the drinking mood as all local drinks are included in the price.

SOFYALI

Sofyalı Sok 9, off İstiklal Cad ⓣ 0212 245 0362. Mon–Sat noon–1am. MAP P.104–105, POCKET MAP A13

A sophisticated *meyhane* with a soothing interior, all white walls, stripped wood floors and antique furniture, this busy place is in heavy demand so best to book ahead – especially for Fri & Sat evenings and for the outside tables. The *meze* are particularly good, with meat mains and fish on request. Also has good range of wines and *rakıs*.

YENİ LOKANTA

Kumbaracı Yokuşu 66 ⓣ 0212 292 2550. Mon–Sat 11:30am–midnight. MAP P.104–105, POCKET MAP B13

Owner/chef Çivan Er was the innovative cook at the famous Changa restaurant before opening his own place at the head of this steep alley. Here he concentrates on traditional Anatolian and southeastern Turkish favourites but gives them a few novel tweaks. For a restaurant that brings droves of well-heel İstanbulites in from wealthy suburbs, it's reasonably priced (mains ₺29-55), and both the cocktail and wine list are sound. Advance reservation essential.

Bars

360

Mısır Apartmanı 311, İstıklal Cad ⓣ 0212 251 1042. Mon–Thurs noon–2am, Fri noon–4pm, Sat 6pm–4am, Sun 6pm–2.30am. MAP P.104–105, POCKET MAP B12

The top floor of this fine nineteenth-century apartment block is home to this up-market bar-restaurant. Take the lift and – if suitably attired – you can enjoy the 360° views and sip a drink whose price reflects the grandeur of the vista.

ARPA BAR

General Yazgan Sok 5 ⓣ 0212 249 0550. Daily 9am–2pm. MAP P.104–105, POCKET MAP A13

Formerly the *Badehane*, this small, corner-plot bar has a pleasant bare-brick interior, jazz soundtrack and reasonably priced beers, but unless the local municipality repeals its strict "no tables in the street policy", it's unlikely to be as popular as its predecessor.

BÜYÜK LONDRA OTELİ

Meşrutiyet Cad 117 ⓣ 0212 245 0670. Daily noon–11pm. MAP P.104–105, POCKET MAP B12

The bar of this hotel (see p.146), little changed since it first opened in the late nineteenth-century to ply drinks to guests arriving on the Orient Express, is all dark wood, gilt and antique furnishings – there's even a parrot in a suitably ornate cage. It's not a place to linger overlong, but there is a very pleasant roof bar that gets much livelier.

BÜYÜK LONDRA OTELİ

CAFE SMYRNA

Akarsu Cad 29 ⓣ 0212 244 2466. Daily 9am–2am. MAP P.104–105, POCKET MAP D13

Cihangir is the abode of choice of vaguely alternative İstanbulites and expats alike, and this laidback café-bar reflects its clientele. The narrow, attractive dark-wood interior is atmospheric, though the street tables are most popular in the summer.

JAMES JOYCE IRISH PUB

Irish Centre, Balo Sok 26 ⓣ 0212 224 2013. Mon–Thurs & Sun 1pm–2am, Fri & Sat 1pm–4am. MAP P.104–105, POCKET MAP B11

Situated in one of the very liveliest parts of Beyoğlu, this rambling place gets packed for big-screen sports events and when there's a band on (most evenings). It's not very Irish – the Guinness is from a can – but it's reasonably priced for the area and a quiet hangout during the day.

KV

Tünel Gecidi 6, off İstiklal Cad ⓣ 0210 251 4338. Daily 8.30am–2am. MAP P.104–105, POCKET MAP A13

Sophisticated place at the Asmalımescit entrance to the very pretty nineteenth-century Tünel passage, especially good in summer when you can sit at outside tables in the potted-plant-lined passageway and enjoy a decent glass of wine and a light meal.

LEB-İ-DERYA

Kumbaracı Yokuşu 57/6 ⓣ 0210 293 4989. Daily 11am–4am. MAP P.104–105, POCKET MAP B13

It's not cheap, but this is one of Beyoğlu's best up-market bars, attracting a well-off but not particularly posey crowd. The lounge has a great picture window with stunning views down to the confluence of the Golden Horn with the Bosphorus, and there's a small roof terrace for warm evenings. Decent cocktails and a (pricey) international-style food menu.

NU TERAS

Meşrutiyet Cad 149 ⓣ 0212 245 6070. June–Oct: Thurs & Sun 6.30pm–2am, Fri & Sat 6.30pm–4am. MAP P.104–105, POCKET MAP B12

Long-established and very chic rooftop bar, with superb views across to the old city and its dramatic skyline – probably best enjoyed around sunset. There's chilled, DJ-spun dance music until the early hours, occasional concerts and a limited menu inside this period building keeps things going as *Nu Pera*, with the *Pop club* in winter and the cafe-bar *Auf and Kauf* year-round.

PASİFİC

Sofyalı Sok, off Asmalımescit ⓣ 0212 292 7642. Daily 11am–2am. MAP P.104–105, POCKET MAP B13

Cheap and cheerful bar on this narrow, busy alley, good bet for an early beer or two, though they also draw in punters with cheap shot deals. The soundtrack is generally rock, the vibe studenty, the flat-screen TV permanently tuned to Akılı TV, a channel devoted to amusing mishaps from around the world.

RHİTİM BAR

Sahane Sok 20, Balık Pazarı ⓣ 0212 249 0252. Daily 10am–2pm. MAP P.104–105, POCKET MAP B11

No-frills bar attracting a good mix of locals and visitors – the owner also runs the popular *World House Hostel* (see p.146) – with reasonably priced drinks. Really gets going on summer weekends when the party-minded pack the rooftop to dance to a mix of favourite dance sounds.

LEB-İ-DERYA

SENSUS

Büyükhendek Cad 5, Galata ⓣ 0212 245 5657, ⓦ sensuswine.com. Daily 10am–11pm. MAP P.104–105, POCKET MAP A14

Unusual and atmospheric semi-basement place nestling in the shadow of the Galata Tower, this wine and cheese bar serves up dozens of different Turk wines. There's a decent in-house deli/wine shop but service can be erratic when it is very crowded - notably weekend evenings.

SOLERA

Yeniçarşı Cad 44, Galatasaray ⓣ 0212 252 2719. Daily 10am–1am. MAP P.104–105, POCKET MAP B12

Wine bars are few and far between in İstanbul, so to come across this tiny, narrow bar serving over 1000 different Turkish and international wines is a near miracle – especially when the prices are quite reasonable too (₺8 per glass, bottles ₺34 and up). The wine is best enjoyed with one of owner Suleyman Er's *meze* sampler plates.

Clubs & venues

BABYLON

Şehbender Sok 3, off Asmalımescıt Sok ⓣ 0212 292 7368, ⓦ babylon.com.tr. Tues–Thurs 9.30pm–2am, Fri & Sat 10pm–3am. MAP P.104–105, POCKET MAP A13

The metropolis's coolest live music venue, this club has been living up to its motto "Babylon turns İstanbul on" for many years. Acts are both local and international, from indie to jazz and electronica to world, with smaller acts being showcased in the attached *Babylon Nublu*. Usually closed July through August. Tickets in advance for live acts from Biletix (ⓦ biletix.com).

BRONX Pİ SAHANE

Terkoz Çıkmazı 8/1, off İstiklal Cad ⓣ 0212 244 6714, ⓦ bronxpisahane.com. Mon–Sat 8pm–4am. MAP P.104–105, POCKET MAP B13

Hosting alternative bands both local and international, this small venue is popular with students and twenty- to thirty-somethings. Cheap(ish) drinks and free entry when there's no band.

GİZLİ BAHÇE

Nevizade Sok 27 ⓣ 0212 249 2192. Daily 9pm–2am. MAP P.104–105, POCKET MAP B11

This upstairs club provides a chilled contrast to the mayhem of Nevizade Sokak (see p.107) below. Lounge on sofas or watch the action below from a balcony listening to an eclectic mix of dance, soul, blues and jazz.

HAYAL KAHVESİ

Büyükparmakkapı Sok 19 ⓣ 0212 244 2558, ⓦ hayalkahvesi.com.tr. Daily 5pm–4am. MAP P.104–105, POCKET MAP D11

Atmospheric venue, all dark wood and bare brick, there's live blues and rock every night from 11pm, though bear in mind that in July and August *Çubuklu Hayal Kahvesi* up the Bosphorus takes over. Tickets in advance for live acts from Biletix (ⓦ biletix.com).

HAYAL KAHVESİ

İNDİGO

Akarsu Sok 1/2, off İstiklal Cad ⓣ 0212 244 8567, ⓦ livingindigo.com. Mon–Thurs & Sun 10pm–4am, Fri & Sat 11pm–5am. MAP P.104–105, POCKET MAP B12

Originally Beyoğlu's venue of choice for lovers of dance and electronica, it now hosts regular live music acts, from jazz to indie and beyond, but club nights remain a staple.

JOLLY JOKER BALANS

Balo Sok 22 ⓣ 0212 251 7020. Mon–Thurs 10pm–2am, Fri & Sat 10pm–4am. MAP P.104–105, POCKET MAP B11

This lively, 1500-capacity venue is a good bet to experience (mainly) mainstream Turkish pop and rock acts, preferably fired-up by a few beers from the in-house German-style microbrewery. Tickets in advance for live acts from Biletix (ⓦ biletix.com).

KASSETTE

Korsan Çıkmazı 6, off İstiklal Cad ⓣ 0536 415 8018. Daily 10pm–4am. MAP P.104–105, POCKET MAP B12

This 'club' is in fact the closed off end of a cul de sac, which transforms after dark into a lively bar/club. Free entry means its gets incredibly busy with a younger crowd, but unaccompanied men won't get in. DJs from Turkey and German play house music, but there's no space for dancing.

LOVE DANCE POINT

Cumhüriyet Cad 349 ⓜ 2 Osmanbey ⓣ 0212 296 3358. MAP P.104–105

Long-running gay club in this prosperous suburb north of Taksim Square, opposite the Military Museum (see p.109), it makes a gentle introduction to the city's gay scene. The music is pop/dance, both domestic and international.

MİNİ MÜZİKHOL

Soğancı Sok 7, off Sıraselvıler Cad ⓣ 0212 245 1996, ⓦ minimuzikhol.com. Wed–Sat 10pm–4am. MAP P.104–105, POCKET MAP D12

The artfully contrived interior and urbane clientele make this one of the best music venues if you're into sophisticated dance and electronica, especially as it attracts a regular supply of well-known international (and local) DJs.

BABYLON

PEYOTE

Kameriye Sok 4 ⓣ 0212 251 4398, ⓦ peyote.com.tr. Daily 10pm–4am. MAP P.104–105, POCKET MAP B11

This is the best place in the city for alternative music, with electronica on the first floor, live bands on the second and an attractive roof terrace where a mixed bag of musical genres are spun.

PIXIE UNDERGROUND

Toşbaşağa Sok 12, off İstiklal Cad. Daily 2pm–4am. MAP P.104–105, POCKET MAP B12

İstanbul's only bass music club, this is the place to head for dubstep, drum'n'bass and jungle. İstanbul's up-and-coming producers cut their teeth in this welcoming place, and entry is free most nights, a nominal ₺10 on bigger occasions.

SALON İKSV

Sadi Konuralp Cad 5 ⓣ 0212 334 0752, ⓦ saloniksv.com. Opening hours vary. MAP P.104–105, POCKET MAP A14

With funding from İstanbul Foundation for Culture and Arts (İKSV), this slightly out of the way venue hosts a variety of acts, from rock, jazz and world music concerts – many reasonably well-known internationally – to contemporary dance and classical music. Tickets in advance from Biletix (ⓦ biletix.com).

TEK YÖN

Siraselviler Cad 63 ⓣ 0212 233 0654. Daily 10pm–4am. MAP P.104–105, POCKET MAP D12

Down canyon-like Siraselviler Caddesi and best approached from the southeast corner of Taksim Square, this "mainstream" gay venue has a large dancefloor, a big garden out back and regular drag-shows – inevitably packed solid on Fri & Sat evenings.

Beşiktaş and Ortaköy

The waterfront Dolmabahçe Palace, a grandiose European-style residence for the Ottoman Empire's last sultans, is the major tourist attraction this side of the Golden Horn. Northeast along the Bosphorus-front is Beşiktaş. Home to the most working class of the city's "big three" football teams, it's rapidly emerging from a cocoon of urban decay and possesses a youthful vibrancy thanks to its huge student population. Further along is Yıldız Park, a vast, wooded park dotted with imperial pavilions. Beyond it, Ortaköy retains some feel of the fishing village it once was. It has a lovely Baroque-style mosque and a lively waterfront lined with posh cafés. Just to the northeast, virtually underneath the continent-spanning Bosphorus Bridge, a handful of glitzy Bosphorus-front clubs play host to the city's glamorous elite and visiting celebrities.

DOLMABAHÇE PALACE
DOLMABAHÇE SARAYI

Dolmabahçe Cad Ⓣ1 Kabataş, buses #25/E, #28 Ⓣ 0212 236 9000, Ⓦ dolmabahce.gov.tr. Tues, Wed & Fri–Sun: April–Oct 8.30am–5pm; Nov–March 8.30am–4pm. Selamlık ₺30, harem ₺20, combined entry ₺40. MAP P.122–123

The apogee of imperial excess and home to the last sultans of the ailing Ottoman Empire after the imperial retinue moved here from Topkapı in 1853, the palace was completed in 1856. Its decidedly European appearance, influenced by the Baroque, Neoclassical and Rococo styles, make it more akin to Versailles than a traditional Muslim palace – although it was divided, according to Islamic precepts, into an area for men only (*selamlık*) and women only (*harem*) as well as administrative quarters. Taking up a whopping 600m of Bosphorus waterfront, the palace's ornate, marble frontage is arguably best viewed from a Bosphorus cruise (see pp.134–135). This grandiose building was primarily the work of two leading Armenian İstanbul architects, Karabet Balian and his son Nikoğos, though the showy interior, gilded with some fourteen tonnes of gold leaf, was masterminded by French decorator Sechan. The palace can only be visited as part of a guided tour, meaning visitors, usually in maximum groups of fifty, are herded through at a brisk pace. Of most interest are the *hamam*, complete with an incongruously luxurious squat toilet, the marquetry-work

GUARD, DOLMABAHÇE PALACE

ÇIRAĞAN PALACE

masterpiece that is the dining hall parquet floor and, in the ceremonial hall, suspended from a ceiling double the height of the other rooms, a magnificently over the top Bohemian crystal chandelier weighing 4.5 tonnes and glowing with 750 lamps, a suitably flamboyant gift from Queen Victoria.

PALACE COLLECTIONS MUSEUM *SARAY KOLEKSİYONLARI MÜZESİ*

Dolmabahçe Cad Ⓣ1 Kabataş, buses #25/E, #28 Ⓣ 0212 236 9000. Tues, Wed & Fri– Sun 9am–5pm. ₺5. MAP P.122–123

If you've baulked at the steep admission price to the palace, it's worth checking out this unusual museum, which will give you a fascinating and more down to earth insight into how the opulent residence functioned. For here, displayed in what were the former kitchens of Dolmabahçe, are over 42,000 items all taken from the palace. They range from those you might expect, like Limoges porcelain tea services and the mother-of-pearl-inlaid wooden clogs used in the *hamam*, through to Singer sewing machines and, dating from the period when Atatürk was resident here, a 1930s Ericcson switchboard so crucial in a labyrinthine complex of over four hundred rooms. The kitchens themselves have been nicely restored too – needless to say, there's no gilt in sight here.

NAVAL MUSEUM *DENİZ MÜZESİ*

Barbaros Meydanı Ⓣ1 Kabataş, buses #25/E, #28, #40, #40/T, #42/T Ⓣ 0212 327 4346, Ⓦ denizmuzeleri.tsk.tr. Wed, Thurs & Fri 9am–5pm, Sat & Sun 10am–6pm. ₺6. MAP P.122–123

Housed in a state of the art new building completed in 2013, this fine museum, with huge windows overlooking the Bosphorus, has over 20,000 m2 of exhibition space. Heart of the museum is a superb collection of restored caïques, elegant boats once used to row the sultans to and from their homes along the Bosphorus. The largest of these caïques, dating from 1648, needed some 144 oarsmen to propel it. Downstairs is an exhibition devoted to woodcarving in the Ottoman navy, featuring some beautiful figureheads. There's also a café and kids play area.

ÇIRAĞAN PALACE *CIRAĞAN SARAYI*

Cırağan Cad Ⓣ1 Kabataş, buses #25/E, #28, #40, #40/T, #42/T. MAP P.122–123

Today, the luxurious *Çırağan Palace Kempinski* (see p.148), this imperial residence was originally constructed in 1855 for Sultan Abdülmecit, and is very much a mini-Dolmabahçe. What you see now, however, is much more recent, as the place burnt down in 1910 and was derelict until its 1990 restoration and conversion to a hotel.

YILDIZ PARK

Çırağan Cad Ⓣ1 Kabataş, buses #25/E, #28, #40, #40/T, #42/T. MAP P.122–123

Sprawling down a steep hillside to busy Çırağan Caddesi and the Bosphorus beyond, this oasis of green, usually entered from the south gates opposite the Çırağan Palace, was the palace complex of Abdülhamit II for thirty years. The notoriously paranoid sultan moved here from the Dolmabahçe Palace as he feared the latter was too exposed to naval attacks. Today, it's a place to escape the city hustle and/or visit the pavilions of the palace, which were designed by the famous Italian architect D'Aronco. The main points of interest are located a ten- to fifteen-minute walk uphill from the park entrance on Çırağan Caddesi. The most visited is the **Yıldız Chalet Museum** (Şale Köşkü; Tues, Wed, Fri–Sun: March–Sept 9.30am–5pm, Oct–Feb 9.30am–4pm; ₺10), an attractive, Swiss chalet-style pavilion dominated by the ceremonial hall which contains a 400m-square Hereke silk carpet. Here, Sultan Abdülhamit entertained Kaiser Wilhelm II in 1889 and 1898 and discussed matters of state. The **Yıldız Porcelain Factory** (Mon–Fri 9am–noon & 1–6pm), downhill to the southeast of the Şale Pavilion, was established in 1890 to produce china for the palace and still churns out quantities of typically florid, nineteenth-century European-style pottery which is sold in the museum shop, should such wares appeal. There are a couple of decent cafés in the grounds, one housed in another of the palace's pavilions, the pretty **Malta Köşkü**. Also worth seeking out is the **Çadır Köşkü**, another

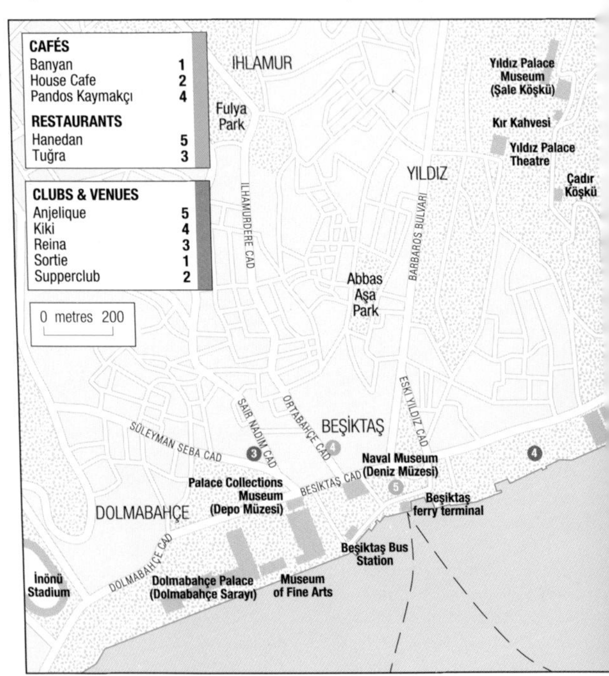

charming pavilion downhill from the Malta Köşkü, beyond the small artificial lake.

ORTAKÖY

Buses #22, #22/RE, #25/E from Kabataş, #40, #40/T, #42/T from Taksim. MAP P.122–123

Despite being dominated by the towering Bosphorus suspension bridge, built in 1973, and surrounded by urban sprawl, Ortaköy has not entirely lost its former fishing village charm. The waterfront area, the so-called boardwalk, is today all cool cafés frequented by well-heeled İstanbulites, who come to see and be seen – and perhaps browse the artsy-craftsy Sunday morning market. The waterfront mosque, the Büyük Mecidiye Camii, is a Baroque gem built in 1854, while in the streets behind are a couple of reminders of the village's cosmopolitan past, the (invariably locked) **Ezt Ahayim synagogue** and the attractive, nineteenth-century Greek Othodox **church of Aya Fokas** (St Phocas), the door to the walled-compound of which is occasionally open.

ORTAKÖY BOARDWALK

Beşiktaş & Ortaköy

ACCOMMODATION	
Çırağan Kempinski	2
Four Seasons Bosphorus	4
Les Ottomans	1
W Hotel	3

Cafés

BANYAN

Salhane Sok 3. Buses #25/E, #28, #40, #40/T, #42 ☎ 0212 259 9060. Daily noon–2am. MAP P.122–123

Like its near neighbour and rival the *House Café*, this place concentrates on giving its loyal, largely youthful local clientele something a bit different, with Asian-fusion cuisine taking centre stage – from Indian to Vietnamese. It's not cheap (mains ₺29 and up) but it's decent quality and the views of the Bosphorus Bridge and boardwalk are great. Licensed.

HOUSE CAFÉ

Salhane Sok 1. Buses #25/E, #28, #40, #40/T, #42 ☎ 0212 227 2699. Mon–Thurs 9am–1pm, Fri & Sat 9am–2am, Sun 9am–midnight. MAP P.122–123

A stylish, upmarket café whose concept has proven so popular there are now nine spread across the city. This has to be the best located, with views over the waterfront and Ortaköy's Baroque-style mosque, and it is housed in a lovingly-converted turn-of-the-nineteenth-century building. Posh pastas, burgers and the like are the staple, Sunday brunch a metropolitan's favourite. Licensed.

BANYAN

PANDOS KAYMAKÇI

Mumcu Bakkal Sok. Buses #25/E, #28, #40, #40/T, #42 ☎ 0212 258 2616. Daily 8am–7pm. MAP P.122–123

A Beşiktaş institution established in the late nineteenth century, this is the place to try a traditional breakfast (just as good at lunch or as a snack) of clotted, buffalo milk cream and sticky honey mopped-up with fresh bread. *Pandos'* existence was threatened in late-2014 by huge rent rises so check its status before visiting. Unlicensed.

Restaurants

HANEDAN

Ciğdem Sok 27. Buses #25/E, #2,8 #40, #40/T, #42 ☎ 0212 259 4017. Daily 11am–2pm. MAP P.122–123

Established in 1983 and with a lively location right next to Beşiktaş pier, the downstairs is given over to grilled meat dishes, the upstairs to seafood. There's a great selection of *meze* and a wide choice of fish, both farmed and wild caught. It's not as swish as some Bosphorus-front places and consequently better value, with fish mains from ₺24, though the decor is nothing to write home about. Licensed.

TUĞRA

Çırağan Palace Kempinski Hotel, Çırağan Cad 32. Buses #25/E, #40, #40/T, #42 ☎ 0212 236 7333. Daily 7pm–midnight. MAP P.122–123

Appropriately expensive place located in this former palace, but worth it for the lovely Bosphorus views from the candle-lit terrace, attentive service and quality Ottoman-style dishes. Also in the *Çırağan Palace Kempinski* is the *Laledan* restaurant (same phone) noted for monumental breakfasts (300-plus items), Sunday brunches and seafood evening meals. Licensed.

REİNA

Clubs & venues

ANJELIQUE

Salhane Sok 5, off Muallim Naci Cad. Buses #25/E, #28, #40, #40T, #42 ⓣ 0212 327 2844, ⓦ anjelique.com.tr. Daily 6pm–4am. MAP P.122–123

Spread over three floors in a Bosphorus-facing mansion, with an interior overhauled by cool design company Autobahn, you'll need to be smartly attired to get into this popular club. There's different music on each floor, from Turkish pop to house. There's no cover charge so drinks are expensive.

KİKİ

Osmanzade Sok 8, Ortaköy. Buses #25/E, #28, #40, #40T, #42 ⓣ 0212 258 5524, ⓦ kiki.com.tr. Wed–Sat 8pm–4am. MAP P.122–123

Unlike near neighbours *Reina*, *Sortie* et al, there's no Bosphorus bling down at understated *Kiki*, a cool club attracting a younger crowd here for the deep house DJs. The club is on three floors and is best in summer when the roof terrace is the place to be. Drinks are dear at ₺14 for a small beer, but entry is free.

REİNA

Muallım Nacı Cad 44. Buses #25/E, #28, #40, #40/T, #42 ⓣ 0212 359 1500, ⓦ reina.com.tr. Daily 6pm–4am. Admission Fri & Sat ₺70, weekdays free. MAP P.122–123

Glitzy waterfront venue with hefty admission charges justified by some punters for the chance to glimpse a celebrity or two. The dancing is to Euro-pop, though much of the action is centred around the bars and six themed restaurants.

SORTİE

Muallım Nacı Cad 141/2. Buses #25/E, #28, #40, #40/T, #42 ⓣ 0212 259 5919, ⓦ sortie.com.tr. Daily 6pm–4am. Admission Fri & Sat ₺70, weekdays free. MAP P.122–123

Slightly more sophisticated and less celebrity-obsessed than rival *Reina*, this Bosphorus-front place plays a mix of house and pop; the steep admission fee at weekends includes one free drink. A series of themed restaurants – Mediterranean, sushi, South American, fish etc – are all part of the concept.

SUPPERCLUB

Muallım Nacı Cad 65. Buses #25/E, #28, #40, #40/T, #42 ⓣ 0212 261 1988, ⓦ supperclub.com. Thurs–Sun 6pm–2am. Admission Fri & Sat ₺40, weekdays free. MAP P.122–123

One of two Turkish ventures by an Amsterdam-based group, this place might strike some as on the pretentious side – lounging around on white sofas listening to local and international DJs mix their stuff, embellished with "spontaneous" performance art and video on occasion.

Asian İstanbul

Worth it for the bargain-priced ferry-ride from Europe to Asia alone, a few hours spent exploring conservative Üsküdar or bustling Kadıköy will enhance your İstanbul experience. The former of these suburbs, known to nineteenth-century visitors such as Florence Nightingale as Scutari, has several impressive Ottoman mosques within easy walking distance of the ferry terminal or Üsküdar Maramaray line metro stop as well as the Maiden's Tower, an offshore lighthouse that figured in Bond thriller *The World is Not Enough*. Kadıköy has transformed itself into a mini-Beyoğlu over the last few years and is great for shopping, eating and night-life. It's also home to the pretty 1920s Süreyya Opera House and one of the city's best restaurants, *Çiya Sofrası*. Adjoining Kadıköy to the north is Haydarpaşa, with its imposing, early twentieth-century railway station, Florence Nightingale Museum and British Crimean War Cemetery.

ÜSKÜDAR AND ITS OTTOMAN MOSQUES

Regular ferries from Eminönü: daily 6.35am–11pm, last ferry back 10.30pm. ₺4 one way. Alternatively Marmaray line metro trains run under the Bosphorus from Sirkeci for ₺4. MAP P.128–129, POCKET MAP N4

Üsküdar ferry terminal is more or less opposite the **Mihrimah Camii**, built in 1547–1548. Like its namesake out by the city's land walls (see p.87) this fine mosque was designed for the favourite daughter of Süleyman the Magnificent, Mihrimah, by the skilled and prolific architect, Sinan (see p.67). It was built on a raised terrace and is curious in design terms because, rather than using the conventional central dome flanked by two or four semi-domes, the Mihrimah Camii has three semi-domes. Around 500m to the southwest, on the far side of the Üsküdar stop of the trans-Bosphorus Marmaray metro line (see p.156), is the very attractive **Şemsi Paşa Camii**. Built in 1580, again a work of Sinan, it is set right on the water's edge. The tomb of the grand vizier for whom it was constructed, Şemsi Paşa, is located in the grounds. A little over half a kilometre inland, the **Yeni Valide Camii**, built at the behest of Ahmet III for his mother, was completed

ŞEMSİ PAŞA CAMİİ

Üsküdar's major sights are all within easy walking distance of the ferry terminal and Marmaray metro stop. Everything worth seeing or doing in Kadıköy lies just a short walk from the ferry terminal. But if you come for an evening meal or drink, double-check the times of the last ferry or metro back. Note that you can reach Kadıköy from Üsküdar by taking the metro one stop to Ayrılk Çeşmesi then changing to the M4 metro for Kadıköy.

in 1710. Its most distinguished feature is the valide sultan's tomb, encased in an aviary-like mesh. Further inland is the **Atik Valide Külliyesi**, a mosque complex once again attributable to the ubiquitous Sinan, dating to 1583. Its courtyard is particularly attractive and there's a small, traditional teahouse where you can sip sweet black tea with mosque-going regulars. Further east is the **Çinili Camii** and its associated *hamam*. Dating to 1640, the mosque is generally locked, but look helpless and the caretaker should appear to let you into the prayer hall. The historic **Çinili Hamamı** is just below the mosque (Çavuşdere Cad 204 ⓣ 0212 553 1593; daily men 6am–10pm, women 8am–8pm; ₺15 plus extra for scrub and massage). The building dates back to 1684, is clean without being antiseptic and the prices a fraction of those in the old city's tourist-orientated bath-houses – but don't expect any English to be spoken. A taxi back to the waterfront ₺12.

THE MAIDEN'S TOWER
KIZ KULESİ

Salacak. Museum Tues–Sun noon–7pm. Free.
MAP P.128–129, POCKET MAP M4

A little over a kilometre south of the Üsküdar ferry terminal is a small pier where boats (noon–6.45pm; ₺5 return) take visitors to the landmark tower. Also known as Leander's Tower, it was built in the fifth century BC to control ships using the Bosphorus. The Byzantines stretched a chain between it and another tower at the tip of the peninsula to block enemy ships and in the Ottoman era it became a lighthouse. There's a café for drinks and snacks and in the evenings a restaurant (7.30pm–1am) with a free private boat service (see ⓦ kizkulesi.com.tr.) to ferry diners to and fro. The views from the tower, up and down the Bosphorus and back across to the old city, are great.

THE MAIDEN'S TOWER

KADIKÖY

Regular ferries: from Eminönü: daily 7.30am–9pm, last ferry back 8.30pm; from Karaköy 6.30am–11pm, last ferry back 11pm; both ₺4 one way. MAP P.130

The heart of this lively suburb is south of the heaving waterfront, in the narrow grid of streets beyond Söğütlüçeşme Caddesi. Look out for older buildings among the more recent concrete ones, notably the cream-curves of the Art Deco *Kurukhaveci Mehmet Efendi* coffee outlet. Pedestrianized **Güneşlibahçe Sokak** is well known for its quality delis and fruit, vegetable and fish stalls, and nearby a couple of churches, one Greek Orthodox, the other Armenian, attest to the area's cosmopolitan nineteenth-century past, when İstanbul's Christian minorities and foreigners lived here in numbers. Vaguely alternative clothing outlets mix with antique and bric-a-brac shops and there are some good restaurants, notably *Çiya Sofrası* (see p.132). Further inland is the beautiful **Süreyya Opera House** (Bahariye Cad 29 ⓣ 0216 346 1531, ⓦ sureyyaoperasi.org), a 1920s gem with a regular winter programme of opera, ballet and classical music. A little further east is the Rüştü Saraçoğlu stadium, home to Turkey's richest club, **Fenerbahçe**.

TOY MUSEUM
OYUNCAK MÜZESİ

Dr Zeki Zeren Sok, Göztepe. Buses #GZ1, #GZ2, #10, #10/B from Kadıköy. Tues–Fri 9.30am–6pm, Sat & Sun 9.30am–7pm. ₺10.

Appropriately housed in what was, until the 1950s, one of the city's best toyshops, this museum has a fine collection of toys drawn mainly from Western Europe and North

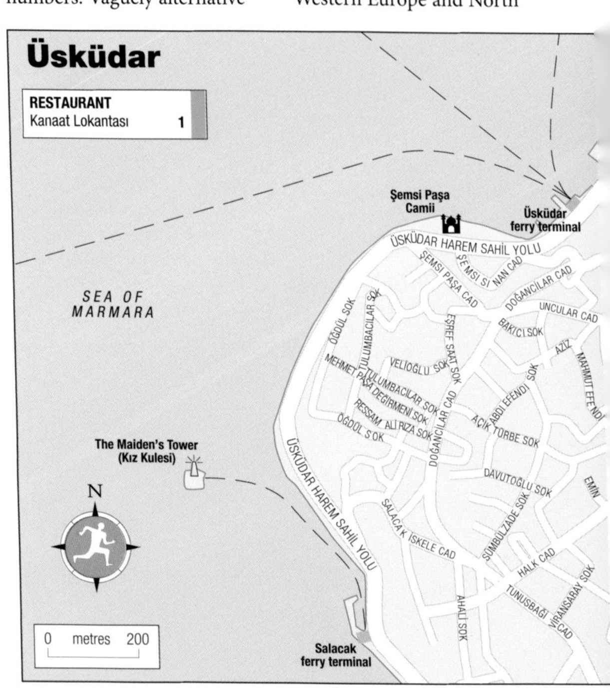

America. Many exhibits are displayed in themed rooms, and there is everything here from teddy bears to Barbies, though best are the tin toys.

TOY MUSEUM

HAYDARPAŞA STATION

A handful of ferries from Eminönü call here – consult the timetables. ₺4 one way. MAP P.130

Haydarpaşa station is well-remembered by millions of Turks who arrived in the big city from villages and towns across Anatolia in the big waves of rural–urban migration between the 1950s and 1990s. German Gothic in style, it was built in 1908 as part of the ambitious Berlin-to-Baghdad railway, a gift from Kaiser Wilhelm II to Sultan Abdülhamit II, and is built on 1100 piles sunk into the Bosphorus. The station has been bypassed by the Marmaray metro project and its future is uncertain.

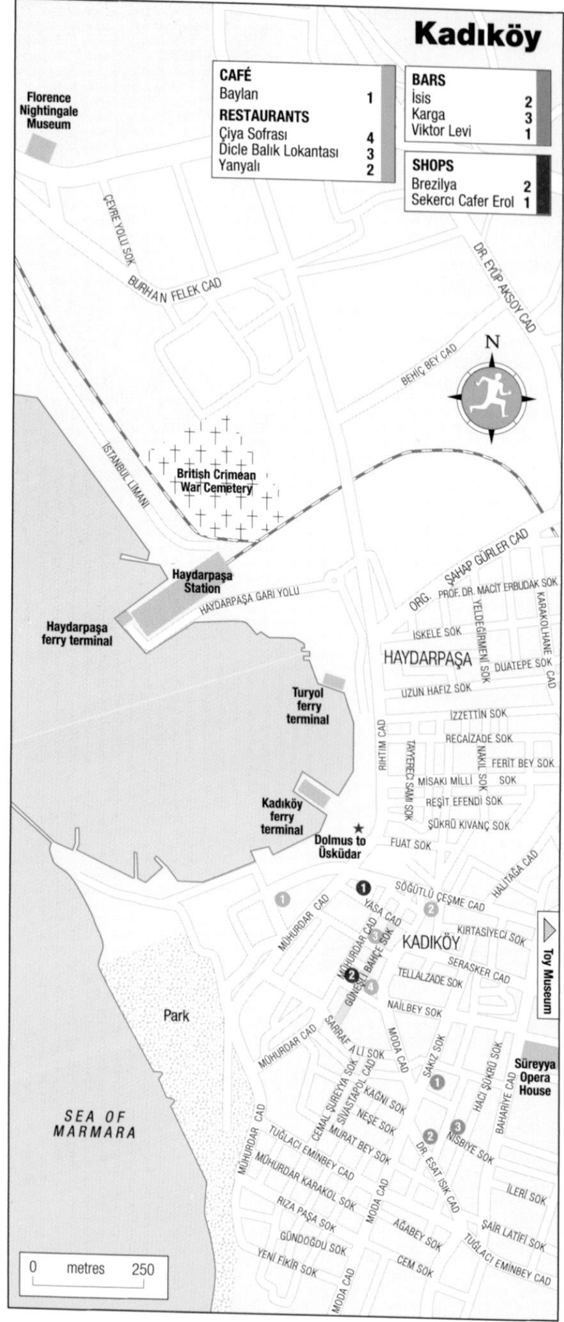
Kadıköy
CAFÉ
Baylan 1
RESTAURANTS
Çiya Sofrası 4
Dicle Balık Lokantası 3
Yanyalı 2
BARS
İsis 2
Karga 3
Viktor Levi 1
SHOPS
Brezilya 2
Sekercı Cafer Erol 1
Florence Nightingale Museum
British Crimean War Cemetery
Haydarpaşa Station
Haydarpaşa ferry terminal
Turyol ferry terminal
Kadıköy ferry terminal
Dolmus to Üsküdar
HAYDARPAŞA
KADIKÖY
Park
SEA OF MARMARA
Süreyya Opera House
Toy Museum
0 metres 250

BRITISH CRIMEAN WAR CEMETERY

TİBBİYE /Burhan Felek Cad, GATA yanı. Buses #12, #1/A from Kadıköy. MAP P.130

Attractively laid-out beneath elegantly tapering cypress and spreading plane trees are the graves and tombs of some 6000 British soldiers who lost their lives in the Crimean War (1853–56). Most were victims of cholera which swept through the nearby military hospital in Scutari (today's Selimiye) barracks established by Florence Nightingale rather than battle-ground casualties. As well as victims of the Crimean War, there are over 700 civilians, and 450 Commonwealth soldiers from both world wars. The single most obvious monument is an obelisk decorated with four angels holding wreaths at each corner, erected at the behest of Queen Victoria in 1857. The cemetery, beautifully maintained by the Commonwealth War Graves Commission, is tricky to find on your own – it may be best to get a taxi in Kadıköy or Haydarpaşa. The entrance is by the *Acıl* (emergency) department of the GATA military hospital (*GATA Asker Hastanesi*).

FLORENCE NIGHTINGALE MUSEUM

Kavak İskele Cad. Buses #12, #12/A from Kadıköy T 0216 553 1009, F 0216 310 7929 or F 0216 553 8000. Mon–Fri 9am–5pm. Free. MAP P.130

Housed in the monumental nineteenth-century Selimiye army barracks, strictly guarded by the Turkish military, this interesting museum can only be visited by applying at least 24 hours in advance – to be certain considerably more. Fax your passport details and expected date and time of arrival and hope for the best. The museum is actually on the site of the original hospital set up by Nightingale, in the northwest wing of the barracks, and contains two of the lamps she so famously used when doing her rounds. Although the cholera epidemic that swept through what was the world's first military hospital killed thousands (now buried in the British Crimean War Cemetery), it was here that Nightingale and her helpers established the precepts of modern nursing and eventually helped reduce the patient death rate from twenty to two percent.

OBELISK, BRITISH CRIMEAN WAR CEMETERY

Shops

BREZİLYA

Guneşlibahçe Sok 42, Kadıköy. Daily 9am–9pm. MAP P.130

Much cheaper than the famed *Kurukhaveci Mehmet Efendi* coffee purveyors in Eminönü and Kadıköy, this place has been grinding coffee since 1920. It's also great for the healthy Turkish delicacy *pestil*, sheets of dried fruit molasses (usually apricot, grape, plum and mulberry) and other deli delights.

ŞEKERCİ CAFER EROL

Yasa Cad 19, Kadıköy. Daily 9am–9pm. MAP P.130

Even if you don't buy it's worth visiting this time-warp sweet shop for its wonderful window and counter displays, which accurately reflect the foundation date of this branch of the store in 1945 (though the family business has been going for over 200 years). Try the exquisitely attractive marzipan fruits, which in fact look far too precious to eat, or the more prosaic *alkide*, boiled sweets.

CAFER EROL

Café

BAYLAN

Muvakithane Cad 19, Kadıköy ⓣ 0216 336 2881. Daily 10am–10pm. MAP P.130

A relic of a bygone era but still going strong, this patisserie has a narrow, 1950s wood-and-chrome frontage and is famous for its eye-catching mini-macaroons, each a different pastel shade. There's respite from the hurly-burly outside in the vine-shaded garden. The perfect afternoon tea stop after a shopping expedition in Asia.

Restaurants

ÇİYA SOFRASI

Guneşlibahçe Sok 43, Kadıköy ⓣ 0216 330 3190. Daily 10am–midnight. MAP P.130

Offering one of the most varied menus in İstanbul this superb restaurant – actually three separate places either adjacent to or opposite each other on this pedestrianized street – *Çiya* has become a major incentive to visit the Asian side of the metropolis. Most popular at lunchtimes is the outlet on the east side of the alley, where you choose from a tempting array of *meze*, salads and *sulu yemek* (stew-type dishes), and have your plate weighed to find out the damage – usually ₺10–15. The two outlets on the other side of the street do superb kebabs. The dishes on offer are drawn from all over Turkey and adjacent Middle-Eastern countries. Unlicensed.

DİCLE BALIK LOKANTASI

Muvakithane Cad 31/A, Kadıköy ⓣ 0216 233 8474. Daily 10am–10pm. MAP P.130

Handily located next to Kadıköy's busy fish-market – where the proprietors have

ÇIYA SOFRASI

their own highly regarded fish-stall – this good-value, unpretentious place does what Turkish fish restaurants do best, fresh-grilled fish mains (from ₺20) accompanied by a simple salad, preceded by an array of fresh *meze* such as fava bean mash or *deniz börülce* (sea samphire). Try to grab a table on the terrace. Licensed.

KANAAT LOKANTASI

Selmanipak Cad 25, Üsküdar ⓣ 0216 341 5444. Daily 6am–11pm. MAP P.128–129. POCKET MAP O3

Established back in 1931 this genteel *lokanta* makes a very worthwhile lunch-stop if you're exploring conservative Üsküdar's backstreets. There's a wide range of starters, both hot and cold, as well as fantastic choice of mains (from ₺6) and desserts – many of them quite different to those found in the average Turkish restaurant – such as Circassian chicken in walnut sauce. Unlicensed.

YANYALI

Yağlıka İsmail Sok 1, Kadıköy ⓣ 0216 336 3333. Daily 9.30am–10.30pm. MAP P.128–129

Similar to Üsküdar's *Kanaat* but even older, having been established by émigrés from Greece in 1919, it's not a place to come for trendy, fusion cuisine – or even pizza or a burger. There are instead some twenty varieties of soup (₺7) on offer, a whole range of different stews including some oven-cooked in clay dishes, and a wide range of desserts including tahini-sauce-drenched candied pumpkin (*kabak tatlisi*). Unlicensed.

Bars

İSİS

Kadife Sok 26, Kadıköy ⓣ 0216 349 7381. Daily 11am–2am. MAP P.130

There's quite an alternative scene on Kadife Sokak and *İsis* is a good example – a café by day and a bar-cum-club by night, it has alternative music, decent-priced beers and other drinks. Plus there's a shady garden out back of this converted, early twentieth-century townhouse.

KARGA

Kadife Sok 16, Kadıköy ⓣ 0216 449 1725. Daily 11am–2am. MAP P.130

Blurring the line between bar, alternative art gallery and café, this is where black-clad students and student wannabes come to drink beer, smoke (in the garden out back), chat and perhaps sample something from the bar-snack menu.

VİKTOR LEVİ

Damacı Sok 4, Kadıköy ⓣ 0216 449 9329. Daily 11am–2am. MAP P.130

Much more mainstream than either *İsis* or *Karga*, *Viktor Levi* is housed in a substantial, late nineteenth-century house ranged around a pleasant garden. It's been making house wines since the 1920s and they are both reasonably priced and palatable enough. Extensive menu, too.

The Bosphorus and Princes' Islands

Few visitors to a city where the sea is so much a part of its being can resist the temptation of a boat trip up the Bosphorus. Over 31km long but a mere 700m wide at its narrowest point, the strait connects the Black and Marmara seas as well as separating Europe from Asia. Many of the impressive sights along the Bosphorus can be seen from the water; to explore them the intrepid can take a bus from the city centre. The pretty Princes' Islands' are just 35 minutes away by sea bus, a little longer by regular ferry. Here you can admire fin-de-siècle villas, ride in a horse-drawn carriage through pine-scented hills, hire a bike and, in summer, swim in the Sea of Marmara.

BOSPHORUS CRUISES

The long, six-hour Bosphorus cruise run by Şehir Hatları (see p.155) is a highlight of any visit to İstanbul. Tickets (₺25 round trip) can be bought from the Boğaz Ferry Terminal just east of the Galata Bridge in Eminönü, boats departing daily at 10.35am year-round, 10.35am and 1.35pm May to September. An extra noon departure is usually added between June 9 and August 31. Drinks and snacks are available on board, as the only lengthy stop is a 2.5hr layover at peaceful Anadolu Kavağı village, on the strait's Asian side. En route, brief stops are made at Beşiktaş (Europe), Kanlıca (Asia), Sariyer and Rumeli Kavağı (both Europe). You can get off at any of these points (₺15 one-way tickets are available) but you'll have to take a bus back to the city centre. Travelling north, on the European shore you'll see Dolmabahçe Palace and Ortaköy

VIEW OF THE BOSPHORUS FROM RUMELI HISARI

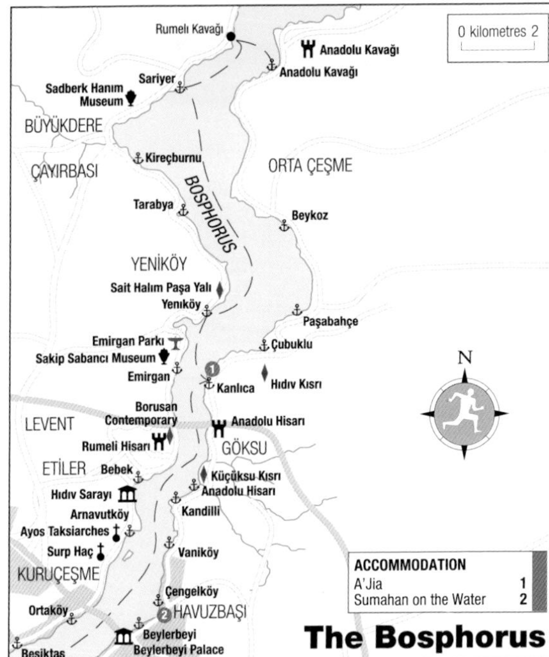

before passing under the first Bosphorus Bridge, with **Beylerbeyi Palace** (see p.136) on the Asian shore virtually under the bridge. Back on the European side you'll pass **Arnavutköy** and **Bebek**, once sleepy fishing villages turned prosperous suburbs. Before the second bridge rises, the landmark **Rumeli Hisarı** fortress (see p.136) and on the Asian side a good example of a *yalı* (Ottoman-era waterfront mansion), the **Köprülü Amcazade Hüesyin Paşa Yalı**. Beyond the second bridge is the **SakIp Sabancı Museum** (see p.136). Try the sugared yoghurt brought on by vendors at **Kanlıca**, then on the European side look out for **Sait Halim Paşa Yalı** at Yeniköy, an Art Nouveau delight. Sariyer is home to the **Sadberk Hanım Museum** (see p.136). The strait becomes less built up as you approach the layover point at **Anadolu Kavağı**, where most visitors are content to stretch their legs and enjoy a cheap fish meal in green, quiet surroundings, though there's a Byzantine fortress to clamber up to for the energetic.

Other cruises include Şehir Hatları's short tour from Eminönü to Ortaköy departing daily at 2.30pm (₺10 round trip) and private operator Turyol have 1.5hr-long tours up to the second, Fatih Mehmet Sultan, bridge at least hourly between 10am and 9pm, more frequently summer weekends (₺12 round trip). Alternatively from mid-June to the end of September only there's a Şehir Hatları Saturday-night cruise (Mehtaplı) departing Eminönü at 6.35pm (₺20 round trip), which goes as far as Anadolu Kavağı.

BEYLERBEYİ PALACE

Abdullah Ağa Cad 12. Buses #15, #15/B from Üsküdar ⓣ 0216 321 9320. Tues, Wed & Fri–Sun 9.30am–6pm. ₺20. MAP P.135

An even grander take on the grand *yalıs* (waterfront mansions) lining the Bosphorus, this nineteenth-century marble pile was the summer residence and guesthouse of late Ottoman sultans. Entrance is expensive, but if European-style palace architecture is your thing it may appeal – and it has attractive gardens (₺1).

BORUSAN CONTEMPORARY

Perili Köşk, 5 Hisar Cad. Buses #40, and #40/T from Taksim, #22, #22/RE and #25/E from Kabataş. ⓣ 0212 3935 200, ⓦ borusancontemporary.com. Sat & Sun 10am–8pm. ₺10. MAP P.135

This unique contemporary arts centre operates as the headquarters of Borusan Holdings during the week, but is open on Saturday and Sunday for art lovers, with all kinds of installations, sculptures and photographs. The building itself, in the shadow of the second Bosphorus Bridge, is a striking ten-storey brick-built mansion begun in 1910, which soon became known as the Perili Köşk ("Haunted Mansion").

SAKIP SABANCI MUSEUM

RUMELİ HİSARI

Yahya Kemal Cad 42. Buses #22, #25/E, #40, #40/T ⓣ 0212 263 5305. Daily except Wed 9.30am–6pm. ₺3. MAP P.135

Superb fortification of six towers joined by curtain walling just before the second, Fatih Sultan Mehmet, suspension bridge, Rumeli Hisarı was built in 1452 as part of Sultan Mehmet's plans to capture Constantinople. Working in tandem with the **Anadolu Hisarı** fort, still visible across the strait in Asia, it effectively blocked the Bosphorus to enemy ships and cut off aid to the beleaguered Byzantines.

SAKIP SABANCI MUSEUM

Saklp Sabancı Cad. Buses #22, #25/E, #40, #40/T ⓣ 0212 277 2200, ⓦ muze.sabanciuniv.edu. Tues & Sun 10am–6pm, Wed–Sat 10am–8pm. ₺12. MAP P.135

Housed in a beautifully restored 1920s waterfront villa, this superb museum-cum-gallery hosts major exhibitions, which in the past have included the likes of Dalí and Picasso. In addition there's a good permanent collection of Ottoman-era calligraphy and works by nineteenth- and twentieth-century Turkish artists, and it's home to the trendy *Müzedechanga* restaurant (ⓣ 0212 323 0901) with a lovely terrace. Just up the waterfront is **Emirgan Parkı** (daily 8am–5pm), the city's most attractive park.

SADBERK HANIM MUSEUM

Büyükdere Cad 27–29. Buses #25/E, #40, #40/T ⓣ 0212 242 3813, ⓦ saberkhanimmuzesi.org.tr. Daily except Wed 10am–5pm. ₺7. MAP P.135

This pair of turn-of-the-nineteenth-century waterfront houses have been lovingly converted into a satisfying museum. The house on the right as you enter is given over

Getting to the Princes' Islands

In Byzantine times home to monasteries and banished royalty, and at the turn of the nineteenth century to the city's wealthy Christian minorities, today the islands (Adalar in Turkish) are a popular escape from the hectic city. Jump-off point is the Adalar ferry terminal at Kabataş, last eastbound stop on the T1 tramline, from where **Şehir Hatları** ferries run, 15 times a day in summer, to the four main islands for ₺5 one way, ₺3.5 with İstanbulkart (see p.153). Winter departures (late Sept to late June) are less frequent. Several private companies operate smaller boats for a slightly higher price. All these boats take around an hour and a half to reach Büyükada, biggest of the islands, fifty minutes to the smallest and nearest, Kınalıada. Alternatively **İDO sea buses** – *deniz otobüs* in Turkish – take just 35 minutes to Büyükada but the fare is ₺10 one way, ₺7.80 with İstanbulkart. Up to 12 daily run in summer, much less frequently in winter.

to mainly Ottoman-period artefacts, including some fine ceramics, as well as rooms mocked-up as they would have been in the nineteenth century. The house on the left is home to a private collection of small but top-quality artefacts collected from Anatolia, from Urartian bronze-work to Attic red-figure vases and Hellenistic gold jewellery to Roman figurines.

KINALIADA

Ferries and sea buses dock at the island's sole settlement on the east coast, where there are plenty of cafés and restaurants. There's little to see on this rather barren outcrop, bar the church of **Surp Krikor Lusavoriç**, up the hill behind the waterfront. Built in 1857, it is notable for its windows, painted nostalgically with famous churches from the Armenians' homeland in what is now Eastern Turkey. The İstanbul Armenians, who make up most of the island's (mainly summer-only) community, keep this symbol of their faith in immaculate condition. The island takes its Turkish name Kınalıada or "Henna Island" from its red cliffs. Rent a bike near the jetty and cycle around the island in under an hour.

BURGAZADA

Again essentially a single settlement clustering around the ferry terminal, Burgazada is green and partially forested. The little town is dotted with some nice wooden villas, mostly shrouded by oleander, fig and palm trees, and is home to the large, nineteenth-century Greek Orthodox **Church of St John the Baptist**. Also in the backstreets you'll find the **Sait Faik Museum** on Burgaz Çayırı Sok 15 (T 0216 381 2132; Tues–Fri 10am–noon & 2–5pm, Sat 10am–noon; free). The house of Sait Faik, a bohemian whose short stories chronicled the harsh lives of the poor, has been wonderfully preserved – down to the pyjamas folded on his bed. If you're feeling energetic, hire a bike and explore – one worthwhile stop is **Kalpazankaya**, where you can swim and eat in a decent restaurant of the same name. Alternatively, ride here in a horse-drawn carriage (phaeton; *fayton* in Turkish) as part of an island tour (from ₺5). There's decent accommodation at *Mehtap 45* (see p.148).

HEYBELİADA

PHAETON

Larger and more popular as a day or weekend outing than either Kınalıada or Burgazada, this attractive island gets its name Heybeliada or "**Island of the Saddlebag**", from the twin hills that dominate it. The small settlement where the ferry docks, on the east coast, has numerous pretty fin-de-siècle villas, including one where the family of novelist Orhan Pamuk (see p.108) summered. Again, there are plenty of places to eat and drink in town and a limited choice of places to stay (see p.148). In town is an imposing **Naval School** (Deniz Harp Okulu) and the Greek Orthodox **Church of Aya Nikola**, curiously adorned with a clock tower. Like all the islands, it's traffic-free so the best way to get around is by phaeton (tours start from Ayyıldız Caddesi behind the waterfront), though a bicycle hired from one of several outlets near the jetty works out much cheaper and gives more flexibility. Best of

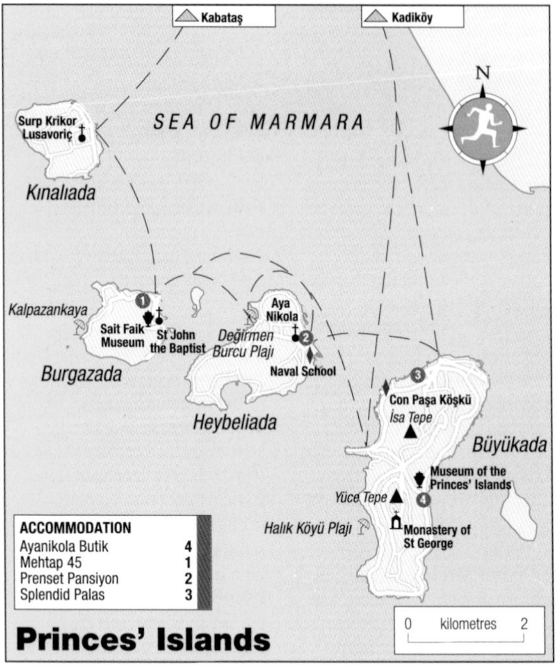

Kabataş
Kadiköy
N
SEA OF MARMARA
Surp Krikor Lusavoriç
Kınalıada
Kalpazankaya
Sait Faik Museum
St John the Baptist
Burgazada
Aya Nikola
Değirmen Burcu Plajı
Naval School
Heybeliada
Con Paşa Köşkü
İsa Tepe
Büyükada
Museum of the Princes' Islands
Yüce Tepe
Halık Köyü Plajı
Monastery of St George

ACCOMMODATION	
Ayanikola Butik	4
Mehtap 45	1
Prenset Pansiyon	2
Splendid Palas	3

0 kilometres 2

Princes' Islands

the three beach clubs is **Değirmen Burcu Plajı** (9am-dusk; ₺13 weekdays, ₺15 Sat & Sun) on the northwest coast, a shingle strip at the foot of cliffs in pine forest.

BÜYÜKADA

By far the most visited of the Princes' Islands, the visitors milling around the ferry terminal of the main settlement can be off-putting, but hire a bike or walk and you're soon away from the crowds. The most sumptuous of the islands' wooden mansions, once owned by wealthy Jewish and Greek families, are on Büyükada, many on the shore west of the Art-Nouveau **Splendid Palas** hotel (see p.148). One roofless and abandoned house below the splendid wooden mansion **Con Paşa Köşkü** on Çankaya Caddesi, was home to **Trotsky**, who started the *History of the Russian Revolution* while exiled here between 1929 and 1933. Again, you can explore by phaeton or bicycle (try Trek on Nisan Cad 23, behind the clock tower), with a round island trip taking about an hour and a half. There's plenty to see, not least the **Monastery of St George** (usually open; free) on **Yüce Tepe**, a prominent pine-covered hill. It's about a fifteen-minute walk to the summit and bikes are not allowed. On the east of the island the **Museum of the Princes' Islands** (Tues–Sun 9am–5pm; ₺5) has an exhibition about the island's writers and poets and nearby is the charming boutique *Ayanikola Butik* hotel (see p.148). There are several places to swim, by far the most peaceful is the **Halik Köyü Plajı** (8am–dusk; ₺15), reached by steep steps from the road running around the island some 3km south of the town. Many views from the islands inevitably at least partially include the urban sprawl of the metropolis, but here you have lovely, uninterrupted views across the Sea of Marmara to its distant, wooded south shore.

HEYBELİADA

NECLA
AKBAYRAK
Cafe
&

ACCOMMODATION

Accommodation

Accommodation is seldom in short supply in İstanbul but to secure a high-season room in one of the more popular places you'll need to reserve well in advance. The majority of visitors choose to stay in or around Sultanahmet, the heart of the old city, where there is a tremendous concentration of hotels, pensions and hostels, and the major sights are on the doorstep. Inevitably given the demand, many more establishments have opened on the fringes of Sultanahmet – in Sirkeci and towards the Grand Bazaar. Ever more visitors, particularly those where nightlife and contemporary arts and culture are as important as historical sights, are basing themselves across the Golden Horn in trendy Galata and Beyoğlu. For those with a big wallet looking for exclusivity, a Bosphorus-front hotel may well appeal, while those looking to spend a night of their İstanbul break on an island retreat may be tempted by the Princes' Islands.

All accommodation prices are for the cheapest double room in high season, which for most establishments is mid-March to mid-November and Christmas/New Year – though many places have reductions in July and August. Low-season rates are usually fifteen to twenty percent less than high. Don't be afraid to ask for a reduction – bargaining is part of the culture – and some smaller places will offer a discount (usually between five and ten percent) for payment in cash. Breakfast is included in all the places listed except apartments; the vast majority have air-conditioning to cope with the city's sultry summers, and double-glazing and central heating for the sometimes cold, damp winters. Free wi-fi is also a given in all but the more expensive international chain hotels.

Sultanahmet

AGORA GUEST HOUSE & HOSTEL > **Amiral Tafdil Sok 6 Ⓣ1 Sultanhamet Ⓣ 0212 458 5547, Ⓦ agoraguesthouse.com.** MAP P.34–35, POCKET MAP H12. A hip and successful cross between a guesthouse and hostel in a quiet street off busy Akbıyık Caddesi, one of its best points is the stylish communal lounge fronted by a terrace. There are ten en-suite double rooms and dorms ranging from four to ten beds – including one female only. The one downside is the small number of shared bathrooms. **Dorms from €17, doubles €80**

ALP > **Akbıyık Cad, Adliye Sok 4 Ⓣ1 Sultanhamet Ⓣ 0212 517 9570, Ⓦ alpguesthouse.com.** MAP P.34–35, POCKET MAP J12. Period-style hotel down a quiet alley off bustling, tourist-central Akbıyık Caddesi. The rooms are on the small side but tastefully done-out with wood floors, rugs, pale walls with dark-wood trim – and some have four-poster beds. The partly enclosed roof terrace has good views of the entrance to the Bosphorus, as do a few of the rooms. **€80**

AYASOFYA KONAKLARI > Soğuk Çeşme Sok 2 Ⓣ1 Sultanhamet Ⓣ 0212 513 3660, Ⓦ ayasofyakonaklari.com. MAP P.34–35, POCKET MAP H10. Great location on lovingly-restored Soğuk Çeşme Sokağı (see p.38) and just a stone's throw from the Topkapı Palace grounds and the Haghia Sophia, this lovely hotel comprises a series of artfully converted nineteenth-century townhouses. There's a wide range of rooms to choose from, perhaps the most authentic being in the detached wooden mansion house, the Konuk Evi, delightfully set in its own grounds. **€170**

CHEERS > Zeynepsultan Camii Sok 21 Ⓣ1 Sultanhamet Ⓣ 0212 526 0200, Ⓦ cheershostel.com. MAP P.34–35, POCKET MAP H10. More subtle than its Sultanahmet rivals, this hostel is nicely located on a quiet side street in a characterful early twentieth-century house. It has a range of well-kitted-out rooms, from doubles to four- and ten-bed dorms. One major plus is the upstairs bar, with a terrace affording a picture-postcard view of the Haghia Sophia. Friendly and well-managed, too. **Dorms from €18, doubles €60**

CHEERS LIGHTHOUSE > Çayıroğlu Sok 18 Ⓣ1 Sultanhamet Ⓣ 0212 458 2324, Ⓦ cheershostel.com. MAP P.34–35, POCKET MAP G9. Part of a new wave of hostel accommodation in the city, it provides hotel-like facilities without losing the communal hostel feel. The five rooms here range from a six-bed dorm to a luxury penthouse, with some facing a quiet street, others the sea, a stone's throw away across the defunct suburban railway line. There's free wi-fi and coffee and an excellent in-house restaurant. **Dorms from €18, penthouse suite €120**

DENİZ HOUSES > Çayıroğlu Sok 14 Ⓣ1 Sultanhamet Ⓣ 0212 518 9595, Ⓦ denizkonakhotel.com. MAP P.34–35, POCKET MAP G9. Two adjoining period buildings, down a quiet alley below the major concentration of hotels on and around Akbıyık Caddesi, make up this well-run establishment. Rooms in A block are small but homely, with stripped wood floors and Turkish rugs. Front rooms have sea views but get some noise from the suburban railway below. B Block rooms are larger and quieter but there are no sea views – go up to the pleasant roof terrace for these. **€65**

EMPRESS ZOE > Akbıyık Cad, Adliye Sok 10 Ⓣ1 Sultanhamet Ⓣ 0212 518 2504, Ⓦ emzoe.com. MAP P.34–35, POCKET MAP J12. You can't get much more historic than a hotel built over the remains of an Ottoman bath-house, which itself stands on the basement wall of a Byzantine palace. The American owners have stamped their distinctive mark on this treasure of a boutique hotel which, despite the rather small rooms and tricky layout, makes for a wonderfully atmospheric stay in the heart of the old city. **€140**

FOUR SEASONS SULTANAHMET > Tevfikhane Sok 1 Ⓣ1 Sultanhamet Ⓣ 0212 638 8200, Ⓦ fourseasons. MAP P.34–35, POCKET MAP H12. For anyone with a desire to spend a night in a former prison (*not* the one Billy Hayes was incarcerated in *Midnight Express*), this luxury hotel may fit in the bill. The rooms are palatial, with all the mod-cons you'd expect. The Neoclassical architecture is splendid, the situation excellent – it backs, controversially, onto Byzantine substructures being turned into an "archeology park" – and you don't have to slop out. **€560**

HANEDAN > Akbıyık Cad, Adliye Sok 3 Ⓣ1 Sultanhamet Ⓣ 0212 516 4869, Ⓦ hanedanhotel.com. MAP P.34–35, POCKET MAP J12. One of the best affordable hotels in Cankurtaran, run by a knowledgeable partnership of four friends, the standard rooms have king-sized beds sitting on dark-wooden boards, pastel-coloured walls and dark wood furniture. The triple and family rooms have four-poster beds and there are good views from the roof terrace. **€60**

İBRAHİM PAŞA > Terzihane Sok 5 ⓣ1 Sultanhamet ⓣ 0212 518 0394, ⓦ ibrahimpasha.com. MAP P.34–35, POCKET MAP G12. Superb blend of old and new in this lovingly converted pair of nineteenth-century townhouses, quietly located just off the Hippodrome. Bare boards, tasteful rugs and a successful blend of antique furniture and contemporary fittings are the basics of the mix of standard and deluxe rooms. Fabulous roof terrace with sweeping sea and old city views, a charming lounge with open fire downstairs and friendly, professional staff. **€99**

KYBELE > Yerebatan Cad 35 ⓣ1 Sultanhamet ⓣ 0212 511 7766, ⓦ kybelehotel.com. MAP P.34–35, POCKET MAP G11. One of the old city's first boutique hotels run by three outgoing brothers, the *Kybele* has been fashioned from a distinctive rendered-brick terraced house. Forget it if minimalism is your thing because this place is crammed with vintage artefacts and has over 4000 antique/period-style light fittings. The sixteen rooms have brass beds and stripped wood floors, while out back is a quiet garden and reading area. **€110**

NOMADE > Ticarethane Sok 15 ⓣ1 Sultanhamet ⓣ 0212 513 8172, ⓦ hotelnomade.com. MAP P34–35, POCKET MAP G11. One of the old city's few designer boutique hotels, the *Nomade* is run by twin sisters who have given their prodigy a distinctive stamp – white floors, striking colour schemes, blonde wood contemporary furniture mixed with ethnic artefacts like kilims. Great roof-terrace bar, too, with superb views of the Haghia Sophia. **€100**

OTTOMAN HOTEL IMPERIAL > Caferiye Sok 6/1 ⓣ1 Sultanhamet ⓣ 0212 513 6151, ⓦ ottomanhotel imperial.com. MAP P.34–35, POCKET MAP H11. A well-run period-style hotel right in the heart of Sultanahmet, offering a wide range of plush rooms conservatively kitted-out with dark wood furniture and shiny bedspreads. The views from the premium rooms especially are stunning, with the magnificent Haghia Sophia dominating the scene. Attached is the *Matbah* restaurant (see p.48), well-known for its Ottoman cuisine. **€125**

PENINSULA > Adliye Sok 6 ⓣ1 Sultanhamet ⓣ 0212 458 7702, ⓦ hotelpeninsula.com. MAP P.34–35, POCKET MAP J12. A small double here is less than one in many of the city's hostels, so it's a good budget option. Newly built in traditional style, it sticks largely to the convention hereabouts of bare floor (laminate in this case), pastel walls and vaguely Ottoman-period decor. Tidy bathrooms and a range of rooms from small singles to a two-room family suite. **€45**

SİDE HOTEL & PENSION > Utangaç Sok 20 ⓣ1 Sultanhamet ⓣ 0212 517 2282, ⓦ sidehotel.com. MAP P.34–35, POCKET MAP H12. A hybrid pension-cum-hotel, this place has been getting good reviews since 1989 – due in no small part to the very friendly trio of brothers who run it. Rooms in the hotel section are en-suite and have a/c, those on the pension side rely on fans for cooling. The six rooms on the upper floor have (spotless) shared bathrooms. The pension rooms are better value than the hotel. **Pension €40, hotel €80**

SULTAN HOSTEL > Akbıyık Cad 21 ⓣ1 Sultanhamet ⓣ 0212 516 9260, ⓦ sultanhostel.com. MAP P.34–35, POCKET MAP H12. The city's biggest hostel and main rival to the equally mammoth *Orient* virtually next door, it offers a wide range of rooms, from doubles to a 26-bed dorm. It's got a good reputation for cleanliness and the friendliness of its staff. Dorm rooms are good value but you can find doubles in pensions nearby for the same, or even less, money. **Dorms from €12, doubles €46**

TURKOMAN > Asmalı Çeşme Sok 2 ⓣ1 Sultanhamet ⓣ 0212 516 2956, ⓦ turkomanhotel.com. MAP P.34–35, POCKET MAP G12. Right opposite the

Egyptian Obelisk on the Hippodrome, this long-established boutique hotel, housed in a tall, narrow nineteenth-century building, has bags of character. All the rooms have brass beds, stripped boards and high ceilings, and there's a pleasant roof terrace for breakfast, with views across to the Blue Mosque. **€109**

UYAN > Utangaç Sok 2 Ⓣ1 Sultanhamet Ⓣ 0212 518 9255, Ⓦ uyanhotel.com. MAP P.34–35, POCKET MAP H12. One of the more stylish mid-range options in the heart of Sultanahmet, the rooms in this converted 1920s corner-plot residence are bright, light and clean (bar ground-floor rooms) with white walls, light-wood floors and crisp, white bed linen. There are good views of the Haghia Sophia from the roof terrace, while suite-room 405 is named the "Blue Mosque Room" for obvious reasons. **€99**

WHITE HOUSE > Çatalçeşme Sok Ⓣ1 Sultanhamet Ⓣ 0212 526 0019, Ⓦ istanbulwhitehouse.com. MAP P.34–35, POCKET MAP G11. On the north side of the main tramline, this beautifully appointed hotel won't suit those looking for a genuine period or boutique hotel – but it's hard to beat for reliable comfort. Rooms are faux-Ottoman, all patterned wallpapers, cream, gilt, ornate furniture and bold bedspreads. Breakfasts are excellent and views from the roof terrace expansive. **€139**

Topkapı Palace to the Golden Horn

NEORION > Orhaniye Cad 14 Ⓣ1 Sultanahmet Ⓣ 0212 527 9090, Ⓦ neorionhotel.com. MAP P.52–53, POCKET MAP G6. There's nothing flash about this 53 room hotel, but it goes to considerable lengths to keep guests happy. There is a roof terrace where you can enjoy a free drink nightly whilst gazing across the Bosphorus, as well as a free basement pool, jacuzzi, sauna and Turkish bath. Rooms are pristine, with subtle Ottoman-style decor and LCD TV's. **€196.**

SİRKECİ MANSION > Taya Hatun Cad 5 Ⓣ1 Gülhane Ⓣ 0212 528 4344, Ⓦ sirkecikonak.com. MAP P.52–53, POCKET MAP H6. Tucked-away down a side street off the main tramline and overlooking the walls of Gülhane Park, this popular hotel is impeccably run. The rooms are comfortable without being overly ornate, there's a fitness centre in the basement and nice touches like free afternoon tea and cake for guests. The roof terrace commands grand vistas over the park and Topkapı Palace beyond. **€189**

Grand Bazaar and around

NILES > Dibekli Camii Sok 13 Ⓣ1 Beyazit Ⓣ 0212 517 3239, Ⓦ hotelniles.com. MAP P.68–69, POCKET MAP E8. Good-value hotel on a steep street running down to the sea from the tramline and just a few minutes' walk from the Grand Bazaar. This area is more workaday than Sultanahmet, a real bonus if you want to be a little away from your fellow visitors. The standard rooms are smallish but were upgraded with consideration in 2013. There's a green and pleasant patio garden plus a roof terrace with sea views. **€105**

PRESIDENT (BEST WESTERN) > Kadriga Liman Cad 85 Ⓣ1 Beyazit Ⓣ 0212 515 6980, Ⓦ thepresidenthotel.com. MAP P.68–69, POCKET MAP E8. Better than average large, chain hotel minutes from the Grand Bazaar and handy for the Beyazit tram. There is a range of different rooms, from standard doubles and twins to suites, the decor restrained. Those with Sea of Marmara views carry a premium. The circular, year-round rooftop pool is a plus for some, as is the gym. **€130**

The Northwest quarter

KARİYE > Kariye Camii Sok 6 Ⓜ1 Ulubatlı Ⓣ 0212 534 8414, Ⓦ kariyeotel.com. MAP P.82, POCKET MAP A2. Like the *Daphnis*, this place is out of the way and a visit to Sultanahmet requires a metro and a tram ride, but this fine period hotel is in a fascinating area – right next to the land walls and the superb Kariye Museum (see p.80). One of the first İstanbul mansion houses to be converted to a hotel, it's showing a few signs of wear but is extremely good value – plus it's got one of the city's best restaurants, *Asitane* (see p.91), attached. **€70**

Galata

ANEMON GALATA > Büyükhendek Cad 11 Ⓜ 2 Şishane or Tünel İstiklal Ⓣ 0212 293 2343, Ⓦ anemonhotels.com. MAP P.92–93, POCKET MAP A15. Excellent location on the square at the foot of the landmark Galata Tower, this place is in the heart of the district's bohemian action. The hotel itself is part of a chain, however, with mock Art Nouveau/Victoriana-style decor and maximum comfort – including tubs in the bathrooms. **€170**

BADA BING > Serçe Sok 6, Karaköy Ⓣ1 Karaköy Ⓣ 0212 249 4111, Ⓦ badabinghostel.com. MAP P.92–93, POCKET MAP B15. As of 2014 Karaköy was the hippest part of the capital and this great hostel is perfectly poised to take advantage. A/c dorm rooms range from four- to ten-bed, with an eight-bed female-only option, and several private doubles. Great views, too, from the roof terrace. **Dorms from €12, rooms from €50**

EKLEKTİK GUESTHOUSE > Kadribey Çıkmaz 4 Ⓜ 2 Şişhane or Tünel İstiklal Ⓣ 0212 243 7446, Ⓦ eklektikgalata.com. MAP P.92–93, POCKET MAP B14. Hard to find but well worth it if you want something truly individual; the name says it all as each of the seven rooms in this period house is decorated and furnished in a different style – so make sure you peruse their website before choosing. **€130**

RAPUNZEL GUESTHOUSE > Bereketzade Camii Sok 3 Ⓜ 2 Şişhane or Tünel İstiklal Ⓣ 0212 292 5034, Ⓦ rapunzelistanbul.com. MAP P.92–93, POCKET MAP A15. A well-run designer hostel in the heart of Galata, with the nineteenth-century brick walls exposed in places. Dorms are en-suite six-bedders, with individual reading lights and hairdryers and there are a few doubles. Breakfast is substantial and the young staff very helpful. **Dorms €20, doubles €70**

VAULT KARAKÖY > Bankalar Cad 5, Karaköy Ⓣ1 Karaköy or Tünel Karaköy Ⓣ 0212 244 3400, Ⓦ thehousehotel.com. MAP P.92–93, POCKET MAP A15. Occupying an imposing bank building dating back to 1863, this hotel has been converted into a hotel by one of İstanbul's leading architects, Sian Kaadar. Original features abound, including subtly-patterned granite floors, high ceilings and the vaults themselves. South-facing rooms have great views over the Golden Horn, and rooms have mod-cons like i-pod docks and big-screen LCD TVs. Part of the well-regarded House brand. **€175**

WORLD HOUSE HOSTEL > Galipdede Cad 85 Ⓜ 1 Şişhane or Tünel İstiklal Ⓣ 0212 293 5520, Ⓦ worldhouseistanbul.com. MAP P.92–93, POCKET MAP B14. More traditional than either *Rapunzel* or *Sumo Cat*, for a rock-bottom stay this side of the Golden Horn it's hard to beat. The rooms are spotless if a little spartan, its great location on happening Galipdede Caddesi only tempered slightly by the call to prayer from the next-door mosque. **Dorms €14, doubles €68**

Beyoğlu

BÜYÜK LONDRA > Meşrutiyet Cad 117 Ⓜ 2 Şişhane or Tünel İstiklal Ⓣ 0212 249 1025, Ⓦ londrahotel.net. MAP P.104–105, POCKET MAP B12. The lowest priced rooms in this once extremely grand fin-de-siècle hotel are as cheap as you'll find in any part of the city you'd want to stay in, and despite the tiny bathrooms and slightly worn decor, are more than adequate. The real pull here, though, is the location, time-warp bar (see p.116), roof bar and general untouched, period ambience. Decent breakfast, too. **€50**

DEVMAN > Asmalımescit Sok 52 Ⓜ 2 Şişhane or Tünel İstiklal Ⓣ 0212 245 6212, Ⓦ devmanhotel.com. MAP P.104–105, POCKET MAP B13. One of a slew of cheapish options on bustling Asmalimescit Sokak, a narrow alley lined with *meyhanes* and bars, it's great if you're looking for basic, no-frills but clean accommodation right in the thick of the nightlife and shopping. Can be noisy, especially on weekend nights. €60

HOUSE HOTEL GALATASARAY > Bostanbaşı Cad 19 Ⓜ 2 Taksim Ⓣ 0212 252 0422, Ⓦ househotel.com. MAP P.104–105, POCKET MAP C12. Located on a quiet side street, this elegant hotel has been fashioned from a very tastefully restored 1870's apartment block. Rooms combine the nineteenth-century charm of high ceilings and wooden floors with free-standing chrome showers and gleaming espresso machines. There's a top-floor dining area, with views to the Galata Tower. €155

MAMA SHELTER > İstiklal Cad 50-54 Ⓜ 2 Taksim Ⓣ 0212 252 0100, Ⓦ mamashelter.com. MAP P.104–105, POCKET MAP C11. This French-Turkish concept hotel, located atop a mall, won't be everyone's ideal. But for confirmed metropolitans this place is perfect. Rooms are white, light and bright, with a sense of fun in the cartoon mask light shades, and there is a cool bar-restaurant run by a Michelin-starred Turkish chef, which attracts hip locals on the Thurs-Sun DJ set nights. €79

MARMARA PERA > Meşrutiyet Cad 21 Ⓜ 2 Şişhane or Tünel İstiklal Ⓣ 0212 251 4646, Ⓦ themarmarahotels.com. MAP P.104–105, POCKET MAP A13. Twelve-storey high-rise towering over neighbouring nineteenth-century apartment blocks and hotels, this smart establishment has stylishly modern rooms, a rooftop pool and bar with sensational views – plus the famed *Mikla* restaurant (see p.115). €145

PERA PALACE > Meşrutiyet Cad 52 Ⓜ 2 Şişhane or Tünel İstiklal Ⓣ 0212 377 4000, Ⓦ perapalace.com. MAP P.104–105, POCKET MAP A13. This historic hotel (see p.106) trades on its reputation and you pay a hefty premium to stay in the recently (2010) refurbished rooms, some occupied in grander times past by the likes of Agatha Christie and Ernest Hemingway. €230

RICHMOND HOTEL > İstiklal Cad 227 Ⓜ 2 Şişhane or Tünel İstiklal Ⓣ 0212 252 5460, Ⓦ richmondhotels.com.tr. MAP P.104–105, POCKET MAP B13. Not the most stylish hotel in Beyoğlu, it's nonetheless a reliable mid-range option, with standard rooms conservatively done out in neutrals, but it is well-located right on İstiklal Caddesi, some upper rear rooms have great Bosphorus views (at a premium) and there's the cool *Leb-i-Derya* bar-restaurant (see p.114). €148

TOM TOM SUITES > Boğazkesen Cad, Tomtom Kaptan Sok 18 Ⓜ 2 Şişhane or Tünel İstiklal Ⓣ 0212 292 4949, Ⓦ tomtomsuites.com. MAP P.104–105, POCKET MAP B13. Opposite the beautiful nineteenth-century Italian Consulate, this similarly dated property is a superbly presented series of suites, all subtle whites and soft browns. It's hard to know what the Franciscan nuns who once lived here would have made of the under-floor heated bathrooms and jacuzzis. €175

TRİADA RESIDENCE > İstiklal Cad, Meşelik Sok 4 Ⓜ 2 Taksim Ⓣ 0212 251 0101, Ⓦ triada.com.tr. MAP P.104–105, POCKET MAP D11. Pretty boutique hotel converted from a grand period dwelling on a narrow alley off İstiklal Caddesi, overlooking the Aya Triada church (see p.109). The large (40 square metre) rooms are very stylish and all have an American-style kitchen with coffee-making machine and fridge – and there's a wonderful roof terrace. €120

VILLA ZURICH > Akarsu Yokuşu Cad 44-46, Ⓜ 2 Taksim Ⓣ 0212 293 0604, Ⓦ hotelvillazurich.com. MAP P.104–105, POCKET MAP D13. Well-established, traditional hotel in the backstreets of now trendy Cihangir, with large, well-equipped doubles. There's a smart rooftop terrace where you can eat a substantial breakfast while admiring the Bosphorus. €96

Beşiktaş and Ortaköy

ÇIRAĞAN KEMPİNSKİ > Çırağan Cad 28. Buses #25/E, #28, #40, #40/T, #42/T T 0212 326 4646, W kempinski.com. MAP P.122–123. As opulent as you'd imagine from a hotel fashioned from a Bosphorus-front, European-style Ottoman palace. There's a huge outdoor pool, several restaurants and the inevitable designer boutiques. Every room has a balcony and the decor rooms a safe blend of the traditional and contemporary. **€420**

FOUR SEASONS BOSPHORUS > Çırağan Cad 42. Buses #25/E, #28, #40, #40/T, #42/T T 0212 381 4000, W fourseasons.com. MAP P.122–123. Like rival the *Çırağan Kempinski*, this upmarket chain hotel is set in a former palace on the Bosphorus and offers similar levels of comfort and luxury. The rooms and suites are very elegant and most have fabulous Bosphorus views – and there's a great pool and Turkish bath. **€490**

LES OTTOMANS > Muallim Naci Cad 68. Buses #25/E, #28, #40, #40/T, #42/T T 0212 359 1500, W lesottomans.com. MAP P.122–123. Beautiful hotel that was once a grand *yalı* (waterfront mansion), prices here make the *Four Seasons* and *Kempinski* look like budget options. This is the last word in exclusive luxury on the Bosphorus so you probably wouldn't want to arrive here by one of the public buses listed above. **€800**

W HOTEL > Süleyman Seba Cad 22. Buses #25/E, #28, #40, #40/T, #42/T T 0212 381 2121, W whotels.com/istanbul. MAP P.122–123. Upmarket, self-consciously hip chain hotel, the *W* in Beşiktaş is appropriately set in the posh Akaretler shopping centre – no mere mall but a series of period townhouses converted into boutiques and the like. Aimed largely at prosperous males up for some sophisticated clubbing and shopping. **€198**

Bosphorus and Princes' Islands

A'JİA > Çubuklu Cad 27, Kanlıca T 0216 413 9300, W ajiahotel.com. MAP P.135. Stunningly beautiful conversion of a splendid nineteenth-century waterfront mansion house, it's all period charm on the outside and stylish white is right minimalism on the inside. The roof-rooms are the best value and have lovely little balconies overlooking the Bosphorus. **€180**

AYANİKOLA BUTİK > Aya Nikola Mevki 104, Büyükada. Ferry or sea bus from Kabataş T 0216 382 4143, W ayanikolabutikpansiyon.com. MAP P.138. Popular with well-heeled but slightly alternative İstanbulites as a weekend retreat, each room is individually furnished with antique bits and pieces and has stripped boards and exposed brick. The "special" rooms are literally right by the sea and you can lounge back in bed and take in the view through the picture windows. **€105**

MEHTAP 45 > Burgazada. Ferry or sea bus from Kabataş T 0216 381 2660. MAP P.138. Quiet island, quiet boutique-style hotel with grand views across the Sea of Marmara back to the metropolis. Plain, simple but comfy rooms that were good enough for Bobby Charlton's four-day stay. Note that here, and at most Princes' Island hotels, you pay a fifty percent premium for Saturday-night stays. **€90**

PRENSET PANSİYON > Ayyıldız Cad 40–42/A, Heybeliada. Ferry or sea bus from Kabataş T 0216 351 0039, W prensetpansiyon.com. MAP P.138. Cheap and cheerful pension close to the ferry terminal and in the middle of the village close to all the restaurants and cafés. Few rooms have views. **€45**

SPLENDİD PALAS > Nisan Cad 23, Büyükada. Ferry or sea bus from Kabataş T 0216 382 6950, W splendidhotel.net.com. MAP P.138. A grand, white-painted wooden fin-de-siècle hotel, complete with cupolas and balconies, this period gem, lovingly restored in 2013, once hosted Edward VIII and Mrs Simpson. There's a pool out back and great sea views from the front rooms. Closed Nov–March. **€145**

SUMAHAN ON THE WATER > Kuleli Cad 51, Cengelköy **T** **0216 422 8000**, **W** **sumahan.com.** MAP P.135. A distillery converted into an award-winning hotel right on the Asian side of the Bosphorus, in the attractive suburb of Cenegelköy, this very stylish place blends the traditional and the modern with verve and makes an ideal retreat from the city hubbub. **€295**

Apartments

Apartments are becoming extremely popular in İstanbul, even for short breaks. With some exceptions, they tend to be concentrated in Galata and Beyoğlu and are often part of a converted period townhouse. Websites worth looking at include W istanbul-flats.com, with a number of cheaper apartments, W thehouseapart.com, with a much more expensive range of properties, W perfectplace.com or W crosspollinate.com. Below are a few recommended apartments, with prices given for one-night, high-season stays.

Apartments

DIVAN TAKSIM SUITES > **Cumhüriyet Cad 49** **T** **0212 254 7777**, **W** **divan.com.tr.** MAP P.104–105. Chic open-plan Scandinavian-style suites on Taksim Square, complete with work-stations, wi-fi and lcd TVs. **Twin or doubles from €190**

İSTANBUL SUITE HOME > **Dizdariye Çeşmesi Sok 51** **T** **0212 458 5255**, **W** **istanbulsuitehome.com.** MAP P.34–35, POCKET MAP G8. Just five stylish apartments in a period house in the quiet backstreets below the tramline and close to Sultanahmet's sights, with all the facilities you'd expect and a shared roof terrace. **From €125 for a four-bed apt.**

PASHA > **Serdar-I Ekrem Cad, Galata Tünel İstiklal** **W** **istanbulplace .com.** MAP P.92–93, POCKET MAP B14. Looking south across the Golden Horn, the sitting room and main bedroom of this beautifully-restored nineteenth-century apartment have great old city skyline views. There are three good-sized bedrooms, a stylish kitchen, and separate shower room and w.c. Perfect combination of period features and contemporary white decor and furnishings. **€300**

ROOMS GALATA > **Kumbarcı Yokuşu 37** **T** **0212 293 3186**, **W** **roomsgalata .com.** MAP P.92–93, POCKET MAP B14. sixteen cool rooms in a beautiful period house, linked by a swish spiral staircase. Kitchenette, wi-fi and king, queen or single beds. **Doubles from €130**

Letting agencies

ARSU LIVING İSTANBUL APARTMENTS Beyoğlu **T** **0531 221 7156**, **W** **living-istanbul.com.** Five reasonably-priced apartments either in, or close to, Beyoğlu, run by a German-Turkish couple.

İSTANBUL APARTMENTS Tel Sok 27, Beyoğ **T** **0212 249 5065**, **W** **istanbul .com.** This well-organised Turkish operation has a wide range of apartments on İstiklal Caddesi and down in Cihangir.

ISTANBUL!PLACE APARTMENTS **T** **0531 221 7156**, **W** **istanbulplace .com.** Anglo-Turkish run company offering fifteen beautifully restored period townhouse apartments in and around Galata.

MANZARA İSTANBUL Tatarbeyi Sok 26b, Galata **T** **0212 252 4600**, **W** **manzara-istanbul.com.** Run by a German-born Turkish architect, and offering forty quality properties, mainly in Galata and Beyoğlu.

ALYANS
KÖKLER
&
SIGARA
İÇILMEZ

ESSENTIALS

Arrival

The vast majority of foreign visitors reach İstanbul by air, though there are good road links, and rather less useful rail connections, with the rest of Europe. The city is also a major stop on Mediterranean cruises.

By plane

İstanbul has two major airports, *Atatürk International* (T 0212 465 3000, W ataturkairport.com) on the European side of the city, and Sabiha Gökçen (T 0216 585 5000, W sgairport .com) across the Bosphorus in Asia. The former is used mainly by scheduled airlines; the latter, considerably further from the city centre, by budget European carriers.

ATATÜRK INTERNATIONAL AIRPORT

Around 24km west of the city centre, the airport comprises two interconnected terminals, one international, the other domestic. Shuttle buses run by Havataş (W havatas .com) run from both terminals to the city centre every half-hour between 4am and 1am for ₺10, stopping at Aksaray (for Sultanahmet, though it's a 400m walk from the stop up to the T1 Aksaray tram stop) and Taksim Square (for Taksim and north Beyoğlu). Journey time is around 45min, a conductor collects fares on board. A cheaper alternative is to use a combination of the **M1 Metro** and **T1 tram** (approximately every 10min, 6am–midnight). Follow the "**M**" signs to the metro and purchase two plastic tokens (*jetons*) for ₺4 each from the *jetonmatik* machines (see opposite). The metro and tram systems connect at Zeytinburnu; get off here and, using the second *jeton*, board the T1 tram which will take you to Sultanahmet or across the Golden Horn to Karaköy, where you can take the Tünel funicular (see p.155) to Galata/Beyoğlu or continue to the last stop at Kabataş and take the modern funicular (see p.155) to Taksim Square. It is also possible to buy an İstanbulkart (see box opposite) from a machine at the airport for ₺10, top-it up with credit and use that instead of the tokens. Journey time to Sultanahmet should be 30min to 45min. A taxi is around ₺40 to Sultanahmet, ₺50 to Beyoğlu/Taksim.

SABIHA GÖKÇEN AIRPORT

Havaş buses (₺13) take around an hour and a half to reach Taksim Square from the airport, departing half-hourly between 4am and 1am. It's also possible to purchase an İstanbulkart travel pass (see box opposite) at the airport and thus take a public bus (₺4), the #E10, or #E/11 to Kadıköy, from where you can board a Turyol ferry (6.45am–8.30pm; ₺4) to Eminönü (for Sultanahmet and the old city) or Karaköy (Galata and Beyoğlu). Total journey time will likely be similar to the Havataş bus. Another choice is the #E/3 bus to Levent and change to the M2 metro to Taksim. A taxi will cost ₺80–100.

By train

Reaching İstanbul by train today is far from the pleasure it must have been in the Orient Express days and is only for the patient and committed rail buff. The most straightforward route from London is via Paris, Munich, Vienna, Budapest and Bucharest. At the time of writing, rail maintenance work meant the last part of the trip, from the Bulgarian/Turkish border to İstanbul was by bus. Trains from Europe no longer arrive at historic Sirkeci station. When work on the Marmaray line (see p.156) is complete, they will terminate at Hakalı, 16km west of the centre, from where there will be a metro to Yenikapı (change for Galata/Beyoğlu) or Sirkeci (old city). For the best information, see rail enthusiasts' delight seat61.com.

By bus

Coaches run by several Turkish companies link İstanbul to various other European cities. Ulusoy (ulusoy.com.tr) has buses to twelve German cities, Varan (varan.com.tr) to Budapest, Vienna and several other destinations. Metro (metroturizm.com.tr) runs coaches to Athens and Sophia. Buses arrive at Esenler *otogar* (bus station; otogaristanbul.com), linked to the city centre by the M1 metro – switch to the T1 tram at Aksaray. Buses from all Turkish destinations also terminate at Esenler, though some also stop at Harem on the Asian side of the Bosphorus, from where regular ferries cross the strait to Eminönü.

By sea

Cruise ships dock at Karaköy International Maritime Passenger Terminal, on the north side of the Golden Horn not far northeast of the Galata Bridge, from where it's a short walk to the Karaköy T1 tram stop (for Sultanahmet) or the Tünel (for Galata/Beyoğlu).

Getting around

It's fortunate that, despite İstanbul's huge sprawl, most areas of interest to the visitor are compact enough to explore on foot. Judicious use of the city's metro, tram, bus and ferry network will, however, enable you to get to slightly out of the way places and save your legs. For all of these forms of transport, you use *jeton*s, purchased from the *jetonmatik* machines located at many stops. *Jetonmatik* machines accept Turkish notes and coins and there's a flat-rate charge for most modes of transport of ₺4. The turnstiles at the entrance to tram, metro, train and ferry stops have a slot to accept the *jeton*s. Far superior to *jetons* is the İstanbulkart travel pass (see box below).

Buses and dolmuşes

The most daunting of İstanbul's public transport options, visitors often find it difficult to know which bus to get on or where to get off – plus they can be uncomfortably crowded and the drivers know no English. Having said that, they are a cheap way of getting around and reaching places other modes of transport (bar taxis) don't. **Municipality buses** have IETT written on them (İstanbul Elektrik

İstanbulkart

This credit card-sized smartcard is available from machines and kiosks near major transport stops. The official price is ₺6 but kiosk vendors usually add a ₺1 mark-up. Bought from a machine the cost is ₺10, which includes ₺4 credit. It can be topped-up when necessary from either a machine or kiosk. Not only does it mean you don't waste time looking for a *jetonmatik* machine, it also saves a substantial ₺1.85 per journey, much more on Princes' Islands ferries and sea buses. Another advantage over jetons is that for journeys taken within 90minutes of the last the charge is only ₺1.45 It can be used on buses, the metro and tram, ferries and sea buses – plus the suburban train and funiculars.

Tramway ve Tünel) though there are some private ones. Most run daily 6.30am to 11pm. The most useful bus stations in the old city are Beyazıt, Edirnekapı and Eminönü, across the Golden Horn Taksim Square and Kabataş, and there are several bus routes that may be useful for visitors (see box below). **Dolmuşes** are a kind of shared taxi (either a car or minibus) but the only really useful routes for visitors are the yellow minibuses departing the Taksim-end of Tarlabaşı Bulvarı for the old city and Yedikule (see p.87) or connecting Kadıköy and Üsküdar in Asia. Note that you need cash for *dolmuşes*.

Trams

The single most useful transport route for most visitors is the T1 tramline which runs from Zeytinburnu

Useful bus routes

For information in English on the bus network in İstanbul, check Ⓦ iett.gov.tr/en. It's tricky to use – on the home page click on "How to go there" for details of routes, stops and maps.

İstanbul in Asia

#12 and **#12/A** Kadıköy to Üsküdar

#15 Üsküdar along the Bosphorus to Beylerbeyi, Kanlıca and Beykoz

#15/A Beykoz to Anadolu Kavağı

European İstanbul

#22 Kabataş along the Bosphorus to İstiniye via Beşiktas, Ortaköy, Arnavutköy, Bebek and Emirgan

#25/A Haciosman metro to Rumeli Kavağı via Tarabya and Sariyer

#25/E Kabataş to Sariyer via Beşiktas, Ortaköy, Arnavutköy, Bebek and Emirgan

#28 Beşiktas to Edirnekapı via Eminönü Transit and Fatih (for Fatih and Yavuz Selim mosques, land walls and Kariye Museum)

#28/T Beşiktas to Topkapı via Karaköy, Eminönü Transit and Fatih

#36/V and **#37/Y** Vezneciler to Edirnekapı via Fatih (for Fatih and Yavuz Selim mosques, land walls and Kariye Museum)

#38/E Eminönü to Edirnekapı via Unkapanı Bridge and Fatih (for Fatih and Yavuz Selim mosques, land walls and Kariye Museum)

#38 Beyazıt to Edirnekapı via Aksaray (for Historia Mall, Akdeniz Hatay Sofrası, land walls, Kariye Museum)

#40 Taksim to Sariyer via Beşiktas, Ortaköy, Arnavutköy, Bebek and Emirgan

#55/EB Beyazıt to Eyüp via Aksaray, Fatih and Edirnekapı (for Yavuz Selim mosque, land walls, Kariye Museum and *Pierre Loti* café)

#54/HT Taksim to upper Golden Horn (for Miniatürk, Rahmi M. Koç Industrial Museum and Santralistanbul)

#80/T Taksim to Yedikule (for south end of land walls)

#87 Taksim to Edirnekapı via Fatih (for Fatih and Yavuz Selim mosques, land walls and Kariye Museum)

#96/T Taksim to Atatürk Airport

#99 Eminönü along Golden Horn (for Fener, Balat, north end of land walls, Eyüp and Santralistanbul)

in the west (where it connects with the M1 metro and thus Atatürk airport) to the ferry terminal/bus station and funicular at Kabataş, on the north side of the Golden Horn. Running through the heart of the old city, with stops including the Grand Bazaar, Sultanahmet, Sirkeci, Eminönü (for ferries to Asia), Karaköy (for ferries to Asia and Galata and the Tünel to Beyoğlu) and Kabataş (for the funicular to Taksim, ferries to the Princes' Islands and buses along the European shore of the Bosphorus). The so-called **antique tram** (daily 9am–9pm; ₺4) rumbles up and down İstiklal Caddesi from Tünel İstiklal to Taksim Square.

Metro

There are several metro lines but only the M1, M2 and Marmaray lines will be of use to the majority of visitors. The M1 metro links Atatürk airport with Esenler bus station and Aksaray – though frustratingly doesn't link up perfectly with the T1 tram and you have to walk around 200m, over a bridge, to swap from the Aksaray M1 metro stop to the T1 tram stop at Yusufpaşa. The M1 metro is useful for getting out to the land walls reasonably close to the Kariye Museum (see p.80). The M2 metro runs from Yenikapı in the old city north across the historic peninsula and Golden Horn to Şişhane at the southern end of İstiklal Caddesi in Beyoğlu. From there, it runs north again to Taksim and out to the northern suburbs. At the time of writing, the Marmaray line was running between Kazlıçesme in the west (useful for the southern terminus of the land walls of Theodosius) eastwards to Yenikapı (where it connects with the M2 metro) then to Sirkeci and under the Bosphorus to Üsküdar. Eventually it will be extended to Halkalı in the west, Gebze to the east.

Funiculars

The F1 funicular links the transport hub at Kabataş with Taksim Square, while the cute nineteenth-century underground funicular, the **Tünel** (7am–10pm; ₺4 or İstanbulkart), connects Karaköy on the Golden Horn with Beyoğlu/İstiklal Caddesi at the top of the hill. There's also a **cable car** (₺4 or İstanbulkart) linking the shores of the Golden Horn at Eyüp with the cemetery and *Pierre Loti* café (see p.90).

Ferries

Few people will want to visit İstanbul and not take a ferry ride to Asia and/or up the Bosphorus or Golden Horn. Şehir Hatları (T 444 1851, W sehirhatlari.com) is the main ferry company – make sure you pick up a timetable from a ferry terminal or tourist office as ferry times do change – or check their website. The main city terminal is at Eminönü, just east of the Galata Bridge, from where ferries run across the Bosphorus to Kadıköy (7.30am–9pm; ₺4) and Üsküdar (6.35am–11pm; ₺4) around three to five times an hour (they are primarily for commuters, not tourists). The terminal for the Şehir Hatları Bosphorus Cruise (see p.134) is also here. To the west of the bridge, from Yemiş İskele, Haliç Hattı ferries originating from Üsküdar run (approximately hourly) up the Golden Horn to Eyüp, useful for visits to the Rahmi M. Koç Industrial Museum (see p.97), the northern end of the land walls and Eyüp. From Karaköy, across the Galata Bridge, there are regular ferries to Kadıköy (6.30am–midnight; ₺3). From Kabataş, at the eastern end of the T1 tram line, ferries and IDO (İstanbul Deniz Otobüsleri; T 444 4436, W ido.com.tr) sea buses run to the Princes' Islands – more transport details can be found in Chapter 9 (see p.137). A number of smaller private companies also operate boats across the Bosphorus and to the Princes' Islands, notably Turyol, with boats departing to Asia from terminals just west of the Galata Bridge on both sides of the Golden Horn.

Taxis

Yellow taxis are ubiquitous and are very useful when visiting out-of-the-way sights and, assuming the driver is honest, reasonably cheap (a standing-charge of ₺2.7, then ₺2.7 per km). Make sure the meter is turned on before setting off – ensuring the driver follows the shortest route is trickier. One way to avoid potential disputes is to get your hotel to arrange a taxi for you for an agreed price.

Tourist buses

Big Bus İstanbul (0212 283 1396, bigbustours.com) has a useful hop-on, hop-off open-top bus service with a recorded guide. Departures are from either opposite the Haghia Sophia in Sultanahmet or across the Golden Horn in Taksim, where there are red kiosks selling tour tickets. You can hop on or off at Taksim, Old Pera (Beyoğlu), Edirnekapı (land walls) and Kumkapı and tours take around 1.5hr.

Walking and special intererst tours

İstanbul Walks (T 0216 489 6032) offer guided walks of the city that include all the major, and many minor, historic sites (admission prices not included) for around €60 for a full day. More specialist is **Fest Travel** (T 0212 216 1036, W festtravel.com.tr), with a wide range of strolls around quarters of the city where it's easy to miss the most interesting sights if you are on your own. İstanbul Tour Studio (T 0533 355 4049, W istanbultourstudio.com) offer a range of activities including sailing, rowing on the Golden Horn, cycling in Asia and exploring the city's street art scene.

Directory A–Z

Cinema

Most films are screened in the language in which they were shot, with Turkish subtitles for non-Turkish productions. The exceptions are children's films, which are generally dubbed into Turkish. There are several cinemas on or just off İstiklal Caddesi (between Galatasaray Meydanı and Taksim Square (see p.108), the largest of which is Cinemaximum Fitaş (W intersinema.com), and one in Sultanahmet, the Şafak (W ozenfilm.com.tr). Otherwise head to one of the big shopping malls. Tickets from ₺10.

The Marmaray project

This massive transport infrastructure project includes a rail tunnel under the Bosphorus linking European and Asian İstanbul. The tunnel finally opened in late-2013 after years of delays caused by the uncovering of important archeological finds made while digging the Yenikapı hub. From Yenikapı, the line runs underground to Sirkeci, then under the Bosphorus to Üsküdar, and west to Kazlıçeşme. Eventually it will form a 76km-long line linking the two international airports. Just as important is the bridge across the Golden Horn, which will link the metro systems. A part of the project completed in early 2014 was the construction of controversial bridge across the Golden Horn which allowed the M2 metro line to link up with the Marmaray line.

Emergency numbers

Ambulance ☎ 112
Fire ☎ 110
Police ☎ 155
Traffic Police ☎ 154

Consulates

Australia, Asker Ocağı Cad 15, Elmadağ, Şişli ☎ 0212 243 1333.
Canada, Tekfen Tower, 209 Büyükdere Cad, Levent 4 ☎ 0212 385 9700.
New Zealand, İnönü Cad 48/3, Taksim ☎ 0212 244 0272.
South Africa (Honorary Consul) Alarko Centre, Muallim Naci Cad 113–115, Ortaköy ☎ 0212 260 378.
UK, Meşrutiyet Cad 34, Tepebaşı, Beyoğlu ☎ 0212 334 6400.
US, Kaplıcalar Mevkii Sok 2, İstinye ☎ 0212 335 9000.

Crime

Mugging and assaults are rare, though pick-pocketing increasingly common – take great care on the crowded transport system especially. A couple of areas to be wary of are Taksim Square at night, notably where it joins Tarlabaşı Bulvarı, and the land walls at dusk/evening time. There are several police forces in Turkey but the branch you're most likely to require is the Security Police (*Emniyet Polisi*), recognized by their blue shirts. A subdivision of this branch is the Tourist Police (*Turizm Polisi*) who have a station, open 24hr, at Yerebatan Cad 6 (☎ 0212 527 4503). There are also blue-uniformed Market Police (*Zabitas*) patrolling bazaars and other commercial areas.

Electricity

220V AC. Plugs have two round pins so bring an adaptor if necessary.

Entry requirements

Make sure you have a full passport with at least 6 months validity. Citizens of most countries must buy an e-visa in advance from Wevisa.gov.tr. Fill-in the simple online form, pay by Mastercard or Visa debit/credit card and your visa will be emailed to you. Visas are multiple entry and for citizens of the UK, Ireland, the US, Canada, Australia and New Zealand, are valid for 90 days in 180 days from the date requested on the application. Visas for citizens of the UK, USA and Ireland are $20, Australia and Canada $60. Note that entry requirements change; consult the Turkish Ministry of Foreign Affairs at Ⓦ mfa.gov.tr for the latest regulations.

Gay and lesbian travellers

İstanbul has a very active gay scene despite the ambivalence of Turkish society to homosexuality, and over 10,000 marchers took part in the 2011 Lesbian, Gay, Bisexual, Transvestite and Transsexual march down İstiklal Caddesi. The scene is centred largely on Taksim and Beyoğlu, where there are a fair number of gay and lesbian cafés and clubs. For more information, see Ⓦ istanbulgay.com and Ⓦ hipsultan.com, or, for gay-friendly accommodation, check Ⓦ turkey-gay-travel-com.

Health

For minor complaints visit a pharmacy (*eczane*). Pharmacists are well trained, many speak some English and most antibiotics are available without a prescription. Standard opening hours are 9am–7pm Mon–Sat but there is always a night duty pharmacy (*nöbetçi eczane*) open 24hr including Sundays – the address of the nearest is posted in pharmacy windows.

There are public and private hospitals in İstanbul. Both are usually well equipped, but state hospitals are often overcrowded, run-down, and finding a good English-speaker may be tricky. Private establishments usually have more English-speaking doctors and often a designated translator. Facilities are generally top-notch and they are well-used to dealing with foreign private patients (and relieving them of their cash – make sure you are insured).

The Taksim First Aid Hospital (Taksim İlkyardim Hastanesi) at Sıraselviler Cad 112, Taksim (T 0212 252 4300), is state-run and only treats emergencies. The private German Hospital, at Sıraselviler Cad 119, Taksim (T 0212 293 2150, W almanhastanesi.com.tr), also has a dental and eye clinic. The private American Hospital (Amerikan Hastanesi), Güzelbahçe Sok 20, Nişantaşı (T 0212 311 2000, W amerikanhastanesi.org), is state-of-the-art and also has a dental clinic. The International Hospital, İstanbul Cad 82, Yeşilköy (T 0212 468 4444, W internationalhospital.com.tr), has a full range of medical services and 24hr emergency care. For a regular rather than hospital dentist, Prodent (Can Ergene) at Valikonağı Cad 109/5, Nişantaşı (T 0212 230 4635), is reliable and English speaking. Dental care is generally both excellent and relatively cheap in Turkey.

Internet

Virtually every hostel, pension and hotel in İstanbul offers free wi-fi and often a fixed terminal or two as well. Many upmarket cafés also have free wi-fi, especially those situated in Galata and Beyoğlu. There are also plenty of internet cafés, though many of these are mainly frequented by youths gaming.

Left luggage

There are lockers at both Atatürk and Sabiha Gökçen airports (₺18 for 24hr).

Lost property

For anything lost (or stolen) contact the Tourist Police at Yerebatan Cad 6 (T 0212 527 4503) in Sultanahmet.

Money

Turkey's currency is the Turkish lira (Türk lirası) or TL for short, divided into smaller units known as kuruş. Coins come in denominations of 1, 5, 10, 25, 50 kuruş and 1TL, with notes in denominations of 5, 10, 20, 50, 100 and 200TL. Prices of goods and services are displayed as either eg 25TL, for example or using the symbol ₺, introduced in 2012 to reflect the growing confidence in the stability and worth of the currency. At the time of writing, the ₺ symbol was being used by businesses either in front of the numerical figure or after it; officially it should be placed before.

There are many, many ATMs throughout the city. All have touch-screen English options, those in major tourist areas dispense euros and dollars as well as Turkish lira. Many banks will change money but can be slow and cumbersome – for the best rate use the state-owned Ziraat Bankası (Mon–Fri 8.30am–noon & 1.30pm–5pm), which has a dedicated exchange counter and an automated queuing system. You can also change money at the Post Office (PTT) commission free and at a reasonable rate. The other alternative is an exchange bureau (döviz bürosu). The rate is usually slightly less than the Ziraat Bankası but the procedure much quicker, and opening hours are longer (generally 9am–8pm Mon–Sat) than banks'. There are several around the Sultanahmet tram-stop area on Divan Yolu as well as on İstiklal Caddesi. Credit cards are widely accepted in most tourist-orientated hotels and upmarket restaurants but sometimes attract a surcharge.

Mosque essentials

Turkey is ninety-nine percent Muslim and although İstanbul is a vibrant, cosmopolitan city, many of its inhabitants still take their religion seriously so it pays to be respectful when visiting mosques. The basic rules of entry are:
- Cover your head (women) and shoulders and upper arms (men and women)
- No shorts (either sex) or miniskirts
- Take off shoes before entering (often a plastic bag is provided for you to place your shoes in and carry around; alternatively place them on one of the shelves provided).

Friday midday prayers are the most important of the week and visiting at this time is not advised – indeed visiting at any of the five daily prayer times is best avoided, though in most cases you will not cause offence. Don't speak too loudly (there are often people in the mosque either praying or learning the Koran) and don't point your camera at worshippers. Mosques always have a donation box which you may want to contribute to. Take note that there are no set opening and closing times and many of the big mosques in the old city will be open all day, from first to last prayer call (which varies through the year according to sunrise and sunset). Smaller mosques in more out of the way places are often kept locked outside prayer times and you may need to track down the caretaker or *imam*.

Museum passes

3 or 5 day İstanbul Museum passes can be both cost and time effective. 3 day passes (₺85) gives entry to Haghia Sophia, Topkapı Palace and Harem, Archeolgy Museum, Mosaic Museum, Museum of Turkish and Islamic Art and History of Science and Technology in Islam Museum, a potential saving of ₺40. The ₺115, 5 day pass includes the Kariye Museum. Passes allow fast-track entry to sites – useful as Haghia Sophia and Topkapı often have interminable queues. Passes are available from the first four museums listed above or online from Ⓦ muze.gov.tr.

Opening hours

Although in Turkey state-run museums invariably close on a Monday, some in İstanbul buck this rule, so make sure you check the opening days of a particular museum before visiting. Opening hours are usually from between 8.30am and 9pm to 5pm or 6pm, though the biggest museums/sights stay open in summer until 7pm. For mosques see "Mosque essentials" (opposite). Private museums follow the same general opening hours as their state-run cousins but sometimes shut for lunch. Banks and government offices usually open Mon–Fri 8.30am–noon and 1.30–5pm. Shop opening hours vary widely, with most opening from between 9am or 10am to 7pm, but many more, especially in Beyoğlu, opening until 9 or 10pm. *Bakkals*, small general stores, and kiosks selling papers, gum, tissues etc are often open from 7am to 10pm. The Grand Bazaar is open Mon to Sat 9am to 7pm, modern malls usually 10am to 10pm seven days a week.

Phones

Note that İstanbul has two codes, 0212 for the European side of the city, 0216 for the Asian. Turkey's country code is 90, directory enquiries 118 and 115 for the international operator. To phone overseas, purchase an international calling card, the best of which is the Alocard, available from PTTs and useable at public phones – just dial the access number supplied with the card, scratch to reveal the 12-digit PIN and enter it, then dial the overseas number. A ₺10 card allows over 100 minutes of calling time to the UK or US. There are plenty of public phone booths scattered around the city, often outside major transport hubs such as Sirkeci, and also at PTTs. Assuming you have a roaming facility your mobile will connect with one of the local providers, though US phones won't work here. Calls are predictably expensive, around £1.30 per minute to the UK, plus you pay for incoming calls. Unfortunately, buying a cheap SIM card is not a great option here as legislation is strict and taxes high. The three main providers (Türkcell, AVEA and Vodaphone) have outlets at both Atatürk and Sabiha Gökçen airports where you must complete a registration form and have your passport photocopied. A typical pay as you go package is ₺120, only ₺70 of which is credit, the rest tax. After between 10 days and two weeks your phone will be blocked for use with the Turkish SIM unless you pay a ₺150 fee at a local tax office.

Post

The two main post offices (PTT) of use to visitors are the massive Sirkeci PTT on Büyük Postane Caddesi, Eminönü (T 0212 526 1200; daily 8.30am–7pm), and at Yeniçarşısı Caddesi, Beyoğlu (T 0212 444 1788; Mon–Fri & Sun 8.30am–5.30pm), just off Galatasaray Meydanı.

Smoking

Smoking is banned on public transport and in all indoor places, although the ban is widely flouted in some bars and traditional teahouses. Many bars, cafés and restaurants get around the ban by providing outside or courtyard tables, which are covered with plastic and/or warmed with outdoor heaters in winter. The rule applies to *nargile* (water-pipe) cafés.

Time

Turkey is two hours ahead of GMT year round. There is no am/pm in Turkey, which uses the 24-hour clock.

Tipping

A 10 to 15 percent service charge is standard in fancy restaurants, though as this goes to the establishment, it is customary to tip the waiters here a further 5 percent. Waiters in more basic establishments will also appreciate the same 5 percent tip.

Toilets

In heavily touristed parts of the city there are sufficient public toilets, in less-visited parts like the land walls and northwest quarter far fewer. Virtually all mosques have toilets attached to them, however. At both public and mosque toilets you have to pay a small fee (usually ₺1) and note that they are invariably of the squat variety and provide no paper. Bars, cafés, restaurants and hotels all have western-style toilets.

Tourist information

There are six tourist offices in the city. Most central is at Divan Yolu 3, Sultanahmet (daily 9am–5pm; T 0212 518 8754) near the Haghia Sophia, which has English-speaking staff and hands out tolerable city maps. The other old city offices at Beyazit Meydanı (daily 9am–6pm; T 0212 522 4902) near the Grand Bazaar, and at Sirkeci station (daily 9am–5pm; T 0212 511 5888) are rather less helpful. In Taksim, there's one in the *Hilton*, Cumhüriyet Caddesi (daily 9am–5pm; T 0212 518 8754), plus at Atatürk International Airport (daily 24hr; T 0212 465 3151) and, for cruise ship arrivals, on Kemaneș Caddesi, Karaköy (daily 9am–5pm; T 0212 249 5776).

Travellers with disabilities

The good news is that the useful T1 tram is reasonably disabled-friendly and will save time and effort pushing a wheelchair along busy Divan Yolu. The metro has few accessible stations. Buses have ramps and low doors, but are so crowded using them is tricky, especially given the language barrier, and anyway are not allowed into Sultanahmet. The Topkapı Palace (see p.54), Haghia Sophia (see p.36) and Archeology Museum (see p.51) are partly accessible by wheelchair, as is the Blue Mosque (see p.43). Unfortunately the old city's steep streets and cobbled surfaces can make it difficult to get around between sights, and few mosques allow wheelchairs. Despite friendly and helpful staff, many other museums and sights do not have wheelchair access, with the honourable exceptions of the Rahmi M. Koç Industrial Museum (see p.97), İstanbul Modern (see p.96) and the Pera Museum (see p.106).

Travelling with children

While there are few specifically child-friendly sights in İstanbul, and it can appear dauntingly crowded and hectic at times, most kids will find İstanbul an absorbing place to visit. The boat rides up and down the Bosphorus, across to Asia and out to the Princes' Islands are all great fun with kids, and several of the city's museums/galleries will be of interest. The Military Museum (see p.109) may be a little stuffy but has enough weaponry to keep boys of a certain age quiet for a while, as will the detailed scale models in Miniatürk (see p.97). Then there are the hands-on science machines at Santralistanbul (see p.97) and the plethora of vintage modes of transport and more at the Rahmi Koç Industrial Museum – plus the life-like panorama of the 1453 siege of Constantinople at the Panorama 1453 Museum (see p.88). Both Gülhane Park (see p.56) and Yıldız Park (see p.122) have plenty of green and open space for kids to run off some energy. Turks love kids, the family means everything here and cafés and restaurants are usually very tolerant of them.

Turkish baths (hamam)

Essentially a continuation of the Roman tradition, the Ottoman Turks made the *hamam* a central feature of everyday life and they were often attached to the great imperial mosque complexes such as the Süleymaniye (see p.66). Today the importance of the *hamam* has declined significantly, though they are still used by locals to relax and meet up with friends. For many visitors the *hamam* experience is a must, especially in İstanbul as it boasts many historic *hamams*, worth seeing for their architecture alone. Some have separate sections for men and women, others are segregated according to a schedule. The vast majority have a foyer/changing area, often with a café, and somewhere to leave your valuables. The main event is the steamy, domed *hararet*, where bathers soap-up and sluice themselves with water of varying degrees of hot and cold, or lie on the *göbek taşı* or navel stone, a raised and heated marble platform in the centre of the room. There is a basic charge for this self-service bath, the traditional scrub and massage are extra. Detailed information on seven *hamams* is given in the relevant Places chapters; in the old city the Ayasofya Hürrem Sultan (see p.38), Cağaloğlu (see p.58), Çemberlitaş (see p.72) and Süleymaniye (see p.67); Tophane the Kılıç Ali Paşa (see p.96), in Beyoğlu the Galatasaray Hamamı (see p.108); and in Üsküdar the Çinili (see p.127).

Festivals and events

Public holidays are denoted by PH and banks, schools and government offices close on these days, though most private businesses, including cafés and restaurants, stay open, and all transport runs as normal. Tickets for many events can be bought online from biletix.com and pozitif-ist.com. For more information consult iksv.org/eng or city tourist offices.

NEW YEAR'S DAY (PH)

January 1

İSTANBUL FILM FESTIVAL

April film.iksv.org/en

Two-week film festival featuring a mix of domestic and foreign films. A good chance to see the best new Turkish films with English subtitles.

TULIP FESTIVAL

Mid-April to mid-May

Over fifteen million tulip bulbs planted across the city bloom, and there are associated events. The most convenient places to see Turkey's national flower are Gülhane, Yıldız and Emirgan parks.

CHILDREN'S DAY (PH)

April 23

A celebration of Turkish independence and Turkey's children, school-band marches take place across the city, notably on İstiklal Caddesi.

YOUTH AND SPORTS DAY (PH)

May 19

Marches and celebrations on the anniversary of the day Atatürk launched the Turkish War of Independence.

INTERNATIONAL THEATRE FESTIVAL

Mid-May to early June iksv.org/en

Major festival featuring Turkish and foreign theatre companies performing in venues such as the Rumeli Hisarı fortress on the Bosphorus.

BABYLON SOUND GARDEN

May babylon.com.tr

One-day music festival in Parkorman, organised by İstanbul's hippest club.

CHİLL-OUT

May chilloutfest.com

One-day dance, electronic and pop festival held at Life Park.

CONQUEST CELEBRATIONS

May 29 ibb.gov.tr

Week-long festivities around the anniversary of the fall of Constantinople to the Ottoman Turks, with concerts by the military Mehter Band, parades and fireworks.

SHOPPING FESTIVAL

First three weeks in June istshopfest.com

Ninety or so shopping centres stay open 24hr a day, new fashions go on show and there are big discounts at various locations around the city, as well as a number of special events.

İSTANBUL MUSIC FESTIVAL

Mid-June to mid-July iksv.org/en

Lasting most of the month, concerts, dance and opera performed at some interesting venues by a mix of leading Turkish and international performers.

EFES PILSEN ONE LOVE

Last weekend June or early July efespilsenonelove.com

Weekend-long indie music festival usually held in Parkorman.

İSTANBUL JAZZ FESTIVAL

First two weeks of July iksv.org/en

Music – not all of it is jazz – played at a series of venues across the city.

VICTORY DAY (PH)

August 30

Celebrates the victory of the Turks over the invading Greeks at the Battle of Dumlupınar in 1922.

INTERNATIONAL İSTANBUL BIENNIAL

Mid-September through November

iksv.org/en

Held odd years in venues across the city, this is a major contemporary arts event.

FİLMEKİMİ

End of September to start of October

fimekimi.iksv.org

Week-long international fim festival; most screenings take place in Beyoğlu cinemas.

REPUBLIC DAY (PH)

October 29

Street parade by school children to mark the foundation of the Turkish Republic on this day in 1923.

AKBANK INTERNATIONAL JAZZ FESTIVAL

Second & third weeks in October

akbanksanat.com

Quality jazz festival with leading domestic and foreign artists performing at venues such as Babylon, İKSV Salon and the Lütfi Kırdar Congress Centre.

ATATÜRK'S DEATH (PH)

November 10

The founder of the Republic died at the Dolmabahçe Palace on this day in 1938. At 09.05, the time of his death, people throughout the city and country stop what they are doing and observe a five-minute silence.

CONTEMPORARY İSTANBUL

November contemporaryistanbul.com

Major, week long arts fair in the prestigious Lütfi Kırdar Congress and Exhibition Centre.

Religious holidays

The religious festivals observed throughout the Islamic world also apply to İstanbul. **Ramazan** (Ramadan), the period of fasting for the month preceding **Şeker Bayramı** (Eid ul Fitr in Arabic) is not a holiday, but if your visit coincides with this month you may notice that some cafés and restaurants, especially away from the tourist haunts, are unusually quiet in the day, packed with fast-breakers after sunset. Try to avoid eating and drinking too obviously in front of people in conservative areas like Fatih (Northwest quarter). Şeker Bayram is usually a three-day festival and banks, government offices and many private businesses are closed for the entire period, though transport continues to run. Museums are usually shut only on the first day of the holiday. **Kurban Bayramı** (Eid ul Adha in Arabic) is a four-day festival during which animals are slaughtered to commemorate Abraham sacrificing a ram instead of his son. The same rules regarding closures apply as for Şeker Bayram. As the Muslim calendar is lunar, the festivals occur eleven days earlier each year.

Şeker Bayramı

2015 Şeker July 17–19
2016 Şeker July 4–7
2017 Şeker June 25–27
2018 Şeker June 15–17

Kurban Bayramı

Kurban Sept 24–27
Kurban Oct 12–15
Kurban Sept 1–4
Kurban Aug 21–24

Chronology

c.6500 BC > Neolithic human settlement on the site of İstanbul.

c.667 BC > The legendary foundation of Byzantium (İstanbul) by Greek colonists led by Byzas.

513 BC > Darius, King of Persia, captures Byzantium.

334 BC > Alexander the Great captures Byzantium.

195 AD > Roman emperor Septimius Severus burns the city down, rebuilds it a few years later.

324 AD > Emperor Constantine decides the city will be his new imperial capital, building starts.

330 > Constantine calls the rebuilt city Nova Roma, but it's soon known as Constantinople.

337 > Constantine is baptized a Christian.

392 > Paganism is banned by Emperor Theodosius and the Roman Empire becomes an overtly Christian entity.

447 > The land walls are rebuilt following a massive earthquake.

532 > The Nika riots cause vast damage to the city before 30,000 of the rioters are massacred in the Hippodrome.

537 > A monumental new cathedral, the Haghia Sophia (Aya Sofya) is completed on the site of an earlier incarnation burnt in the 532 riots.

674 > The Arabs besiege Constantinople; the defenders use "Greek fire" against their enemy.

726 > Emperor Leo III forbids icon veneration as idolatry, causing riots across the empire.

1054 > Schism of the Orthodox and Catholic churches.

1071 > The first Turks reach Anatolia and defeat Emperor Romanos IV Diogenes at Manzikert.

1097 > The First Crusade passes through Constantinople.

1204 > The Fourth Crusade captures Constantinople and irrevocably weakens the Byzantine Empire.

1261 > Michael VIII Palaeologus recaptures the city for the Byzantines.

1326 > The Osmanlı (Ottomans to the West), a Turkish tribal group, capture Bursa and further weaken the Byzantine Empire.

1453 > The Ottomans capture Constantinople on May 29 after a two-month siege. The Byzantine Empire is extinguished.

1459 > Construction of the Topkapı Palace, the heart of the Ottoman Empire, begins.

1481 > Beyazit II becomes Sultan.

1492 > Beyazit II sends an Ottoman fleet to Spain to save the Jews from persecution.

1514 > Selim I "the Grim" wins a crucial victory over the Persians.

1517 > Selim I captures Medina, takes the title of Caliph.

1529 > The Ottomans reach the gates of Vienna led by Süleyman the Magnificent.

1558 > The completion of the Süleymaniye Camii by Sinan.

1571 > Don John of Austria defeats the Ottoman navy at Lepanto.

1616 > The monumental Sultanahmet Camii is completed after eight years' toil.

1729 > Sultan Ahmet I establishes the Ottoman Empire's first printing press.

1779 > The Ottomans lose the Crimea to Russia.

1830 > Greece fights off Ottoman control and becomes an independent state.

1839 > Sultan Abdülmecid begins to reform the empire on European lines.

1853 > Tsar Nicholas I of Russia declares the Ottoman Empire the "sick man of Europe".

1854 > Florence Nightingale arrives in İstanbul.

1856 > Abdülmecit leaves Topkapı Palace and moves to European-style Dolmabahçe Palace.

1888 > Visitors from Europe reach İstanbul on the new Orient Express.

1889 > Foundation of The Committee for Union and Progress (CUP) or Young Turks as they are better known.

1909 > Sultan Abdülhamit deposed by the CUP.

1914 > Ottoman Turkey signs an alliance with Germany and enters World War I.

1918 > Britain occupies İstanbul after the Allied victory in World War I.

1919 > Mustafa Kemal lands at Samsun on the Black Sea, triggering the Turkish War of Independence.

1922 > The Sultanate is abolished by Turkish nationalists led by Atatürk.

1923 > The Republic of Turkey is officially founded, Ankara replaces İstanbul as capital.

1934 > Haghia Sophia (Aya Sofya), a church then a mosque, becomes a museum.

1938 > Atatürk dies at Dolmabahçe Palace.

1939 > Turkey remains neutral for most of World War II, İstanbul a centre of intrigue.

1955 > A weekend of rioting destroys many Greek-minority-owned properties on İstiklal Caddesi and across the city.

1960 > Turkey's first military coup.

1971 > Turkey's second military coup.

1977 > Thirty-nine leftist demonstrators shot by extremists at a May Day rally in Taksim Square.

1980 > Turkey's third military coup.

1994 > A pro-Islamic Refah Party wins İstanbul in municipal elections, Tayyip Erdoğan becomes mayor.

2002 > Pro-Islamic AKP sweep to power in general elections led by Tayyip Erdoğan.

2007 > The AKP increases its majority in next elections.

2010 > İstanbul is joint European Capital of Culture.

2011 > The AKP wins the general elections for a record third time.

2013 > Protests erupt in Gezi Park, part of Taksim Square, when the government try to replace a green area with a shopping mall.

2014 > Tayyip Erdoğan confirms the support he has from 50 percent-plus of the electorate in becoming Turkey's first popularly elected president.

Turkish

Few visitors to İstanbul speak any Turkish and only a handful bother to try to learn any. This is a great shame as a very little Turkish can go a long way not only in helping you negotiate your way around the city – particularly its less visited quarters – but also in showing that you have an interest in an intensely proud people who often feel that they are misunderstood by foreigners. Below is a brief guide to pronunciation, some useful words and phrases and a basic glossary for food and drink. For a more comprehensive introduction, see *The Rough Guide Turkish Phrasebook*.

Pronunciation

Turkish is phonetically spelt and, compared to most other languages, grammatically regular. It is lightly stressed, usually on the last syllable. It uses the following letters which do not appear in the English version of the Latin alphabet – ç, ğ, ı, ö, ş, ü – but does not contain the letters q, w or x. Below is a brief pronunciation guide.

Aa	short a, as in c**a**r
Ee	as in p**e**t
İi	as in b**i**n
Iı	an **uh** sound
Oo	as in d**o**te
Öö	like **ur** in ch**ur**n
Uu	as in cl**ue**
Üü	like **ew** in d**ew**
Cc	like j in **j**elly
Çç	like **ch** in **ch**ang
Gg	like **g** as in **g**o
Ğğ	hardly pronounced, but slightly lengthens the preceding vowel
Hh	as in **h**ate
Jj	like the **s** in trea**s**ure
Şş	like **sh** in **sh**op
Vv	between a **v** and a **w**

Words and phrases

BASICS

good morning	günaydın
good afternoon	iyi günler
good evening	iyi akşamlar
good night	iyi geceler
hello	merhaba
goodbye	Allaha ısmarladık
yes	evet
no	hayır
no (there isn't/ aren't any)	yok
please	lütfen
thank you	teşekkür ederim/ sağol
you're welcome	bir şey değil
How are you?	Nasılsınız? Nasılsın?
I'm fine	İyiyim
Do you speak English?	İngilizce biliyormusunuz?
I don't know	bilmiyorum
I beg your pardon	affedersiniz
excuse me	pardon
I'm English/ Scottish/ Irish/ American/ Australian	İngilizim/ Iskoçyalım/ Irlandalıyım/ Amerikalı/ Avustralyalım
today	bugün
tomorrow	yarın
yesterday	dün
now	şimdi
later	sonra
in the morning	sabahleyin
in the afternoon	öğle'den sonra
in the evening	akşamleyin
here/there/ over there	bur(a)da/şur(a)da/ or(a) da
good/bad	iyi/kötü, fena
big/small	büyük/küçük
cheap/expensive	ucuz/pahalı
early/late	erken/geç
hot/cold	sıcak/soğuk
near/far	yakın/uzak
vacant/occupied	boş/dolu
Mr	Bey (follows first name)
Miss	Bayan (precedes first name)
Mrs	Hanım (follows first name)

QUESTIONS AND DIRECTIONS

Where is the...?	...Nerede?
When?	Ne zaman?
What/What is it?	Ne/ne dir?
How much (does it cost?)	Ne kadar/kaç para?
How many?	Kaç tane?
What time is it?	Saat kaç?
How do I get to...?	...'a/e nasıl giderim?
How far is it to...?	...'a/e ne kadar uzak?
When does it open?	Saat kaçta açılıyor?
When does it close?	Saat kaçta kapanıyor?

TRANSPORT

aeroplane	uçak
bus	otobüs
train	tren
car	araba
taxi	taksi
ferry	feribot, vapur
catamaran, sea bus	deniz otobüsü
bus station	otogar
railway station	gar, tren ıstasyonu
ferry terminal/jetty	iskele
A ticket to...	...'a bir bilet
one-way	gidiş sadece
return	gidiş-dönüş
What time does it leave?	Saat kaçta kalkıyor?
Where does it leave from?	Nereden kalkıyor?

SIGNS

açık/kapalı	open/closed
baylar	gentlemen
bayanlar	ladies
çekiniz/itiniz	pull/push
dikkat	beware
dur	stop, halt
giriş/çıkış	entrance/exit
girmek yasaktır	entry forbidden
ilk yardım	first aid
lütfen ayakkabılarınızı çıkartınız	please take off your shoes
sigara içilmez	no smoking
WC/tuvalet	WC

ACCOMMODATION

hotel	otel
pension	pansiyon
Do you have a room?	Boş odanız var mı?
Single/double/triple	Tek/çift/üç kişilik
with a double bed	fransiz yataklı
with a shower	duşlu
hot water	sıcak su
cold water	soğuk su
Can I see it?	Bakabilirmiyim?
I have a booking	Reservasyonum var
Is there wi-fi?	Kablosuz internet var mı?
What's the password?	Şifre nedir?

NUMBERS

bir	1
iki	2
üç	3
dört	4
beş	5
altı	6
yedi	7
sekiz	8
dokuz	9
on	10
on bir	11
on iki	12
on üç	13
yirmi	20
otuz	30
kırk	40
elli	50
altmış	60
yetmiş	70
seksen	80
doksan	90
yüz	100
yüz kırk	140
iki yüz	200
yedi yüz	700
bin	1000

Food and drink terms

BASICS

bal	honey
buz	ice
ekmek	bread
makarna	pasta (noodles)

peynir	cheese
pilav, pirinç	rice
şeker	sugar
su	water
süt	milk
tereyağı	butter
tuz	salt
zeytin yağı	olive oil
yoğurt	yoghurt
yumurta	eggs

COOKING TERMS

acı	hot, spicy
ezme	puréed dip
fırında(n)	baked
haşlama	stew(ed)
ızgarada(n)	grilled
sıcak/soğuk	hot/cold (*meze*)
soslu, salçalı	in red sauce
tava, sahanda	deep-fried, fried
yoğurtlu	in yoghurt sauce
zeytinyağlılar	cold cooked vegetables with olive oil
with/without (meat)	(et)li/(et)siz

SOUP (*ÇORBA*)

ezo gelin	tomato, rice and lentil
işkembe	tripe
mercimek	lentil
tarhana	yoghurt, grain and spice
tavuk	chicken

APPETIZERS (*MEZE*)

Antep or acılı ezmesi	spicy tomato/chilli mash
cacık	yoghurt, cucumber and herb dip
çoban salatası	tomato, cucumber, parsley, pepper and onion salad
haydarı	strained yoghurt and garlic dip
imam bayıldı	cold baked aubergine, onion and tomato
mücver	courgette fritters
patlıcan ezmesi	aubergine pâté
piyaz	white haricots, onions and parsley salad
sigara böreği	cheese-filled pastry rolls
turşu	pickled vegetables
yaprak dolması	rice-stuffed vine leaves
zeytin	olives

MEAT (*ET*) AND MEAT DISHES

Adana kebap	spicy mincemeat kebab on skewer
beyti	minced kebab in flatbread
çiğ köfte	spicy bulgur patties
ciğer	liver
dana eti	beef
döner kebap	meat sliced from a rotisserie
İskender kebap	*döner* in yoghurt and tomato sauce
kanat	chicken wing
karışık ızgara	mixed grill
köfte	meatballs
kuzu	lamb
şiş kebap	shish kebab, lamb or chicken
tavuk/piliç	chicken

SNACK/LUNCH FOODS

börek	pastry with cheese, meat or potato filling
çerez	nut and roasted pulse nibbles
gözleme	stuffed paratha-like flatbread
lahmacun	flatbread with spicy mincemeat
mantı	Turkish "ravioli" in yoghurt sauce
midye dolması	rice-stuffed mussels
pide	Turkish "pizza"
poğaça	soft, often filled, bread roll
simit	bread rings studded with sesame seeds

FISH (*BALIK*) AND SEAFOOD (*DENIZ ÜRÜNLERI*)

barbunya/tekir	red mullet, small/ large
çipura	gilt-head bream
hamsi	anchovy (Black Sea)
kalamar	squid
kalkan	turbot
karides	prawns
kılıç	swordfish
levrek	sea bass
lüfer	bluefish
mercan	pandora/red bream
mezgit	whitebait
palamut/torik	small/large bonito
sardalya	sardine

VEGETABLES (*SEBZE*)

bamya	okra, lady's fingers
biber	peppers
domates	tomato
ıspanak	spinach
kabak	courgette
mantar	mushrooms
maydanoz	parsley
nohut	chickpeas
patates	potato
patlıcan	aubergine
roka, tere	rocket greens
salatalık	cucumber
soğan	onion
taze fasulye	french beans

FRUIT (*MEYVE*) AND NUTS (*FISTIK*)

antep fıstığı	pistachio
armut	pear
badem	almond
ceviz	walnut
çilek	strawberry
elma	apple
erik	plum
fındık	hazlenut
incir	fig
karpuz	watermelon
kayısı	apricot
kiraz	sweet cherry
muz	banana
nar	pomegranate
portakal	orange
şeftali	peach
üzüm	grape
vişne	sour cherry

CHEESE

beyaz	white goat's cheese, like feta
kaşar	yellow cow's cheese
otlu peynir	herb-stuffed goat's cheese
tulum	goat's cheese cured in a goatskin

SWEETS (*TATLILAR*) AND PASTRIES (*PASTALAR*)

acı badem	giant almond biscuit
baklava	nut-filled filo pastry
dondurma	ice cream
helva	sweet made from semolina flour
İrmik helvası	semolina and nut *helva*
kabak tatlısı	baked pumpkin served with tahini
kadayıf	"shredded wheat" in syrup
lokum	Turkish delight
muhallebi	milk pudding with rice flour and rosewater
sütlaç	rice pudding
tahin helvası	sesame paste *helva*
tavuk göğsü	chicken-breast, milk, sugar and rice taffy

DRINKS

ayran	drinking yoghurt
bira	beer
çay	tea
elma çayı	hot apple-flavoured drink
kahve	coffee
maden suyu/soda	mineral water (fizzy)
meyva suyu	fruit juice
rakı	aniseed-flavoured spirit
şarap	wine

PUBLISHING INFORMATION

This second edition published October 2015 by **Rough Guides Ltd**
80 Strand, London WC2R 0RL
11, Community Centre, Panchsheel Park, New Delhi 110017, India
Distributed by the Penguin Random House
Penguin Books Ltd, 80 Strand, London WC2R 0RL
Penguin Group (USA) 345 Hudson Street, NY 10014, USA
Penguin Group (Australia) 250 Camberwell Road, Camberwell, Victoria 3124, Australia
Penguin Group (NZ) 67 Apollo Drive, Mairangi Bay, Auckland 1310, New Zealand
Penguin Group (South Africa) Block D, Rosebank Office Park, 181 Jan Smuts Avenue, Parktown North, Gauteng, South Africa 2193
Rough Guides is represented in Canada by
Tourmaline Editions Inc., 662 King Street West, Suite 304, Toronto, Ontario, M5V 1M7
Typeset in Minion and Din to an original design by Henry Iles and Dan May.
Printed and bound in China

176pp includes index
A catalogue record for this book is available from the British Library
ISBN 978-0-24118-701-2

1 3 5 7 9 8 6 4 2

ROUGH GUIDES CREDITS

Text editor: Sharon Sonam
Layout: Nikhil Agarwal
Cartography: Ed Wright
Picture editor: Aude Vauconsant
Photographer: Lydia Evans
Production: Linda Dare
Proofreader: Norm Longley
Cover design: Roger Mapp and Nikhil Agarwal

THE AUTHOR

Terry Richardson is based in the Mediterranean Turkish city of Antalya. He first visited İstanbul back in 1978 and has been an author of *The Rough Guide to Turkey* for over a decade. He leads history and archeology tours in İstanbul and elsewhere in Turkey, writes regular travel features for an English-language Turkish newspaper and occasional articles for the UK press. He was also involved in setting up Turkey's first two long-distance walking trails. When not researching, travelling or climbing the snow-capped Toros Mountains he's likely to be listening to punk/alternative music or following the fluctuating fortunes of Middlesbrough FC.

HELP US UPDATE

We've gone to a lot of effort to ensure that the first edition of the **Pocket Rough Guide Istanbul** is accurate and up-to-date. However, things change – places get "discovered", opening hours are notoriously fickle, restaurants and rooms raise prices or lower standards. If you feel we've got it wrong or left something out, we'd like to know, and if you can remember the address, the price, the hours, the phone number, so much the better.

Please send your comments with the subject line "**Pocket Rough Guide Istanbul Update**" to mail@roughguides.com. We'll credit all contributions and send a copy of the next edition (or any other Rough Guide if you prefer) for the very best emails.

Find more travel information, connect with fellow travellers and book your trip on roughguides .com

PHOTO CREDITS

All images © Rough Guides except the following:
(Key: a-above; b-below/bottom; c-centre; f-far; l-left; r-right; t-top)

Front cover & spine Tiling in the Topkapı Palace © AWL images/Danita Delimont Stock
Back cover Yeni Camii © AWL Images/ Mauricio Abreu

p.1 Ali Kabas/Corbis
p.2 Gavin Hellier/Robert Harding Picture Library
p.4 Ali Kabas/Corbis
p.5 Gallo Images/Getty Images
p.6 Gallo Images/Getty Images
p.8 Gavin Hellier/Robert Harding Picture Library (tr); Cindy Hopkins/Alamy (cr)
p.9 Gary Yeowell (tr); Gallo Images/Getty Images (br)
p.11 Cubo Images/SuperStock (tr); Salvator Barki/Getty Images (cl)
pp.12–13 Mark Horn/Getty Images
p.14 Tetra Images/Corbis
p.15 Nik Wheeler/Corbis (tl); Turkish Culture and Tourism Office (b)
p.16 DeAgostini/Getty Images
p.17 Dennis Cox/Alamy (cr); Tips Images/ SuperStock (b)
p.19 travelstock44 (t); Riccardo Sala/Alamy (cl)
p.20 AWL Images/ Getty Images
p.21 Fabian von Poserimag/SuperStock (c)
p.22 Gavin Hellier/Corbis
p.23 Steve Outram/Photoshot(tl); LMR Group/ Alamy (tr)
p.27 David Sutherland/Corbis (b)
p.28 Turkish Culture and Tourism Office
p.29 Imagebrokers/Photoshot (t); Tips Image/SuperStock (cl); Rawdon Wyatt/ Alamy (b)
p.32 Hackenberg-Photo-Cologne/Alamy
p.37 Turkish Culture and Tourism Office
p.40 Leyla S. Ismet/Alamy
p.42 TTL/Photoshot
p.43 Alexis Grattier/Getty Images
p.44 Wilmar Photography/Alamy
p.59 Imagebrokers/Photoshot
p.65 LOOK Die Bildagentur der Fotografen GmbH/ Alamy
p.72 Bruno Ehrs/Corbis
p.76 Ali Kabas/ Alamy
p.78 Ali Kabas/Alamy
p.83 Jean-Christophe Godet/Alamy
p.84 Blickwinkel/Alamy
p.100 Images & Stories/Alamy
p.106 Rawdon Wyatt/ Alamy
p.108 Ma Yan/Xinhua Press/Corbis
p.121 Mel Longhurst/Photoshot
p.129 Xinhua/Photoshot
p.134 Slow Images/Getty Images
p.139 Turkish Culture and Tourism Office
pp.140–141 David Sutherland/Corbis
pp.150–151 Bob Krist/Corbis

Index

Maps are marked in **bold**.

D

E

F

G

H

I

J

K

L

M

N

O

P

R

S

T

U

W

Y

Z